Read for the Fun of It

Read for the Fun of It

Active Programming with Books for Children

by Caroline Feller Bauer

Drawings by Lynn Gates Bredeson

THE H. W. WILSON COMPANY 1992

Library of Congress Cataloging-in-Publication Data

Bauer, Caroline Feller.
    Read for the Fun of It / active programming with books for
children / by Caroline Feller Bauer ; drawings by Lynn Gates
Bredeson.
        p.   cm.
    Includes bibliographical references and index.
    ISBN 0–8242–0824––2 ; $40.00
    1. Libraries, Children's—Activity programs. 2. Children's
literature—Appreciation—Problems, exercises, etc. 3. Children—
Books and reading. I. Title
Z718. 1.B38   1992
027.62′5—dc20   91–31450

Printed in the United States of America
First Printing

For Peter,
who has made it all fun . . .
and reads, too.

Contents

Part III   Promoting Poetry

Part IV   Active Programming with Books for Fun

Acknowledgments

The author is grateful for permission to include the following works:

"After English Class" by Jean Little from *Hey World, Here I Am!* Copyright © 1986. Reprinted by permission of HarperCollins Publishers.

"Anansi's Hat-Shaking Dance" from *The Hat-Shaking Dance and Other Ashanti Tales from Ghana* by Harold Courlander, Harcourt Brace and World, Inc. Copyright © 1957, 1985 by Harold Courlander. Reprinted by permission of the author.

"Another Snake Story" from *Auntie's Knitting a Baby* by Lois Simmie. Copyright © 1984 by Lois Simmie. First published by Western Producer Prairie Books with Orchard. Used by permission of Douglas & McIntyre, and Orchard Books.

"April Is A Dog's Dream" from *Turtle in July* by Marilyn Singer. Copyright © 1989 by Marilyn Singer. Reprinted with permission of Macmillan Publishing Company.

"Aunt Roberta" from *Honey, I Love and Other Love Poems* by Eloise Greenfield. Copyright © 1978. Reprinted by permission of HarperCollins Publishers.

"Bad Decision" by Tony Johnston. Reprinted by permission of G. P. Putnam's Sons from *I'm Gonna Tell Mama I Want an Iguana*. Text copyright © 1990 by Tony Johnston.

"Balloon" from *Flashlight and Other Poems* by Judith Thurman. Copyright © 1976 by Judith Thurman. Used by permission of Marian Reiner for the author.

"Beach Stones" from *Something New Begins* by Lillian Moore. Copyright © 1982 by Lillian Moore. Reprinted by permission of Atheneum Publishers, an imprint of Macmillan Publishing Company.

Excerpt based on one series of cartoons from *Blackboard Cartooning for Teachers* by Eric Teitelbaum. Copyright © 1977, 1991 by Eric Teitelbaum. A WE Productions Publication.

"Books" by Johanna Hurwitz. Copyright © 1950 by Johanna Hurwitz. Reprinted by permission of the author.

"Brachiosaurus" by Jack Prelutsky from *Tyrannosaurus Was a Beast*. Copyright © 1988 by Jack Prelutsky. Reprinted by permission of Greenwillow Books, a division of William Morrow & Co.

"Chairs" from *Small Poems* by Valerie Worth. Copyright © 1972 by Valerie Worth. Reprinted by permission of Farrar, Straus and Giroux, Inc.

"Changing" by Mary Ann Hoberman from *Yellow Butter Purple Jelly Red Jam Black Bread*. Copyright © 1981 by Mary Ann Hoberman. Published by Viking. Reprinted by permission of the Gina Maccoby Literary Agency.

''Dessine-Moi Une Maison/Draw Me A House'' from *Dessine-Moi Une Maison* by Helene Ray Bordas. Copyright © 1986 BORDAS Paris.

''The Dog'' by Jeanne Steig from *Consider the Lemming.* Copyright © 1988 by Jeanne Steig. Reprinted by permission of Farrar, Straus and Giroux, Inc.

''Dogs and Cats and Bears and Bats'' by Jack Prelutsky from *The Random House Book of Poetry for Children.* Selected and introduced by Jack Prelutsky. Copyright © 1983 by Random House, Inc. Reprinted by permission of Random House, Inc.

''Eddie's Birthday Present'' text from *The Butterfly Jar* by Jeff Moss. Copyright © 1989 by Jeff Moss. Used by permission of Bantam Books, a division of Bantam Doubleday Dell Publishing Group, Inc.

''Flying a Ribbon'' from *Stilts, Somersaults and Headstands* by Kathleen Fraser. Copyright © 1968 by Kathleen Fraser. Reprinted by permission of Marian Reiner for the author.

''Frying Pan in the Moving Van'' from *A Word or Two with You* by Eve Merriam. Copyright © 1981 by Eve Merriam. Reprinted by permission of Marian Reiner for the author.

Excerpt from *Goodbye My Island* by Jean Rogers. Copyright © 1983 by Jean Rogers. Reprinted by permission of William Morrow & Co.

''Gone'' by David McCord from *One at a Time* by David McCord. Copyright © 1970 by David McCord. By permission of Little, Brown and Company.

''Greedy Dog'' by James Hurley from *If You Should Meet A Crocodile,* published by Kaye and Ward. Copyright by James Hurley. Reprinted by permission of the author.

''Greetings'' by Anne Bell from *Someone Is Flying Balloons: Australian Poems for Children* selected by Jill Heylen and Celia Jellet. First published by Omnibus Books, Adelaide, Australia, 1983. Copyright © 1983 by Anne Bell. Reprinted by permission of the author.

''Guess What I Can Do?'' by Nonie Borba. Used with permission from the author.

''Harrods of London Orders 'Cover-Up''' from *The Los Angeles Times,* June 18, 1989. Copyright © 1989 by Reuters. Reprinted with permission.

''Hello'' by Mary Ann Hoberman from *Nuts to You and Nuts to Me,* published by Alfred A. Knopf, 1974. Copyright © 1974 by Mary Ann Hoberman. Reprinted by permission of the Gina Maccoby Literary Agency.

The High Price of Cat Food by Charlotte MacLeod. Reprinted by permission of Jed Mattes Inc., New York. All rights reserved. Copyright © 1987 by Charlotte MacLeod.

''Hippopotamus'' by Robert Heidbreder from *Don't Eat Spiders.* Copyright © 1985 by Robert Heidbreder. Reprinted by permission of Oxford University Press Canada.

''Honey, I Love'' by Eloise Greenfield from *Honey, I Love and Other Love Poems.* Copyright © 1978. Reprinted by permission of HarperCollins Publishers.

''Hot Food'' by Michael Rosen from *The Hypnotiser,* published by Andre Deutsch. Reproduced with permission of the Peters Fraser & Dunlop Group Ltd.

''Houses from the Sea'' by Alice E. Goudey from *Houses from the Sea.* First published by Charles Scribner's Sons. Copyright by Alice E. Goudey. Reprinted by permission of the author.

''How Long Does It Take You to Read a Word?'' by Marilyn Burns from *This Book Is About Time.* Copyright © 1978 by the Yolla Bolla Press. By permission of Little, Brown and Company.

''How to Make a Yawn'' from *The Birthday Cow* by Eve Merriam. Text copyright © 1978 by Eve Merriam. Reprinted by permission of Alfred A. Knopf, Inc.

''I'm Bold, I'm Brave'' from *The New Kid On The Block* by Jack Prelutsky. Copyright © 1984 by Jack Prelutsky. Reprinted by permission of Greenwillow Books, a division of William Morrow & Co.

Ickle Bickle Robin by Edna Mitchell Preston (Scholastic, 1975). Copyright © 1975 by Edna Mitchell Preston. Reprinted with permission from the author.

''If I Were My Mother'' from *In One Door and Out the Other* by Aileen Fisher. Copyright © 1969. Reprinted by permission of HarperCollins Publishers.

''If you find a little feather . . .'' from *Something Special* by Beatrice Schenk de Regniers. Copyright © 1958, 1986 by Beatrice Schenk de Regniers. Reprinted by permission of Marian Reiner for the author.

''Imaginary Rooms'' by Sylvia Cassedy from *RoomRimes.* Copyright © 1987. Reprinted by permission of HarperCollins Publishers.

''Invisible Dog'' by Nonie Borba. Used with permission of the author.

''Jelly Beans'' text from *In One Door and Out the Other* by Aileen Fisher. Copyright © 1969 by Aileen Fisher. Reprinted by permission of HarperCollins Publishers.

''Last Laugh'' by Lee Bennett Hopkins from *Kims Place.* Copyright © 1974 by Lee Bennett Hopkins. Reprinted by permission of Curtis Brown, Ltd.

''Library'' from *Small Poems Again* by Valerie Worth. Copyright © 1975, 1986 by Valerie Worth. Reprinted by permission of Farrar, Straus and Giroux, Inc.

''R-E-A-D Cheer'' by Lorraine E. Regan. Permission granted by author.

''Life Savings'' from *The Clothes Horse* by Janet and Allen Ahlberg (Viking Kestrel, 1987). Copyright © 1987 by Janet and Allen Ahlberg. Reprinted by permission of the publisher.

''Little Red Riding Dog'' by Beverly Conrad from *Doggy Tales* (Dell, 1980). Copyright © 1980 by Beverly Conrad. Reprinted with permission of the author.

''Long Red Fingernails and Red, Red Lips'' by Patricia L. Gay. Reprinted with permission from the author.

''Mad Dog'' by Grace Cornell Tall. Used by permission of the author.

''Magic'' from *A Song I Sang to You* by Myra Cohn Livingston. Copyright © 1984, 1969, 1967, 1965, 1959, 1958 by Myra Cohn Livingston. Reprinted by permission of Marian Reiner for the author.

''Marbles'' from *Small Poems* by Valerie Worth. Copyright © 1972 by Valerie Worth. Reprinted by permission of Farrar, Straus and Giroux, Inc.

''Marbles'' from *Stilts, Somersaults and Headstands* by Kathleen Fraser. Copyright © 1968 by Kathleen Fraser. Reprinted by permission of Marian Reiner for the author.

''Miraculous Mortimer'' from *The New Kid On The Block* by Jack Prelutsky. Copyright © 1984 by Jack Prelutsky. Reprinted by permission of Greenwillow Books, a division of William Morrow & Co.

''My Journals'' by Jean Little from *World, Here I Am!* Copyright © 1986 by Jean Little. Reprinted by permission of HarperCollins Publishers.

from *A Mouse's Diary* by Michelle Cartlidge, William Heinemann Ltd. Publishers. Reprinted with permission of the Octopus Publishing Group.

''No Dogs Is Not Enough'' by Linda Leopold Strauss. Copyright © 1984 by Linda Leopold Strauss.

''Order'' from *The Way Things Are And Other Poems* by Myra Cohn Livingston. Copyright © 1974 by Myra Cohn Livingston. Reprinted by permission of Marian Reiner for the author.

Excerpt from *Orp* by Suzy Kline. Copyright © 1989 by Suzy Kline. Reprinted by permission of G. P. Putnam's Sons.

''Outside'' by Lillian Moore from *I Feel the Same Way.* Copyright © 1967 by Lillian Moore. Reprinted by permission of Marian Reiner for the author.

''Paperclips'' by X. J. Kennedy. Copyright © 1987 by X. J. Kennedy. Reprinted by permission of Curtis Brown, Ltd.

''The Pear Tree'' by E. Elizabeth Longwell from *Story Parade.* Copyright © 1943 by Story Parade, Inc. Copyright renewed 1971, reprinted by permission of Western Publishing Company, Inc.

''Perfection'' from *The Devil's Storybook* by Natalie Babbitt. Copyright © 1974 by Natalie Babbitt. Reprinted by permission of Farrar, Straus and Giroux, Inc.

''The Playground'' by Carmen Coupe. First published in *Borderland* (English Teachers Association of WA with St. George books), edited by Eric Carlin and Richard Rossiter.

''Please Tree, Don't Die'' from *Time Magazine,* July 10, 1989. Copyright © 1989 The Time Inc. Magazine Company. Reprinted by permission.

''The Princess and Jose'' from *The Boy Who Could Do Anything* by Anita Brenner. Published by William R. Scott & Co., 1942. Copyright © 1942 by Anita Brenner.

''Puzzle'' from *The Birthday Cow* by Eve Merriam. Text copyright © 1978 by Eve Merriam. Reprinted by permission of Alfred A. Knopf, Inc.

''Questions for a Dinosaur'' from *The Tigers Brought Pink Lemonade* by Patricia Hubbell. Copyright © 1988 by Patricia Hubbell. Reprinted with permission of Atheneum Publishers, an imprint of Macmillan Publishing Company.

"Read" from *Street Talk* by Ann Turner. Copyright © 1986 by Ann Turner. Reprinted by permission of Houghton Mifflin Co.

"Ready for Winter" by Clarice Foster Booth from *Away We Go.* Copyright © 1956 by Clarice Foster Booth.

"Riddle Hat" by Nonie Borba. Used with permission of the author.

"The Sack of Diamonds" from *Stupid Peter and Other Tales* by Helen Kronberg Olson. Text copyright © 1970 by Helen Kronberg Olson. Reprinted by permission of Random House, Inc.

"Shells" from *I Thought I Heard the City* by Lillian Moore. Copyright © 1969 by Lillian Moore. Reprinted by permission of Marian Reiner for the author.

"Sing a Song of Pockets" from *Something Special* by Beatrice Schenk de Regniers. Copyright © 1958 by Beatrice Schenk de Regniers. © 1986 renewed. Used by permission of Marian Reiner for the author.

"Slower than the Rest" from *Every Living Thing* by Cynthia Rylant. Copyright © 1985 by Cynthia Rylant. Reprinted with permission of Bradbury Press, an affiliate of Macmillan, Inc.

Excerpt from *Snapshots of Paradise* by Adele Geras. Copyright © 1982 by Adele Geras. Reprinted with permission of Laura Cecil, Literary Agent.

"Sometimes I Wish . . ." by Nonie Borba. Used with permission from the author.

"Souvenir" from JAMBOREE *Rhymes For All Times* by Eve Merriam. Copyright © 1962, 1964, 1966, 1973, 1984 by Eve Merriam. Reprinted by permission of Marian Reiner for the author.

"Stamps" by Linda G. Paulsen. Used with permission from the author.

"Stamps" by Siv Widenberg from *I'm Like Me* (The Feminist Press of CUNY). Copyright © 1968, 1973 by Siv Widenberg; translation © 1973 by Verne Moberg.

"Storytime" from *Midnight Forest* by Judith Nicholls. Published by Faber & Faber. Copyright © 1987 by Judith Nicholls. Reprinted by permission of the author.

"The Tail Who Wagged the Dog" from *The Tail Who Wagged the Dog* by Robert Kraus. Copyright © 1971 by Robert Kraus. Used by permission of Simon & Schuster, Inc., New York, NY.

"Tale of the Telephone Operator" by Marilyn Burns from *This Book Is About Time. Copyright* © 1978 by the Yolla Bolla Press. By permission of Little, Brown and Company.

"Tear-Water Tea" from *Owl at Home* by Arnold Lobel. Copyright © 1975. Reprinted by permission of HarperCollins Publishers.

"The Tiger's Minister of State" from *The Tiger's Whisker and Other Tales From Asia and the Pacific* by Harold Courlander. Harcourt Brace and World, 1959. Copyright © 1959, 1987 by Harold Courlander. Reprinted by permission of the author.

"Those Three Wishes" from *A Taste for Quiet and Other Disquieting Tales* by Judith Gorog. Reprinted by permission of Philomel Books, text copyright © 1982 by Judith Gorog.

"Thoughts on Talkers" from *The Collected Poems of Freddy the Pig* by Walter R. Brooks. Copyright © 1953 by Walter R. Brooks. Copyright renewed 1981 by Dorothy R. Brooks. Reprinted by permission of Alfred A. Knopf, Inc.

"To the Skeleton of a Dinosaur in a Museum" by Lillian Moore. Copyright © 1987 by Lillian Moore. Reprinted by permission of Marian Reiner for the author.

"Tongue Twister" by Bernard Wiseman from *Morris and Boris: Three Stories by Bernard Wiseman.* Copyright © 1974 by Bernard Wiseman. Reprinted by permission of the author.

"Train Whistles," a brief text excerpt from Helen Roney Sattler's *Train Whistles.* Copyright © 1977, 1985 by Helen Roney Sattler. Reprinted by permission of Lothrop, Lee & Shepard, a division of William Morrow & Company, Inc.

"Watch Out!" by Bruce Coville. Copyright © 1987 by Bruce Coville. Reprinted by permission of the author.

"What Teacher Said" by J. Patrick Lewis. Copyright © 1990 by J. Patrick Lewis. Reprinted by permission of the author.

"Yellow, Warm and Friendly" by Julie Fredericksen. Reprinted by permission of the author.

"Yellowstone Grizzly Joins Cookout" from *San Diego Union*, August 28, 1990. Originally published as "Cookout Crasher Rekindles Park Issue" by Robert Reinhold. Copyright © 1990 by The New York Times Company. Reprinted by permission.

Introduction

I like ice cream—any flavor, especially one that has bits of chocolate, pralines, or nuts floating around in it. But, as much as I like ice cream, I like reading better. I need to have a book with me at all times. I suppose it looks a bit odd to carry a best-seller to the opera or a young adult novel to the tennis matches, but I don't care. I know that anyone worth talking to at those events will be wishing that they had had the nerve to bring a book, too.

Just like any addict, I want other people to become as addicted as I am. I tempt dieters into the ice cream shop and try to convert relatives, colleagues, and strangers on tour busses to avid reading.

The adversaries in my reading campaign range from television, a major culprit, to overscheduled children. Television still ranks high as a consumer of children's time. In 1988, the National Assessment of Education Progress, based in Princeton, New Jersey, conducted a survey of 13,000 students attending schools in the United States. They examined students' reading habits in grades 4, 8, and 12, attempting to find a correlation between reading instruction and reading for pleasure. It is still shocking to me that the survey discovered that, for instance, 69 percent of the fourth graders said they watched three or more hours of television daily. Even so, two-thirds of the fourth graders reported that they used the library at least once a week. Only 24 percent of the eighth graders visited the library weekly, and the twelfth graders lagged far behind with only 12 percent making a single visit to the library per week. The findings also showed that students who had easier access to books and periodicals at home and in their schools had higher reading scores than those who did not.

One does not really need a major study such as the one conducted by NAEP to see that Americans are not the voracious readers we wish we were. Nor do they put a priority on owning books. Even adults in the book business—librarians, publishers, book sellers—don't always have a home library. I always enjoy visiting the homes on those open-house tours sponsored by various charities. The houses are always beautifully decorated to the last detail, but I often come away wondering, "Where are the books?" Are the owners of the house (who never seem to be on the premises during the tours) downstairs in the basement cuddled up with a good book while we tramp through the living room gawking at the fireplace andirons?

I do my own informal reading surveys as I journey here and there. Recently, I was on an airplane with twenty-one unchaperoned young people. I walked up and down the aisle to see what they were reading. The Baby-sitters Club series and choose-your-own-adventure books were in evidence. Many children did not seem to have brought any books along. My observations may not be a real survey, but how could any adult send a child on a plane trip without a book?!

However, there is hope. Strolling through the terrace of a local hotel this weekend, I did my usual snooping, trying to see what the sunbathers were reading. The predictable summer mysteries and novels were out in abundance. One woman was reading the newspaper, but on the table in front of her lay a hardcover mystery by Scott Turow and a paperback edition of James Joyce's *Finnegans Wake*. I stopped and commented that it was quite a combination of books and she replied, "The Turow is my husband's. I've been reading this one for twenty years." I chuckled to think that she meant she'd been *trying* to read Joyce on vacation for twenty years. There used to be a cartoon that ran in *The New Yorker* at the beginning of the summer, showing a woman on the beach opening *Moby Dick*, her never-ending summer project. This woman on the hotel terrace certainly looked exactly like the cartoon-lady with her wide-brimmed sunhat and flowered blouse. But she wasn't at all like the woman in the cartoon, for she showed me her copy of *Finnegans Wake* and explained her note-taking system. Every page of the book was covered with complex marginal notes and the endpapers were filled with commentary. That woman really had been reading Joyce for twenty years. I was truly impressed, because even though I like to read better than I like to eat ice cream, I don't read Joyce for fun.

Maybe our children would grow up to enjoy reading authors like Joyce and Proust if we started them on the road to reading earlier and kept showing them the delights of reading all through their school years.

It is encouraging that more school systems are recognizing the importance of literature. The widespread endorsement of literature-based curriculums and the love affair with "whole language" programs in recent years have been a boon to those of us in the field of children's literature. There has been a dramatic increase in the number of teachers who are knowledgeable about children's books, and this translates into more children who are acquainted with and enjoy good literature.

I am worried, however, that the books we consider "good reads" are being used exclusively as training materials for teaching reading and thinking skills. We do want children to learn to read critically. We want them to be able to identify and understand new vocabulary. We also want them to be able to relate their reading to their own experiences and to articulate their responses to higher thinking-level questions. But, do we really need a study manual for a book like *Peter Rabbitt* that has been read and enjoyed by thousands of children and their parents since 1903 who never had access to such a guide?

We can use literature to teach skills, but at the same time, let us encourage children to read just for pleasure. Let's show them the wonders of literature by reading aloud, telling stories, presenting poetry, and promoting reading— without the study questions—just for the fun of it!

Jean Little says it all:

After English Class

I used to like "Stopping by Woods on a Snowy Evening."
I liked the coming darkness,
The jingle of harness bells, breaking—and adding to
    —the stillness,
The gentle drift of snow. . .

But today, the teacher told us what everything stood for.
The woods, the horse, the miles to go, the sleep—
    They all have "hidden meanings."

It's grown so complicated now that,
Next time I drive by,
I don't think I'll bother to stop.

                          Jean Little
                          Hey World, Here I Am!
                          Harper, 1986

This book is a collection of ideas to encourage adults to introduce children to the wonders of the printed word. The ideas range from simple to complex. The point is simply to offer the ideas to adults, who, in turn, will use the ones they enjoy with children.

I'm assuming the readers of this book will be similar to most of my workshop audiences: a mixed group of adults interested in children and books. You may be a library school or education student just beginning a career, or you may be a fourth-grade teacher or public librarian with twenty-four years of service behind you. Perhaps you are a parent of two voracious readers or the aunt of a preteen nephew who has yet to read his first novel just for fun. Whatever your interest in reading or browsing through this book, I hope you will find an idea or two to use with your children. Since I don't know just who each of you is, I have addressed a spectrum of readers. In some chapters, I am speaking particularly to a public library children's librarian; in others, I may seem to be talking to a classroom teacher. I hope you will adapt my ideas to your own specific situation.

This book is really a survey of literature-based promotion ideas in which you will find discussions on subjects ranging from how to reach parents effectively to some thoughts on multicultural, multinational books for children. One chapter outlines a program for teaching beginners, both children and adults, how to tell stories. Visual storytelling and presenting poetry with visual props and illustrations are also suggested, and the easy-to-reproduce graphics are included. In fact, all of the art scattered throughout the book can be reproduced and used as clip art for exhibits, bookmarks, and for storytelling. Simple drawings you can use as patterns for board figures, stick puppets, and picture poetry are also included for those of you who are not artists and as inspiration for those who prefer to draw their own visuals. Lynn Bredeson has created outline drawings that lend themselves to dressing up with your own finishing touches. Of course, if you prefer, all of the stories and poems can be presented without any visual aids. A chapter on creative writing will give you tips for using stories, newspaper articles, and poems to inspire young writers.

In many cases, the entire text of a story or poem is given to make this book a one-stop-shopping center for you, in the hope that you will be able to take this book to camp or to your aunt's house, away from your library's resources and still have everything you need to prepare and tell stories.

On the other hand, the book also has many selected bibliographies meant to send you to the library or bookstore. Use these lists as reading lists for you and for the children. There are lists to duplicate and give to administrators, parents, and children. These lists have been printed so that you may add your library or school imprint before you duplicate them. I hope to visit your town someday and see your principal or your son at the local children's bookstores or the library, list in hand, searching for some of the titles I've included.

Although I like all of the ideas in *Read for the Fun of It*, I realize that you may not want to try every project and program this week. You may want to pick and choose the suggestions that appeal to you for this year and try others next year. I think there are levels of commitment to this "books are fun" game. Not everyone reading this book will be like my former neighbor—one of those impossible people who did everything well. She could cook, bake, sew, paint, and play the piano. She was a whiz at calculus and spoke flawless French—well, you get the idea. . . . As you browse through this book, you will see projects that will take some time to complete. If you love the idea and want to use it tomorrow, you might stop everything to prepare a book program. Or, you might see an idea that would be perfect for next month and use the intervening time to work on the project.

I've identified four or five levels of project-commitment in myself and in colleagues and acquaintances. Perhaps you'll recognize your own approach in one of these levels. For an example of how this works out, consider using the reading poster on page 63 with your children.

Level One: You will duplicate the picture from the book and tack it up on the bulletin board without even trimming the edges; you'll probably use the same push-pin that was holding that important notice.

Level Two: You duplicate the picture and color it with watercolors, mount it on a colorful piece of posterboard and tack it on the bulletin board with a color-coordinated push-pin.

Level Three: You duplicate the poster, color it with poster paint, mount it on poster board, add a stand, so that you can put it on a table along with the books you want to exhibit. You reproduce the picture onto the covers of the folders that contain an extensive bibliography of your own current reading interest for distribution. You advertise a contest to encourage reading the books, and for prizes, you duplicate the poster picture onto reading certificates.

Level Four: You like the idea of reading posters. You design your own posters, reproduce them onto silk banners, and hang them in the school board meeting room. Each member of the board receives a miniature of the poster with a personalized reading list developed by you for them to carry in their wallets for easy consultation.

And then, of course, there's the Level Five person . . . me. I (and maybe you, too) find a talented student to reproduce the posters for you.

The editor of *Read for the Fun of It*, Judith O'Malley, thinks of this as the avocational cook that she is. "Oh, I see what you're saying," she exclaimed, "it's like making peanut butter cookies:

Level One: Buy a package of refrigerated dough and follow the directions on the wrapper for slicing and baking.

Level Two: Sprinkle chopped peanuts on top of the sliced refrigerated dough before baking.

Level Three: Make the cookies from scratch following the recipe on the back of the peanut butter chip package.

Level Four: Make a batch of my Absolutely the Best Crunchy Peanut Butter Cookies that it took years to perfect and that take a bit of time:

Absolutely the Best Crunchy Peanut Butter Cookies

1 cup butter
1 cup brown sugar
1 cup white sugar
1 cup super-crunchy peanut butter
2 eggs, beaten slightly
1 tblspn. milk
2 cups flour
2 tspn. baking soda
½ tspn. salt
½ tspn. sugar
1 tspn. vanilla
½ cup peanut butter chips
½ cup chopped, salted peanuts (optional)

Cream butter with both sugars and add peanut butter. Mix eggs and milk and stir into peanut butter/sugars mixture. Blend flour with salt, baking powder, and add to creamed mixture till thoroughly blended. Stir in vanilla and peanut butter chips last. Roll with moistened hands into balls and, with wet fork, score tops of balls twice, flattening them and making crosshatched lines. Real peanut fanatics can sprinkle the chopped, salted peanuts over the tops of cookies. Bake at 350 degrees for 15 to 20 minutes in center of preheated oven.

Level Five: Stop at the nearest convenience store and buy a box of peanut butter cookies."

Whatever level you see yourself in, share the cookies with your group after reading Sue Alexander's *World Famous Muriel* (Little, 1984).

If this were a book about ice cream, I'd start cheering now to introduce you to chapter one: I SCREAM. YOU SCREAM. WE ALL SCREAM FOR ICE CREAM.

Since this is a book about reading, we need a cheer for books. Start cheering while I fetch a dish of caramel turtle fudge ice cream. I'll be finishing the latest book by Jon Hassler over there, by the tree. . . .

R-E-A-D Cheer
by Lorraine Regan

R-E-A-D   R-E-A-D
You learn to read by going to school
Once you can read you're nobody's fool
R-E-A-D   R-E-A-D
If you need to know it,
A book is gonna show it.
R-E-A-D   R-E-A-D
Give me an R
Give me an E
Give me an A
Give me a D
What's that spell?
   READ
What's that spell?
   READ!
Go to the library and get a book.
Become a magician or a gourmet cook.
R-E-A-D   R-E-A-D
Now do it!
Go to it.
R-E-A-D   R-E-A-D
Additional Verses:
Reading books is really great
It helps you to communicate

Read poetry all day long
and perhaps one day you'll write a song

The poet, Shel Silverstein, is a very funny guy,
but his book, *The Giving Tree*, makes me cry.

If you want to prepare your family tree
Check out a book on gen-e-al-o-gy.

Geography, history, joke books, too,
what you read is up to you.

From plumbing to computers to aerospace,
books will help you set the pace.

PART I

Forming the Reading Habit

Getting the Whole Community Involved in Reading—For Life

Chapter 1

Read Aloud for the Fun of It

Jan Donaldson, Principal of Orting Elementary School,
in Orting, Washington, reads to kindergarteners.

Think about it. Wouldn't it be wonderful if all over the country, every day parents were reading to their children, teachers were reading aloud in their classrooms, librarians were reading aloud in their libraries? That would certainly be a good start, but I'd like to enlist the aid of others in the community to help us in the goal of a read-aloud continent.

Administrators

Administrators! These wretched individuals sitting at their desks surrounded by reports, budgets, complaints, schedules. They need a bit of
worthwhile fun. We need them to read aloud to our children. Ask your
library director, principal, superintendent, or the president of a local company to leave their offices and come to your library or classroom and read
aloud.

What a treat for an administrator to have personal contact with individual
children or a small group of children. When that lucky person gets home and
is asked, "What was your day like today, dear?" I'll bet that he or she does not
relate the conversation with the planning commission, but tells with great
delight how the children reacted to Paul Fleischman's *Rondo in C.*

Most administrators will not have even thought of reading aloud as part
of their job description. However, once approached with the idea, they may
be delighted to try it. I've been giving presentations to school administrators
around the country for the last few years, and I'll admit that, when I'm
scheduled to appear, many may shake their heads in confusion, thinking
something along the lines of "What does storytelling or poetry have to do
with me? Why isn't this talk on discipline, budgets or staff stress, if I'm
supposed to participate?" I can't say that I've converted everyone to the
importance of emphasizing books and leisure reading in the schools, but I've
been amazed at the number of "I'm-really-doing-it" letters I've received.

After all, it won't take much time out from the other daily projects, but
will be so much more satisfying than most of the "must dos" on a typical
administrator's desk. I suggest that each and every principal take a few minutes, and I stress that just a few are necessary, each school day to go into
classrooms and read aloud to a group of children. This activity has positive
value for everyone: The administrator or principal is given a real purpose for
entering each class on a regular basis. The children have a chance to see the
principal, not just in a role of authority, but as a real person in a positively
lovable role. They can also see by example that books are important to someone in a position of authority, and they will be introduced to some of the best
literature available while being entertained in a truly unforgettable way. Even
my husband, whose memories of his own childhood are vague and selective
(to the point of untruthfullness: "I was a very neat little boy"), remembers his
teacher reading aloud in his classroom in Vienna.

The following are a few hints to the reader of this book who wishes to
plan and arrange a read aloud session for administrators:

Hint #1—Since you are probably not the administrator I'm trying to reach with the following information but are more likely to be the librarian, teacher, media specialist, church worker, or parent, you can take this idea to your administrator, along with some books. Don't leave her office until you've convinced her to make an initial visit to a classroom to read aloud. You know your school better than I do; perhaps it would be wise to broach this idea in a staff meeting first, since the principal's visits would affect scheduling of class time. Stress that the mechanics of the project are very simple. The administrator needs only access to the books and a calendar in which to write down a schedule for the class visits. Remind everyone frequently that their office and class time will be disrupted for only a few (say, twelve to fifteen) minutes. Urge your administrator to allow her personality to dictate the style of presentation. A more reserved or traditional individual may want to sit on a chair or just stand in the front of the room, while a more casual person might suggest a circle of desks be formed for the reading. The important point is that everyone can see the book, especially if there are pictures to share.

Hint #2: You may have to do some cajoling (or lecturing) to promote the picture book as a splendid read-aloud choice for classes above the primary grades. Some adults and children do not realize that all books that look like picture books are not necessarily for preschoolers and that some books that are written for young children still have merit for older students.

Hint #3: Don't ignore the potential for read alouds with administrators if you are not in a classroom or school-library situation. You can adapt this idea to a public library by holding a daily read-aloud session in the adult section. Ask the library director to read an occasional poem or picture book for the children in a designated reading corner.

Once your administrator has agreed that it may be a good idea for him to visit the library with a book, you may want to help him choose a book appropriate to read aloud. You will find that many administrators are so busy with all the paperwork that they may not have kept up with the current riches of children's literature. In fact, you may have a principal or director who doesn't read for pleasure at all. This is not as big a sin as it might seem to those of you who live and breathe children's books. It's never too late to be introduced to the pleasures of books. Reading aloud might be the very thing a busy superindendant needs to get interested in reading himself. The list in this chapter will help you and your administrator find titles that might be appealing to a particular group. Obviously, you will not be limited to these books, but it might be a place to start.

Make it easy. Bring a few books from the children's room to the administrator's office so she can choose a book without taking extra time this first time to find a book. Give a little book talk about each title if the books are unfamiliar. Schedule a time for the Read Aloud. As soon as the administrator has read aloud, bring your calendar to her office and schedule the next time.

Grandparents, Retirees

Our nation's workers are retiring earlier. Many of these people are eagerly looking for ways to be useful and enjoy themselves at the same time. They can be a virtual army of volunteers sharing books aloud with children. Los Angeles Public Library in California, and the Dauphin County Library in Pennsylvania are two of the systems taking advantage of this source of people-power. It is important to offer a training program before your honorary grandparents venture into a read-aloud program. You'll find that this idea works best if the volunteers each work with one or two children. You will need someone to take the responsibility of organizing this program, and you may often find that one of the people who signed up first will be happy to organize training and scheduling.

Los Angeles Public Library "Grandparents and Books" Program

Maureen Wade, the current director of the Grandparents and Books program in Los Angeles, a project that was developed and set in motion by Virginia Walter, offers a three part training session to her one-hundred-plus volunteers, who read aloud in Chinese, Japanese, Korean, and Spanish, as well as English. The grandparents learn the techniques of reading aloud, how to listen to children's responses, and also how to present literature using the flannel board and puppets. In addition to such specific training, you will probably want to show your volunteers the varieties of books available to share aloud. The Los Angeles project offers a training manual which you can obtain by mail from: *Grandparents and Books: Trainer's Manual*, Los Angeles Public Library, 630 W. 5th St., Los Angeles, California, 90071.

Children

Children should be encouraged to read aloud to other children. We usually think of older children reading to younger children, but of course anyone who can read, or would like to should be allowed to participate in a read-aloud program. The Share-Aloud team program described in this chapter may appeal to you and your children's group as an ongoing activity.

Community Workers

In school, children learn about the civic roles of the local government, firemen, the police force, and the local merchants. Invite some or all of these people to participate in a read-aloud program at your school or public library.

Lorene Olson of Sherwood, Oregon, uses this idea to celebrate Children's Week. It could be an annual tradition in your institution, too. Approach as many community leaders as possible: the chief of police, the fire chief, the mayor, the postmistress, the president of the Chamber of Commerce or of the Lions Club, and ask them to come to your library or school, sit in a comfortable rocking chair and read aloud a favorite short story, picture book, or selection from a novel. Ideally, this should be a day-long, marathon Read-in. When you run out of such identifiable civic leaders, solicit the participation of patrons of the library. The best readers in all the grades of your school, the teachers, selected parents (those you know are interested, willing, and available during the most convenient hours for such an event), shopkeepers, doctors, dentists, and lawyers in the area, as well as office staff, the school nurse, the custodian, and the maintanence staff might all be delighted to be part of a read-aloud project. Recruit them.

Time

When will you find the time to schedule all these eager readers? Since reading is a leisure-time activity, think in terms of scheduling read-aloud sessions when your children are engaged in other extra-curricular activities. There is time before school, after school, the lunch period. There may be time in the evening. Think about where children tend to gather in your community. Why not schedule a read aloud session before the championship soccer game?

What to Share Aloud

Many libraries have created their own read-aloud lists. Three popular books that have annotated booklists featuring titles for families to read aloud are: *For Reading Out Loud,* by Mary Margaret Kimmel and Elizabeth Segal (Delacorte, 1988), *Read Aloud Handbook* by Jim Trelease (Penguin, 1985), and *Books Kids Will Sit Still For: The Complete Read-Aloud Guide* by Judy Freeman (Bowker, 1990). This chapter also includes a list aimed at the busy person who would like to participate in a read-aloud program, but who doesn't have a lot of time to devote to finding the right book or to reading. And don't forget that sharing a poem, passage, or book is not reserved for children's groups. Read something tonight to your friend, spouse, next door neighbor, or with the whole family gathered together.

Some Read-Aloud Program Ideas

Read-Aloud Assembly—I've been invited to participate in some of these assemblies in various locations. Children are invariably delighted to see authors and other people in positions of authority reading aloud from their own books or their favorite books. Invite two or three prominent townsfolk to read their favorite picture books or selections from longer books in an auditorium setting. Don't expect that all guests will be accomplished readers, though you can also include a local storyteller, actor, or a parent you know can perform well as a final reader. The point is simply to help the children associate reading with the adults they respect.

Daily Readings—Each morning, as you start your school day, assign a child to read a brief passage from a favorite book. This establishes the pattern of regular reading times, and arouses the interest of students who may be "shopping" for their next book to read. You can also help with the book selections and vary the reading so that one week your class is hearing poetry, the next week might be picture books, the following one jokes and riddles, or books on a specific theme or topic. It doesn't take a lot of time from your schedule, and in fact, if you start out the day with something fun, you can be sure that everyone will arrive on time and with a positive attitude.

Lunch-Hour Read Aloud—Schedule time to read a chapter a day from a book that appeals to a large age range. Advertise the book in advance, so that the children will be anticipating the first day of reading. Asking for book suggestions or giving mini-booktalks over the loud speaker, on a bulletin board or in the class and school newspapers are good ways to find popular books and build excitement. Be sure that readers are familiar with the chapter to be read that day, in order to avoid stumbles over words, repeats, or omissions of sections of the book. If the group is fairly small, show any pictures while reading the text. For a larger audience, those who are interested in seeing the illustrations can stay after the reading.

Shopping Mall Read Aloud—This is another opportunity to involve the whole community in a read-aloud program. Set up a microphone and speaker in a booth in a shopping mall or at a school fair. Use signs and announcements to advertise that this is the chance for anyone who wishes to perform in front of a group to do so. Choose short passages of one or two minutes in length from books or periodicals that would interest a broad spectrum of the public and permit anyone who would like to do so to read to passersby. This suggestion is easily adaptable to school, library, or community fairs, carnivals, and other fund-raisers, and may get an even more enthusiastic response when the prospective readers know at least some members of their audience.

Volunteer Dial-a-Read Aloud—Hearing good books read can still be an option for older members of the community who may not be able to visit the library frequently, for shut-ins, or those families who's like to include others in their family book sharing sessions. This program can operate much like cooperative babysitting groups, meals on wheels, or dial-a-ride services. Armed with books, volunteers can be available for community service to those who'd like human and literary companionship.

Reading Aloud Book List for Administrators and Other Busy Persons

Reading aloud is by far the most popular way to introduce children to children's literature. It takes a minimum amount of preparation and can be offered once or many times in a day. You can read aloud for five minutes at a time or for an hour.

Here are a few things to keep in mind before you begin:

1. The selection of the story, book, or poem that you will read is the most important consideration. You don't want your students to halt their work to listen to something that isn't worthwhile or that won't excite them about reading. Your school or public librarian should be able to help you to find the perfect book. Some booksellers, particularly those that are children's specialty store will be able to offer suggestions. Start with this list. Bring it with you to the library so you can find books quickly and spend your time reading-aloud and not searching for the book to read.

Some states, California for example, have found it useful to publish a list of books by grade level that you might find helpful in exploring a wider selection of titles.

2. Try not to limit your reading aloud to any one genre. Explore short stories, picture books, novels, poetry, and non-fiction.

3. PREPARE! Read the selection that you have chosen *before* you present it to your group. Find out how to pronounce any difficult words. Practice on your family, friends and pets.

4. When reading to the group, don't bury yourself in the book. Make sure that you pause after several sentences and make eye contact with your audience.

5. Decide in advance when you will show the pictures. You can choose to show the pictures before, during, or after the reading—or not at all if you don't think the art is worthy of showing. When presenting a picture book, the art is usually shared during the reading, since the graphics are an integral part of the book.

6. Give the author and the title of the selection before and after the reading. You want your children to remember *who* wrote the book so that they can find it or other writings by the author in the library.

7. If possible, leave the book in the classroom, when you finish, so that children can re-read the book and examine the illustrations more closely.

8. Occasionally, you will find that you have chosen the wrong title for a particular group. It may be too difficult or the subject matter may not appeal to those children. Don't feel obligated to continue reading something that you or your group are not enjoying. Just say, "Let's try this one another time." Make the book available for those who would like to finish the story on their own.

9. Once you've introduced a book, feel free to read the whole book or part of it, again and again. If a book is worth reading once it should be worth reading again.

10. *Enjoy!* . . . and bring in a new title to read tomorrow . . . or, perhaps, later today, please.

The list that follows is for anyone who would like a few title suggestions when starting a daily read-aloud program. It was created with the school or library administrator in mind, someone whose busy schedule and interests might keep him or her from looking for the perfect read-aloud choice. The books on this list are put into categories by grade level. As anyone who works with children knows well, there is really no such thing as a "Third Grade Book," but it does make it easier for someone who is not at all familiar with the books to make a choice if there is some indication of reading or grade level. This particular list features selections that are short (to fit into a busy time schedule) and they are books or stories that may not be familiar even to a parent or teacher who tries to keep up with children's books. For a more classic list, with books such as *Charlotte's Web* or *Winnie the Pooh*, please refer to the paperback lists (page 82–91). The books on this list are here just so that you—or the person that you give it to—will not have to spend extensive periods of time in the search for the illusive Best Book.

Read-Aloud Book List for Administrators and Other Interested Adults

A fantastic way of sharing yourself with your students and staff is to take five or ten minutes regularly and read a book aloud. As a rough rule of thumb only, this list of children's books is divided into groupings by classes. Most of the selections are picture books (a 32-page format is standard for these); for other types of books, the total number of pages in the books are given. It takes approximately two and a half minutes to read a full page of text at an enjoyable speed—a lot shorter for the average picture book text. So, you can plan how to estimate your time and divide longer books you wish to read into manageable sections.

Don't attempt to make the read-aloud session into a formal lesson. Learning is implicit in the act of reading. The children will be improving their reading skills, developing their imaginations, and discovering that books can teach, amuse, frighten, and amaze. Themes of self-reliance, loneliness, friendship, the value of humor and creativity, individuality, resourcefulness, independence, self-esteem, respect, and bravery abound throughout the titles on this list.

Whether by a set schedule or as a surprise treat, take time to visit each classroom often to share a book.

Pre-K–1st Grade

Calmerson, Stephanie. *What Am I?* Art by Karen Gundersheimer. Harper, 1989.
    Easy-to-Read riddles.

Carlstrom, Nancy White. *Jesse Bear, What Will You Wear?* Art by Bruce Degen. Macmillan, 1986.
    Rhythmic text featuring a bear and his parents.

Degen, Bruce. *Jamberry.* Art by author. Harper, 1983.
    Nonsense rhyme—just for fun.

Field, Rachel. *General Store.* Art by Nancy Winslow Parker. Greenwillow, 1988.
    Big bold drawings illustrate the poem by Rachel Field, which was first published in 1926.

Hale, Sarah Josepha. *Mary Had a Little Lamb.* Photos by Bruce McMillan. Scholastic, 1990.
    The traditional poem is accompanied here by perfect color photographs.

Hayes, Sarah. *This Is a Bear.* Art by Helen Craig. Lippincott, 1986.
    A bear is lost and found. Rhythmic text.

Kudrna, C. Imbior. *To Bathe A Boa.* Carolrhoda, 1986.
    Big pictures to share shows a child battling a boa into a tub.

Lillebard, Dee. *Sitting in My Box.* Art by Jon Agee. Dutton, 1989.
    A little boy shares a box with a group of wild animals.

Miller, Margaret. *Who Uses This?* Photos by author. Greenwillow, 1990.
    Tools are shown being used by adults and children.

Paterson, Bettina. *My First Wild Animals.* Art by author. Harper, 1989.
    Each page has a single paper collage animal to identify.

Scott, Ann Herbert. *One Good Horse: A Cowpuncher's Counting Book.* Art by Lynn Sweat. Greenwillow, 1990.
    A father and son ride from one to 100 checking on the cattle. Quail, fence posts, and crows are among those counted.

Serfozo, Mary. *Who Said Red?* Art by Keiko Narashashi. McElderry, 1988.
    Color poem with lots of colors in watercolor wash featuring red. Another book of this type to look for is Kathy Stinson's *Red Is Best* (Annick, 1982).

2nd–3rd Grade

Bauer, Caroline Feller. *Midnight Snowman*. Art by Catherine Stock. Atheneum, 1987.
A multi-cultural neighborhood builds a snowman.

Bojunga-Nunes, Lygia. *The Companions*. Art by Larry Wilkes. Farrar, 1989.
Three eposodic chapters tell the tory of a bear, a rabbit, and a dog—one lost and two runaways (58 pages).

Bunting, Eve. *The Wednesday Surprise*. Art by Donald Carrick. Clarion, 1989.
Anna teaches her grandmother to read.

Cameron, Ann. "The Box." In *More Stories Julian Tells*. Art by Ann Strugrell. Knopf, 1986.
The surprise in the box is worth the worry. Other wonderful selections are in *The Stories Julian Tells* (Pantheon, 1981).

Edwards, Patricia Kier. *Chester and Uncle Willoughby*. Art by Diane Allison. Little, 1987.
Four short, friendly stories accompanied by warm watercolors. Try "Nothing" as a first selection.

I Know an Old Lady Who Swallowed a Fly. Art by Glen Rounds. Holdiay, 1990.
Sing or read this familiar song while showing the laugh-out-loud drawings.

Latimer, Jim. *Going the Moose Way Home*. Art by Donald Carrick. Scribners, 1988.
Short stories about a friendly and charming moose.

McKissack, Patricia. *Flossie and the Fox*. Art by Rachel Isadora. Dial, 1987.
Flossie outwits a fox. Practice the dialect and be sure to share the pictures.

Pearce, Phillippa. "Lion at School." In *Lion at School and Other Stories*. Art by Caroline Sharpe. Greenwillow, 1985.
A bully is awed by a visit of a lion to school.

Samuels, Vyanne. *Carry Go Bring Come*. Art by Jennifer Northway. Four Winds, 1988.
Leon is the main "fetch and carrier" on the morning of his sister's wedding. Fast-paced fun.

Schwartz, Henry. *How I Captured a Dinosaur*. Art by Amy Schwartz. Orchard, 1989.
Liz captures a dinosaur and brings him back to Los Angeles.

Simon, Seymour. *New Questions and Answers about Dinosaurs*. Art by Jennifer Dewey. Morrow, 1990.
"How smart were dinosaurs?" "Which dinosaur had the most teeth?" are two of the questions, with one-page answers for each. Share one question at a time or the whole book.

Smith, William Jay. *Ho for a Hat!* Art by Lynn Munsinger. Little, 1989.
A joyous rhyme all about hats.

Snow, Alan. *The Monster Book of ABC Sounds.* Art by the author. Dial, 1991.
> Oversized pages, a short poem, and a chance to make silly sounds makes this lots of fun to present.

Stevenson, James. *National Worm Day.* Art by the author. Greenwillow, 1990.
> Three short stories with lots of conversation. The featured players are a worm, a rhinoceros, and a snail, who are variously big, little, strong, brave.

Tafuri, Nancy. *Junglewalk.* Art by author. Greenwillow, 1988.
> This is a wordless picture book, but don't worry—you won't need text for this look at jungle animals in double spreads.

4th–5th Grades

Brittain, Bill. *Devil's Donkey.* Art by Andrew Glass. Harper, 1981.
> Daniel didn't believe that Old Magda would turn him into a donkey. With eight chapters (120 pages), this is two weeks of reading, but worth it.

Calmenson, Stephanie. *The Principal's New Clothes.* Art by Denis Brunhees. Scholastic, 1989.
> An updated version of "The Emperor's New Clothes" in a school setting.

Day, Alexandra. *Frank and Ernest.* Art by author. Scholastic, 1988.
> A bear and an elephant run a diner for three days and learn such diner language as "Eve with a lid and moo juice." You'll also enjoy these characters in *Frank and Ernest Play Ball* (Scholastic, 1990.)

Dutton, Cheryl. *Not in Here, Dad!* Art by Wendy Smith. Barrons, 1989.
> An anti-smoking story, but with a bit of humor.

Haswell, Peter. *Pog.* Art by author. Orchard, 1989.
> These are fully-illustrated story-jokes in a picture-book format. Share one or all.

Hurwitz, Johanna. "Ali Baba and the Mystery of the Missing Circus Tickets." In *Hurray for Ali Baba Bernstein.* Art by Gail Owens. Morrow, 1989.
> In this story, one of six in this collection featuring a nine-year old, a mix-up of raincoats results in lost tickets. More tales of Ali Baba can be found in *The Adventures of Ali Baba Bernstein* (Morrow, 1985).

Jukes, Mavis. *Like Jake and Me.* Art by Lloyd Bloom. Knopf, 1984.
> Alex's "real cowboy" stepfather is afraid of spiders.

Kinsey-Warnock, Natalie. *The Canada Geese Quilt.* Art by Leslie W. Bowman. Cobblehill/Dutton, 1989.
> A short novel of, six chapters (60 pages), this deals with a young girl's coming to grips with a new baby in the family and a grandmother's failing health.

Martin, Rafe, *Will's Mammoth.* Art by Stephen Gammel. Putnam, 1989.
> Will doesn't believe his parents who tell him mammoths don't exist. Full color, wordless art, shows Will cavorting with mammoths.

Page, Michael. *The Great Bullocky Race.* Art by Robert Ingpen. Dodd, 1988.
 Two Australian bullock teams race to the port.

Park, Ruth. "When the Wind Changed." In *Windy Day,* ed. by Caroline Bauer. Lippincott, 1988.
 Josh is a whiz at making scary faces.

Ringgold, Faith. *Tar Beach.* Art by the author. Crown, 1991.
 In this story, based on a quilt made by the author, a young girl flies and dreams over her Harlem home.

Yorinks, Arthur. *Company's Coming.* Art by David Small. Crown, 1988.
 Moe and Shirley invite visitors from outer space for dinner.

Young, Ed. *Lon Po Po: A Red Riding Hood Story from China.* Art by the author. Philomel, 1989.
 Three brave children outwit a wolf in this award-winning version of Little Red Riding Hood.

6th Grade

Adoff, Arnold. *Chocolate Dreams.* Art by Turi MacCombie. Lothrop, 1989.
 Poems about chocolate.

Arnold, Caroline. *The Terrible Hodag.* Art by Lambert Davis. Harcourt, 1989.
 Tall-tale lumberjack story.

Ballard, Robert D. *Exploring the Titanic.* Scholastic, 1988.
 Photos and paintings chronicle the history of the famous ship.

Cowcher, Helen. *Antarctica.* Art by author. Farrar, 1990.
 A subtle plea for saving Antartica from human intrusion, with glorious graphics.

Foreman, Michael. *War Boy.* Art by author. Arcade/Little, 1990.
 Vignettes of a boy's childhood during World War II. Browse, read and reminisce about your own childhood. Also of interest on this theme is Deborah Kogan Ray's *My Daddy Was a Soldier: A World War II Story* with art by the author (Holiday, 1990)

Freedman, Russell. *Buffalo Hunt.* Holiday, 1988.
 Nonfiction at its best. Describes the history of American buffalo hunting and includes fine art illustrations. There are five chapters (one to read each weekday).

Gorog, Judith. "Oh, Louis!!!" In *In a Messy, Messy Room and Other Strange Stories.* Art by Kimberly Bolkan Root. Philomel, 1990.
 Louis worries that his relatives won't recognize him at the end of a train trip. This is one of five share-aloud stories in this volume.

Kimmel, Eric. *Charlie Drives the Stage.* Art by Glen Rounds. Holiday, 1989.
 Charlie outruns an avalanche, Indians, and an ambush to get Senator McCorkle to Washington on time.

Lester, Julius. *How Many Spots Does a Leopard Have?* Art by David Shannon. Scholastic, 1989.
African and Jewish myths, such as, "The Monster Who Swallowed Everything."

_____. *More Tales of Uncle Remus: Further Adventures of Brer Rabbit, His Friends, Enemies and Others.* Art by Jerry Pinkney. Dial, 1988.
Brer Rabbit is retold in style in these tales and in those in *Tales of Uncle Remus: The Adventures of Brer Rabbit* (Dial, 1987). There is some dialect.

Little, Jean. *Hey World, Here I Am!* Art by Sue Truesdell. Harper, 1989.
Thoughts, memories, and poems are included. Try "About Old People" and "About Notebooks".

Lyon, George Ella. *Come a Tide.* Art by Stephen Gammell. Orchard, 1990.
A rollicking account of a hometown flood.

Mahy, Margaret. *Nonstop Nonsense.* Art by Quentin Blake. McElderry, 1977.
Short, wacky stories. Try "The Ghost Who Came Out of the Book."

Moss, Jeff. *The Butterfly Jar.* Bantam, 1989.
Humorous and poignant poems begging to be shared.

Sanders, Scott Russell. *Aurora Means Dawn.* Art by Jill Kastner. Bradbury, 1989.
The Sheldens conquer the wilderness in a beautifully illustrated pioneer story.

Scheffler, Ursel. *Stop Your Crowing, Kasimir!* Art by Silke Brix-Henker. Carolrhoda, 1988.
The neighbors win a case against a noisy rooster but "lose the war".

Schroeder, Alan. *Ragtime Tumpie.* Art by Bernie Fuchs. Little, 1989.
The story of Josephine Baker as a child in a gloriously illustrated picture book.

Schwartz, David M. *How Much Is a Million?* Art by Steven Kellogg. Lothrop, 1985.
Graphically depicts million and billions. For a look at higher finance in picture-book style, try *If You Made a Million* by the same author (Lothrop, 1989).

7–8 Grade

Cummings, Betty Sue. *Turtle.* Art by Susan Dodge. Atheneum, 1981.
This short (42 page) novel tells of an old woman's friendship with a turtle she bought years ago for 39 cents.

DeFelice, Cynthia C. *The Dancing Skeleton.* Art by Robert Andrew Parker. Macmillan, 1989.
Aaron walks out of his grave and sits in his favorite rocking chair until he is only bones. It is bizarre, but the junior high folks will love it.

Fisher, Leonard. *The ABC Exhibit.* Art by the author. Macmillan, 1991.
An alphabet book for junior high? This is a series of lovely paintings, one for each letter, to share a group.

Gardiner, John Reynolds. *Stone Fox*. Art by Marcia Sewall. Harper, 1980.
An extraordinary tale of grit and courage. Appeals to boys, girls, and adults. Its 81 pages could be split in three parts.

Gorog, Judith. "Dr. Egger's Favorite Dog." In *No Swimming in Dark Pond*. Philomel, 1987.
A dog saves a child in this ghost story.

Hutton, Warwick. *Theseus and the Minotaur*. Art by author. McElderry, 1989.
Theseus kills a monster, in picture-book format.

Jennings, Paul. "There Is No Such Thing." In *Unbelievable! More Surprising Stories*. Penguin, 1986.
On his grandad's behalf, Chris sets off to prove that there really is a dragon in Donovan's Drain.

Lewin, Ted. *Tiger Trek*. Art by author. Macmillan, 1990.
Watercolors illustrate a tale about tigers in an Indian jungle.

Murphy, Jim. *The Last Dinosaur*. Art by author. Scholastic, 1988.
Poignant fictionalized speculation. Full page art. Another book of interest by this author is *The Call of the Wolves* (Scholastic, 1989).

Porte, Barbara Ann. *Jesse's Ghost*. Greenwillow, 1983.
Collection of off-beat stories short enough to learn to tell, if you wish, rather than read aloud.

Rogow, Zack. *Oranges*. Art by Mary Szilagyi. Orchard, 1988.
Oranges from field to you via many nationalities.

Sanfield, Steve. *The Adventures of High John the Conqueror*. Art by John Ward. Orchard, 1989.
Short stories feature a black folkhero who often outwits Old Master. Try "Tops and Bottoms," "In a Box," and "John Wins a Contest" for some good read-aloud sessions.

Scieszka, Jon. *The True Story of the Three Little Pigs*. Art by Lane Smith. Viking, 1989.
Even the toughest middle schooler will think this is funny. The wolf tells his side of the classic story.

Seligson, Susan. *Amos: The Story of an Old Dog and His Couch*. Art by Howie Schneider. Little, 1987.
Hilariously funny portrait of an old dog (with cartoon art at it best) who travels in a couch through town.

Soto, Gary. *Baseball in April and Other Stories*. Harcourt, 1990.
Eleven short stories featuring Mexican-Americans. Try "The Marble Champ" and "Seventh Grade".

Steptoe, John. *Mufaro's Beautiful Daughters*. Art by author. Lothrop, 1987.
Contemporary fable about the trap of pride.

Thayer, Ernest Lawrence. *Casey at the Bat: A Ballad of the Republic, Sung in the Year 1888*. Art by Patricia Polacco. Putnam, 1988.
The 100-year-old poem is updated with splashy art.

Tsuchiya, Yukio. *Faithful Elephants*. Art by Ted Lewin. Houghton, 1988.
> A true account of the elephants in the Tokyo Zoo during World War II. A painful account but worth sharing for its message about the costs of war.

Wisniewski, David. *The Warrior and the Wise Man*. Art by author. Lothrop, 1989.
> A contest between "blind force" and reasoned action depicted in a picture-book format with dramatic paper cuttings.

All Ages

These are books you can present to a mixed-age group or carry from one class to another.

Durell, Ann, ed. *The Diane Goode Book of American Folk Tales and Songs*. Dutton, 1989.
> Tales from different ethnic origins. All are good to share aloud.

Gray, Nigel. *A Country Far Away*. Art by Philippe Dupasquier. Orchard, 1989.
> A boy in an African village and a boy in a western town share the same text, but with different pictures.

Martin, Bill Jr. and John Archambault. *Listen to the Rain*. Art by James Endicott. Holt, 1988.
> Sophisticated words and art with a memorable cadence.

McMillan, Bruce. *One Sun: A Book of Terse Verse*. Photos by author. Holiday, 1990.
> Excellent photographs illustrate two line poems.

Rosen, Michael. *We're Going on a Bear Hunt*. Art by Helen Oxenbury. McElderry, 1989.
> Large format makes it easy to share this storyteller's game.

Shaw, Nancy. *Sheep in a Jeep*. Art by Margot Apple. Houghton, 1986.
> Exuberant rhyming text accompanied by delightful art.

Novels to Share

Avi. *Romeo and Juliet—Together (and Alive!) at Last*. Orchard, 1987.
> Laugh aloud with a seventh grade class putting on Shakespeare. Seventh graders and older will enjoy this.

Bauer, Marion Done. *On My Honor*. Clarion, 1986.
> The question of responsibility is explored when one boy drowns. For fourth grade and above, this one is worth sharing (90 pages).

Dahl, Roald. *Matilda*. Art by Quentin Blake. Viking, 1988.
> Literate Matilda and her friends foil some dreadful adults at home and at school. This is a good choice for fifth grade and above.

Taylor, William. *Agnes the Sheep.* Scholastic, 1990.
A hilarious romp with an old woman and a sheep with a mind of her own.

Staff

Ahlberg, Janet and Allan. "Life Savings." In *The Clothes Horse.* Viking, 1987.
A woman saves bits and pieces of her life to spend in her old age.

Fleischman, Paul. *Rondo in C.* Art by Janet Wentworth. Harper, 1988.
Each person in the audience thinks of something different as a young girl plays Beethoven. An illustrated poem.

Fox, Mem. *Wilfred Gordon McDonald Partridge.* Art by Julie Vivas. Kane/Miller, 1985.
Explores memories with some older folks and a small boy.

Glenn, Mel. *Back to Class.* Photos by Michael J. Bernstein. Clarion. 1988.
Poetry featuring the thoughts of students and school staff. Right on!

Mosley, Francis. *The Dinosaur Eggs.* Art by author. Barrons, 1988.
Dinosaur children grow up to take care of their parents.

Adults

Grossman, Bill. *The Guy Who Was Five Minutes Late.* Art by Judy Glasser. Harper, 1990.
The guy is always late and he finds a princess who is always late, too. "They think that we're late, when really it's they who are early."

Heide, Florence Parry. *The Problem with Pulcifer.* Art by Judy Glasser. Lippincott, 1982.
And the problem is: Pulcifer likes to read instead of watching television. Horrors! This is 50 pages, with 25 pages of text.

_____. *Tales for the Perfect Child.* Lothrop, 1985.
Seven short stories about naughty children who outwit their parents.

Children Reading to Children

There's no doubt that some of my observations of the world, often made at 30,000 feet above the ground while on airplanes headed to various destinations, may be less than representative of the "real world." However, I am happy to report that during a recent trip from San Diego to Chicago, I overheard a nine-year old named Neil reading to his older sister. As professionals in libraries and schools, it just takes a bit of organization on your part to make this scene of children sharing books with other children a daily occurrence. Encouraging children to read younger children, to those in their own class, to older students and friends, and even to adults can be a useful way to introduce young people to good juvenile literature and to demonstrate that peers can be positive role models.

There are many ways to organize a student exchange reading group, but start where you work. In a school, you might want to select a particular class as your pool of "designated readers." In this case, the idea is for an older student to read to children at least one grade younger. Children can be guided in their book selections and monitored to be sure that they can read the books they choose with confidence and understanding. Teachers of younger grades can be alerted that readers are ready to come into their classes for read-aloud sessions, but it is not necessary for children to reach an entire class at once. In fact, they may be more comfortable reading in small groups, say two or three children at a time.

In a public library, you might find it more efficient to start with an existing book club or enlist interested volunteers from among your faithful young patrons.

In either school or library setting, you might want to set up a more formal Share-Aloud Team. In this case, interested readers would apply for a position on the team by filling out a Share-Aloud job application and being interviewed. If accepted, the child would be given a schedule of read-aloud times for practice and presentation.

A training session is important, as it can demonstrate such skills as

SHARE ALOUD

Application form

NAME: _____

Class: _____ Teacher: _____

I would enjoy reading aloud because:

_____

_____

The last book I read was:

_____

Requirements:

1. Attend orientation session and practice reading aloud with expression
   to the Reader's Group

2. Interview

Fill out brief application form

Permission from teacher to participate in Read Aloud

Report to: The Librarian

Compensation: Satisfaction that you entertained others

A free book at the end of the program

Position: Read aloud to children

Hours: Before school, during
                                  1st period on Wednesdays

Where: Latchkey room, first grade

Requirements: Choose a book in the library.
                     Practice reading aloud at home.

reading aloud with good, but natural expression, enunciating clearly, and showing pictures effectively. Since, in many cases, children will be reading to one other child, it can be suggested that the book be laid between them on a table, so that the reader and listener can both see and enjoy the art and the text. For larger groups, you can start with instructions to read the text to the group first, then share the pictures. As your readers gain experience in reading aloud, some of them might want to experiment with displaying artwork while reading.

The more seriously the children approach their jobs as Share-Aloud readers, the more successful the project will be. Emphasize that "practice makes perfect," and work on teaching your group to read expressively, without the "singsong" manner that many children adopt as soon as they are asked to recite. Let all of the members of a team help identify the good points in each presentation, as constructive critical response and peer approval will help to polish the team's efforts.

Selecting the books to be read aloud is extremely important, and when time allows, the initial orientation meetings of the Share Aloud Team can include a book talk approach to some of the recommended choices as a way of introducing children to some of the best of children's literature. When this isn't feasible, create a pre-selected collection or list from which the members of the team can choose their books.

Be sure to reward your readers for a job well done. A certificate might be the perfect prize; if funds are available for extra books, give keepsake copies of their first read-aloud choices to those members of the team who persevere. On the previous and following pages you'll find a sample Share-Aloud Team kit, including an application form for prospective members, reminders to teachers, a Share-Aloud Team badge to make and a certificate of participation. I've also provided two Share-Aloud book lists to start your team out.

Dear Teacher:

Our trained Read Aloud students are ready with outstanding picture books to read to two or three students at a time. Please let us know if you would like to be part of this program.

Share Aloud Team.

Dear Teacher:

This is to remind you that a member of the Share Aloud Team will be visiting your class today.

We are looking forward to reading to your students.

Share Aloud Team

Two Share-Aloud Book Lists for Children

Children will enjoy browsing through the library for the perfect book to present to other children. However, it can be a bit overwhelming when picking that first book to have such a wealth of choices. They just might find book lists as useful as you do. The first of the two lists here, Short and Wonderful Picture Books to Share with a Friend, features books with brief text and great pictures to explore. The annotations are directed to the young readers (micro-mini booktalks), but the bibliographic form is similar to the other book lists in this book. This is an excellent opportunity to show your students how to use a bibliography. The library may not have all of these titles, making this a chance to explain that there are many more books published than the library can possibly buy. You can demonstrate that an efficient way to use the list is to first look in the catalog to see if the library owns a particular book. If you are the librarian you might want to check those titles that your library owns or can borrow through an interlibrary loan.

Some of your young readers might want to encourage their audiences to help tell the story when the book uses sounds or repetitive phrases. The books with such participation possibilities are starred and the annotations often suggest how the listeners can take part.

The second booklist, Picture Books to Think About, is directed to older children who may want to read aloud to each other. These books have texts and pictures that are challenging and fun.

Short and Wonderful Picture Books to Share with a Friend

*Ahlberg, Janet, and Allan Ahlberg. *Peek-a-Boo!* Art by authors. Viking, 1981.
  Look through the peek hole and tell us what you see.

*Allen, Pamela. *Who Sank the Boat?* Art by author. Coward, 1982.
  Which animal sank the boat?

Anderson, Peggy Perry. *Time for Bed, the Babysitter Said.* Art by author. Houghton, 1987.
  Joe, a frog, won't go to bed.

*Baer, Gene. *Thump, Thump, Rat-a-Tat-Tat.* Art by Lois Ehlert. Harper, 1989.
  Rat-a-tat-tat. Sing along with a marching band.

*Benjamin, Alan. *Rat-a-Tat, Pitter Pat.* Photos by Margaret Miller. Crowell, 1987.
  Ding dong, ping pong; a book of sounds to make and photographs to share.

*Brandenberg, Franz. *Cock-a-Doodle-Doo.* Art by Aliki. Greenwillow, 1986.
  Woof! Woof! Gobble gobble! Animal sounds to imitate as the day begins.

*Brooke, L. Leslie. *Johnny Crow's New Garden.* Art by author. Warne, 1986.
  This book was first published in 1935. Read it and find out why it's still popular.

Burningham, John. *Wobble Pop.* Art by author. Viking, 1984.
  Share this with one friend. Repeat the words together.

*Carlstrom, Nancy White. *Better Not Get Wet, Jesse Bear.* Art by Bruce Degen. Macmillan, 1988.
  Jesse can't wait to get wet.

*Causley, Charles. *"Quack!" Said the Billy Goat.* Art by Barbara Firth. Lippincott, 1986.
  Hens oink. Goats quack. What is wrong in the barnyard?

Daugherty, James. *Andy and the Lion.* Art by author. Viking, 1938.
  Would you help a lion in trouble?

*Deming, A. G. *Who Is Tapping at My Window?* Art by Monica Wellington. Dutton, 1988.
  It's not I, but who is it?

Ehlert, Lois. *Color Zoo.* Art by author. Lippincott, 1989.
  Bright and bold, these animals are seen through cut out shapes.

Ernst, Lisa Campbell. *Up to Ten and Down Again.* Art by author. Lothrop, 1986.
  Count up and down while on a picnic.

Gerstein, Mordicai. *William, Where Are You?* Art by author. Crown, 1985.
  Lift the flap and look for William. Just big enough to share with one friend.

Hale, Sarah Josepha. *Mary Had a Little Lamb.* Photos by Bruce McMillan. Scholastic, 1990.
  You already know this nursery rhyme. Now, meet a real lamb and . . . Mary.

Home Before Midnight: A Traditional Tale. Art by Bobby Lewis. Lothrop, 1984.
  Help Nellie Bones get home.

Hill, Eric. *Spot's Birthday Party.* Art by author. Putnam, 1982.
  Play hide-and-seek with the birthday dog.

Kaza, Keiko. *When the Elephant Walks.* Art by author. Putnam, 1990.
  Most of the animals are scared of the elephant, but one animal scares him.

*Keats, Ezra Jack. *Whistle for Willie.* Art by author. Viking, 1964.
  Can you whistle? Try it with your friends.

Kitchen, Bert. *Animal Numbers.* Art by author. Dial, 1987.
  Count the animals and their babies.

Kudrna, C. Imbior. *To Bathe a Boa.* Art by author. Carolrhoda, 1986.
  Ever tried to give a bath to a boa constrictor? It's not easy.

Marshall, James. *Red Riding Hood.* Art by reteller. Dial, 1987.
  You've heard this before, but . . .

Martin, Rafe. *Will's Mammoth.* Art by Stephen Gammell. Putnam, 1989.
  Your chance to meet a mammoth.

Miller, Margaret. *Who Uses This?* Photos by author. Greenwillow, 1990.
  Guess the use of an object. Turn the page and see people using it.

Morris, Ann. *Hats, Hats, Hats.* Photos by Ken Heyman. Lothrop, 1989.
  Hats of all types from around the world.

Parker, Nancy Winslow, and Joan Richards Wright. *Bugs.* Art by Nancy Winslow Parker. Greenwillow, 1987.
  Read the bug riddles on the left side of the page; examine an insect on the right-hand side.

*Serfozo, Mary. *Who Said Red?* Art by Keiko Narahashi. McElderry, 1988.
  "I said red," insists a little girl.

*Shannon, George. *Lizard's Song.* Art by Jose Aruego and Ariane Dewey. Greenwillow, 1981.
  "Zoli-Zoli-Zoli." Bear wants lizard's song.

*Sis, Peter. *Waving, A Counting Book.* Art by author. Greenwillow, 1988.
  Count the fireman, the boys walking dogs, and everyone else on the street, and wave to them all.

Tafuri, Nancy. *Who's Counting?* Art by author. Greenwillow, 1986.
  Count the Animals.

*Voake, Charlotte. *Tom's Cat.* Art by author. Lippincott, 1986.
  Click, click; vroom vroom. Lots of noises to make Tom look for his cat.

Ziefert, Harriet. *Andy Toots His Horn.* Art by Sanford Hoffman. Viking, 1988.
  Andy's family misses the noise he makes with his horn.

Picture Books to Think About

Aliki. *The King's Day: Louis XIV of France*. Art by author. Crowell, 1989.
 What was it like to be a king?

Bang, Molly. *The Grey Lady and the Strawberry Snatcher*. Art by author. Four Winds, 1980.
 Will the strawberry snatcher succeed? Find out in this wordless picture book.

Browne, Anthony. *Piggybook*. Art by author. Knopf, 1986.
 Mrs. Piggott tells her family, "You are pigs."

_____. *Willy the Wimp*. Art by author. Knopf, 1984.
 Willy takes body building classes so he won't be a wimp. However, once a wimp. . .

Bunting, Eve. *The Man Who Could Call Down Owls*. Art by Charles Mikolaycak. Macmillan, 1984.
 A great snowy owl avenges the death of the man who could call down owls.

_____. *The Wall*. Art by Ronald Himler. Clarion, 1990.
 Visit the Vietnam Veterans Memorial with a father and his son.

Drescher, Henrik. *Look Alikes*. Art by author. Lothrop, 1985.
 "Please get us out of this crazy place!"

Fiday, Beverly, and David Friday. *Time to Go*. Art by Thomas B. Allen. Harcourt, 1990.
 Say goodbye one last time.

Grossman, Bill. *The Guy Who Was Five Minutes Late*. Art by Judy Glasser. Harper, 1990.
 Read this to a friend who is always late . . . or always on time.

Hirst, Robin, and Sally Hirst. *My Place in Space*. Art by Roland Harvey with Joe Levine. Orchard, 1990.
 Do you know exactly where you live?

Leaf, Margaret. *Eyes of the Dragon*. Art by Ed Young. Lothrop, 1987.
 The dragon seemed almost alive.

Martin, Bill, Jr., and John Archambault. *Listen to the Rain*. Art by James Endicott. Holt, 1988.
 The wonders of rain in sound and pictures.

Miller, Edward. *Frederick Ferdinand Fox*. Art by author. Crown, 1987.
First person account, by a fox, of his rise to fame.

Oxenbury, Helen. *Pig Tale*. Art by author. Morrow, 1973.
Two bored pigs think it would be more interesting if they could live like people.

Spier, Peter. *We the People: The Story of The United States Constitution*. Art by author. Doubleday, 1987.
Enjoy an artist's interpretation of the U. S. Constitution. Examine the many mini-pictures with a friend.

Romanova, Natalia. *Once There Was a Tree*. Art by Gennady Spirin. Dial, 1983.
There's life in a tree stump. Originally published in the Soviet Union.

Rupprecht, Siegfried P. *The Tale of the Vanishing Rainbow*. Tr. by Naomi Lewis. Art by Jozef Wilkon. North-South, 1989.
When a rainbow disappears the wolves and bears almost go to war.

Say, Allen. *The Bicycle Man*. Art by author. Houghton, 1982.
"We howled with wonder" when an American soldier does tricks on a bicycle in Japan.

Scheffler, Ursel. *Stop Your Crowing, Kasimir!* Art by Silke Brix-Henker. Carolrhoda, 1988.
Take that rooster to court. He's too loud.

Siebert, Diane. *Mohave*. Art by Wendell Minor. Crowell, 1988.
The desert tells its tale in text and full color paintings.

Vagin, Vladimir, and Frank Asch. *Here Comes the Cat*. Art by authors. Scholastic, 1989.
A Russian artist and an American artist have a surprise ending for you.

Wisniewski, David. *The Warrior and the Wise Man*. Art by author. Lothrop, 1989.
Who will rule the kingdom? The wise son or the warrior.

Read Aloud Together: Reader's Theater

We have adults reading to children, children reading to children, and now, children and adults reading aloud together. Sharing a book out loud together is the perfect way to hone reading skills while introducing children to the joys of good literature. There are several ways to do this effectively. You can choose a book and take alternate turns reading with a child, paragraph by paragraph, page by page. Several children and adults can also participate in a reading round-robin in which each person is assigned a portion of the selection to read aloud. When this basic idea is formalized a bit, it becomes reader's theater, a method of scripting a published narrative for oral reading. Children and adults can enjoy reader's theater informally, at home, or the approach can be used to present a show to an audience. The selections following these tips and guidelines can provide an introduction to this popular technique for presenting literature orally. They are short plays for children to present in school, to their reading clubs, or at home with and for their families. I've included an easy-to-read selection for beginning readers (or for presenting with and to young readers), a folktale from Mexico, a nonfiction piece, poems, and even jokes. Children and adults can choose their favorites in preparing entertaining intergenerational programs.

Just What Is Reader's Theater?

"Who wants to be in a play?" Whenever I ask this question of a group of children, almost every hand goes up. In my work with children of all ages in schools and public libraries, I've found children are eager to use their read-aloud skills in performance situations. The pieces can be used informally to present "instant plays," or rehearsed (with costumes and props added, if you wish) and brought up to a more polished performance level.

Start simply. Children who read with some degree of proficiency should be comfortable reading these plays. Make enough photocopies of the script you choose so that every reader has a personal copy. This is really a one-time chore, as the copies can be used for repeated performances by the same children or by different groups of readers. Highlight each player's role on his script, making it easier for everyone to come in to a scene on cue. Assign the parts and have all cast members sit in a circle to read the play through aloud together for the first time. On subsequent readings, players can stand or move around when it's appropriate to the action to create a more realistic effect. Artwork has been provided by Lynn Bredesen for each play, which you can reproduce and use, as you choose, for covers for the scripts, or as posters and fliers to advertise the performance, if it's to be presented to another class, to friends, or to a PTA meeting or parents' group. This art can also become "instant certificates" if you type the title of the play, the date of the presentation, and the name of the player on each copy of the picture. They can be kept by the readers as souvenirs to hang or the wall or put into a memory book. To add an authentic flair to your production (and another memento for the children) reproduce the ticket drawing in this chapter, adding the name and date of your group's performance. On the day of the performance, collect the tickets, letting the audience keep their stubs.

While these scripts were written to be used as an oral reading activity, they can, of course, be memorized for performance as a traditional scripted play. If you enjoy this sampling of reader's theater, you may want to check for additional scripted material from contemporary stories, folktales, poems, and jokes in *Presenting Reader's Theater* (The H. W. Wilson Company, 1987).

The Audience

If part of the class is serving as the audience, be sure to give them a part in the proceedings, too, by rehearsing their applause for the end of the reading. Or, have them pretend to be a studio audience for a taping of a television show. As the camera person, you can ask for "reaction shots," and pantomime taping the audience as they laugh, groan, applaud, or even give a standing ovation. This extra effort helps to make everyone, even those who don't have a scripted part in today's play, feel that they have an integral role in the presentation.

An excellent audience warm-up activity is a silly game to play called "animal sounds." You'll need seven cardboard rectangles, cut into 4-by-10 inch cards. Prepare for this game by printing the names of the following animals on one side of the cards:

DOG, CAT, COW, DONKEY, DUCK, PIG, RABBIT

On the other side, print the sounds these animals make (print or glue these words upside down, so that you can simply flip the card and the word will be readable):

BOW WOW, MEOW, HEE-HAW, QUACK, OINK

Leave the reverse side of the card that reads RABBIT blank. Choose seven volunteers from the audience and tell them that each will receive a card that should be held in front of his or her chest. After giving each person a different animal card, demonstrate how the audience should make the appropriate animal sound when you tap each animal-card carrier on the shoulder, but overlook the rabbit card. Now, you are ready to play. As the volunteers stand in a line, holding their signs, you move back and forth, tapping each shoulder. Each person flips his card, the audience responds with the required sound, then the volunteer turns his card back to its original position. After a few rounds, always ignoring the rabbit, tap the person holding the rabbit card. The confused silence will give way to laughter at the trick.

The audience can also double as your chorus. I sometimes explain, "We need music in case there's a delay back stage." I tell the audience they'll be singing "Jingle Bells" (or some other very familiar tune), and that they are to sing loudly when I raise my right hand, and sing softly when I raise my left. We try this a few times, and when they're alert and involved in their singing, I raise both hands at once to foil them. Again, the laughter that results relaxes everyone and players and audience are attentive and ready to listen to the reading.

LOGIC LESSON

Players: 5

Narrator   Teacher   Student One   Student Two   Student Three

NARRATOR: Greetings. Our skit is called "THE LOGIC LESSON" by Caroline Feller Bauer.

My name is _____.
I play the Narrator.

TEACHER: My name is _____.
I play Teacher.

STUDENT 1:   My name is _____.
I play a Student.

STUDENT 2:   My name is _____.
I play a Student.

STUDENT 3:   My name is _____.
I play a Student.

NARRATOR: A Teacher is holding a class.

TEACHER: Attention Students! It's time for a problem. Listen carefully. Two cows were walking on a narrow bridge. They jostled, pushed and bumped. At last, one of the cows forced her way in front of the other cow and said, "I'm the leader." The question is—which cow said, "I'm the leader?" Cow number one or cow number two?

NARRATOR: The students looked puzzled, but one of them took a chance and guessed.

STUDENT 1:   The first cow.

TEACHER: No. It was not the first cow.

STUDENT 2:   The second cow.

TEACHER: No. It was not the second cow.

NARRATOR: The third student was sure to answer correctly.

STUDENT 3:   Both cows.

TEACHER: No. You are all wrong.

NARRATOR: The students were puzzled.

TEACHER: You are all wrong because you have all forgotten that cows can't talk.

ALL: The End.

AN ABRAHAM LINCOLN JOKE

Players: 4

Narrator Abraham Lincoln Boy Farmer

NARRATOR: Abraham Lincoln was coming home from a day of work at his law office. The road was blocked by a load of hay. A boy was standing in front of the hay looking very sad.

LINCOLN: Hello. Don't look so sad. I'll take you down the road to a farmer's house. He'll help you get your hay back on the cart.

BOY: My father won't like this.

LINCOLN: Don't worry. We'll get the hay back on the cart.

NARRATOR: The farmer was happy to help out, but first he suggested that Lincoln and the boy have dinner.

FARMER: You'll feel a lot better after you've eaten something.

BOY: My father won't like this.

LINCOLN: Don't worry. You'll feel better after you eat dinner.

BOY: My father won't like this.

FARMER: Where is your father?

BOY: Under the pile of hay.

Children will love Morris the moose and Boris the bear. They will be familiar with the popular tongue twister and will identify with Boris' teasing. This piece can introduce the other stories of Morris and Boris.

THE TONGUE TWISTER
By Bernard Wiseman

Players: 3

Morris   Boris   Narrator   Bird

NARRATOR: Hello! We would like to present The Tongue-Twister by Bernard Wiseman.

My name is _____
I play the Narrator.

MORRIS: My name is _____
I play Morris the Moose.

BORIS: My name is _____
I play Boris the bear.

BIRD: My name is _____
I Play a bird.

BORIS: Can you say a tongue-twister?
MORRIS: A tongue-twister.

BORIS: That is just the name of it. What you must say is: Peter Piper picked a peck of pickled peppers.

MORRIS: What is a peck?

BORIS: A peck is a lot of something. Go on, say it.

MORRIS: A peck is a lot of something.

BORIS: No! No! Say the whole thing!

MORRIS: The whole thing.

BORIS (shouting): No! No! NO! Say: Peter Piper picked a peck of pickled peppers!

MORRIS: What are pickled peppers?

BORIS: Come with me. . . These are peppers. Pickled peppers are peppers you put in a pot and pickle. To pickle means to make sour. Now say the tongue twister.

MORRIS: Peter Piper picked a peck of peppers and put them in a pot and pickled them.

BORIS: NO! Peter Piper picked a peck of pickled peppers!

MORRIS: How could Peter Piper pick a peck of pickled peppers? Pickled peppers are peppers you put in a pot and pickle!

BORIS: (shouting) I KNOW THAT! But in the tongue-twister, Peter Pepper . . .

MORRIS: You mean Peter Piper.

BORIS: (yelling) YES! Peter Piper! In the tongue-twister, Peter Piper pecked a pick . . .

MORRIS: You mean picked a peck!

BORIS: (roaring) YES! YES! Picked a peck! In the tongue-twister, Peter Piper picked a peck of pickled pots! No! I mean Peter Piper picked a pot of pickled pecks! No! No! Oh, You got me all mixed up! You will never to learn to say a tongue-twister!

NARRATOR: And Boris went away. A bird asked Morris,

BIRD: Why was Boris yelling?

MORRIS: Because I could not say: Peter Piper picked a peck of pickled peppers.

STORYTIME
by Judith Nicholls

Players: 2

STORYTELLER:	STORYTIME by Judith Nicholls Once upon a time, children, there lived a fearsome dragon. . . . .
CHILD:	Please miss, Jamie's made a dragon. Out in the sandpit.
STORYTELLER:	Lovely, Andrew. Now this dragon had enormous red eyes and a swirling, whirling tail. . . . .
CHILD:	Jamie's dragon got yellow eyes, miss.
STORYTELLER:	Lovely, Andrew. Now this dragon was as wide as a horse as green as the grass as tall as a house. . . . .
CHILD:	Jamie's would JUST fit in our classroom miss!
STORYTELLER:	But he was a very friendly dragon. . . . .
CHILD:	Jamie's dragon ISN'T, miss. He eats people, miss. Especially TEACHERS, Jamie said.
STORYTELLER:	Very nice, Andrew! Now one day, children, this enormous dragon rolled his red eye, whirled his swirly green tail and set off to find. . . . .
CHILD:	His dinner, miss! Because he was hungry, miss!

STORYTELLER: Thank you, Andrew.
He rolled his red eye,
whirled his green tail,
and opened his wide, wide mouth
until

CHILD: Please miss,
I did try to tell you, miss!

JELLY BEANS
by Aileen Fisher

Two Voices

VOICE ONE: Jelly Beans by Aileen Fisher
VOICE TWO: I like white ones.
VOICE ONE: Here are two.
VOICE TWO: I like blacks.
VOICE ONE: But there are so few!
VOICE TWO: I want pink ones.
VOICE ONE: Two for you.
VOICE TWO: I like orange.
VOICE ONE: What shall we do—
there isn't an orange,
I've looked them through.
VOICE ONE: Wait! here's a red,
and a yellow too—
THAT'LL make orange
when you get through.

CHANGING
by Mary Ann Hoberman

Players: 2

VOICE ONE: Changing

VOICE TWO: by Mary Ann Hoberman

VOICE ONE: I know what I feel like;

VOICE TWO: I'd like to be you
And feel what you feel like.

VOICE ONE: And do what you do.

VOICE TWO: I'd like to change places
For maybe a week

VOICE ONE: And look like you look like
And speak as you speak

VOICE TWO: And think what you're thinking
And go where you go

VOICE ONE: And feel what you're feeling
And know what you know.

BOTH: I wish we could do it;
What fun it would be

VOICE ONE: If I could try you out

VOICE TWO: And you could try me.

THOUGHTS ON TALKERS
by Walter R. Brooks

Players: 6

VOICE ONE: Thoughts on talkers

VOICE TWO: by Walter R. Brooks

TALKER ONE: Some people talk in a telephone

TALKER TWO: And some people talk in a hall;

TALKER THREE: Some people talk in a whisper,

TALKER FOUR: And some people talk in a drawl;

ALL: And some people talk-and talk-and talk- and talk and talk
And never say anything at all.

EDDIE'S BIRTHDAY PRESENT
by Jeff Moss

Players: 3

NARRATOR: Eddie's birthday present by Jeff Moss.

Aunt Kay said,

KAY: "Here's your present dear.
A birthday comes but once a year."

EDDIE: "Wow!" thought Eddie, "Am I in luck.
I'll bet it's a pony or a big toy truck!
Or maybe a robot or a ten-speed bike
Or a Ping-Pong table that I'd really like
Or an encyclopedia all my own
Or a chemistry set or a big trombone!
Oh, boy, am I a lucky kid!"

NARRATOR: He tore off the paper and opened the lid
And reached inside the birthday box
And said . . .

EDDIE: "Thanks so much for this . . .
pair of socks."

OPTIONAL: On the last line, Eddie can pull out a pair of socks from a paper bag or box.

GREETINGS
by Anne Bell

Readers: 6

Anyone who has ever conversed with a cat or a dog will be able to relate to this poem.

Wife   Husband   Dog   Cat   Two Sons

WIFE: "Good morning, my husband," I said,
"Where have you been and what have you seen,
What's new?"

HUSBAND: "Hmmm?" said husband, "Hmmm?"

WIFE:	"Good morning, my sons," I said, "Where have you been and what have you seen, What's new?"
SONS:	"Excuse us, please," said sons, "We've things to do."
WIFE:	"Good morning, my dog," I said, "Where have you been and what have you seen, What's new?"
DOG:	"Why, everything's new," said dog, "The sun that bounced into the sky Is quite a different sun To the one that rolled behind the hills Last night, just as darkness fell; And the grass is full of brand-new scents, Most marvellous and interesting; And birds are singing different songs— Oh, everything's new," said dog.
WIFE:	"Good morning, my cat," I said, Where have you been and what have you seen, What's new?"
CAT:	But cat only narrowed his golden eyes And asked if the milk was there.

THE PRINCESS AND JOSE
by Anita Brenner

This story features a classic riddle.

PLAYERS: 8

Narrator 1   Soldier 1   Soldier 3   Princess
Narrator 2   Soldier 2   King   Jose

NARRATOR 1:	I am _____ and I am one of the narrators.
NARRATOR 2:	I am _____ and I am also a narrator.
SOLDIER 1:	I am _____ and I play a soldier.
SOLDIER 2:	I am _____ and I play a soldier.
SOLDIER 3:	I am _____ and I play a soldier.

KING:	I am _____ and I play the king.
PRINCESS:	I am _____ and I play the Princess.
JOSE:	I am _____ and I play Jose.
NARRATOR 2:	We would like to present The Princess and Jose by Anita Brenner
NARRATOR 1:	Jose was a good boy and very polite. He liked to learn about other places. So one day he decided to go and see the world.
NARRATOR 2:	He was walking along the road when he was arrested. Some soldiers arrested him.
JOSE:	Why do you arrest me? I haven't done anything wrong.
SOLDIER 1:	You look like a thief. Besides, we need prisoners to build the roads.
JOSE:	I am not a thief. And I don't see why I should work on the roads if I don't want to, especially if I am not paid for it.
SOLDIER 2:	Prisoners aren't paid.
NARRATOR 1:	Jose stood in the middle of the road and the soldiers stood around him, and he made a speech. They took their guns off their shoulders and listened.
JOSE:	It is not fair to make people work and not pay for it. I will not do it.
SOLDIER 3:	If you won't work, then you go to jail.
NARRATOR 2:	And there he was. In jail.
SOLDIER 1:	And if you don't work, you don't eat.
NARRATOR 2:	So, there he was in jail, and hungry.
NARRATOR 1:	Now the king of this place had a daughter. She was the princess. She was very beautiful and also very kind. When she heard about Jose she took a basket and packed it full of things to eat, enough for breakfast and dinner and supper. She covered it up with a fine white napkin and she got into her golden coach and went to the jail.
NARRATOR 2:	There were many prisoners in the jail. They were all going to be shot, one by one. This was because the king had nothing to do. He loved games and riddles but they were all old ones and he was tired of them, so he was

peevish. Every time he was peevish he always had some-body shot. That is the way kings are.

NARRATOR 1: Every morning the princess came to the jail with a basket on her arm. It had Jose's food in it. The soldiers let her in. They winked and smiled and said,

SOLDIER 1: This princess must be in love with Jose.

SOLDIER 2: But it is very sad, they cannot marry because Jose has to be shot.

SOLDIER 3: Yes, he will be the very first one because he wouldn't work on the roads.

SOLDIER 1: The next time the king feels like shooting someone, it will be Jose's turn. Too bad.

NARRATOR 1: But the princess said to Jose,

PRINCESS: I am looking for a way to save you.

NARRATOR 2: One morning the king woke up feeling very cross. He had nothing to do and so he was cross. He decided that Jose would be shot that day. The princess saw how cross he was so she ran to Jose and whispered something, and then she ran out again to where the soldiers were all lined up ready to shoot him.

NARRATOR 1: Everybody was watching. Suddenly the princess spread out a sheet that was nine feet long. Four soldiers had to hold it up. It had something written on it in big red let-ters. It said,

PRINCESS:	Father, if he tells you a riddle that you can't guess, will you spare his life?
KING:	Yes, certainly I will. Of course. Naturally. If you tell me a riddle that I can't guess, I will spare your life.
NARRATOR 2:	There was Jose in the middle of all the soldiers. He looked at the king, then he looked at the princess, then he looked wise.
JOSE:	What is it that goes first on four legs, then on two legs, and then on three legs?
NARRATOR 1:	The king thought. He thought and thought. He scratched his head until his crown fell off and then he thought some more, but he couldn't guess.
KING:	All right, your life is saved. But what is the answer?
JOSE:	Why, it's very simple. It is yourself. When you were a baby you crawled on all fours. Now you are a man and you walk on two legs. When you grow old, you will have a cane. That will be three. See? First four, then two, then three.
NARRATOR 2:	The king was surprised. It was so simple.
KING:	Jose must be pretty clever to think of something like that. It is all right if he wants to marry the princess.
NARRATOR 1:	So they married. They had a big party and they all ate and sang and danced and Jose opened the jail and let all the other prisoners out. And Jose lived happily in the palace with the princess.
ALL:	The End.

READER'S THEATER AS BOOK TALK

The reader's theater technique can also be used to introduce books on a particular theme to children. Here is an example using picture books that feature the author's childhood memories. No doubt, after taking a part in this piece, adults will want to share memories of their own childhoods. Children, no matter how young, can start to pinpoint what they will someday want to tell their children about the time they fell in the canal, or got lost in the department store.

Memories

Readers: 7

READER ONE: We would like to introduce you to some memories of childhood.

READER TWO: We are certain that you will want to borrow these books from the library.

READER THREE: Listen carefully. We will give you the author and title of the books so you can find and read them.

READER FOUR: Maybe you will want to write your own book of memories.

READER ONE:

"When I was young in the mountains, we walked across the cow pasture and through the woods, carrying our towels. The swimming hole was dark and muddy, and we sometimes saw snakes, but we jumped in anyway." From: *When I Was Young in the Mountains* by Cynthia Rylant.

READER TWO:

"In the storeroom, the sight of the pillows and eiderdown quilts gives us an idea. My brother throws a pillow at Richard, who throws one back. I try to join in, but the weight of the quilt makes me clumsy, and, Crack! The material of the quilt tears under my foot. Out from the rip, a cloud of goose feathers flies up to the ceiling. The feathers fall gently down again, changing the three of us into snowmen." From: *One Summer at Grandmother's House* by Poupa Montaufier.

READER THREE:

"The last morning we looked across the water. There were two islands near each other. One of them had a statue on it—a lady with a crown. Everyone got very excited and waved to her. I did too." From: *Watch the Stars Come Out* by Riki Levinson.

READER FOUR: "Back in the twenties a penny was not to be sneezed at, and a nickel was a highly respectable coin. A nickel was the price of a chocolate bar, a hot dog, a sack of peanuts, an ice cream cone, a box of Cracker Jack with a prize in it, a root beer, or a Coke, and for me the best of all nickel bargains was a box of crayons." From: *Bill Peet: An Autobiography* by Bill Peet.

READER FIVE: "One day Ben Allen dared me onto a yearling mule that had never had anything on his back before. When that mule felt me there, he started bucking and running around like crazy. I whooped and hollered like a rodeo rider as I hung onto his mane, while Priss and Ben Allen laughed till they cried." From: *On Granddaddy's Farm* by Thomas B. Allen.

READER SIX:  "On a few very special afternoons he would load us all into a car for a hot, sweaty trip to Pittsburgh and a double header Pirates game at Forbes Field. We sat in the bleachers way out in left field, eating popcorn and drinking lemonade that we brought from home, yelling our heads off for the Pirates." From: *No Stars Tonight* by Anna Egan Smucker.

READER SEVEN: 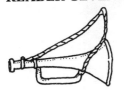 "My father had boots and a bugle from when he was in the army in the first World War, and a mandolin from when he was in school. Sometimes when he came home from work, he would play taps for us. At night our mother would read to us." From: *When I Was Nine* by James Stevenson.

READER ONE: Do you have a memory to share?

ALL: The end.

The Books:

Allen, Thomas B. *On Granddaddy's Farm*, art by the author (Knopf, 1989).

Levinson, Riki. *Watch the Stars Come Out*, art by Diane Goode (Dutton, 1985).

Montaufier, Poupa. *One Summer at Grandmother's House*, tr. from the French by Tobi Tobias; art by the author (Carolrhoda, 1985).

Peet, Bill. *Bill Peet: An Autobiography*, art by the author (Houghton, 1989).

Rylant, Cynthia. *When I Was Young in the Mountains*, art by Diane Goode (Dutton, 1982).

Smucker, Anna Egan. *No Stars Tonight*, art by Steve Johnson. (Knopf, 1989).

Stevenson, James. *When I Was Nine*, art by the author (Greenwillow, 1986).

Chapter 2

Reading All Year

We want our children to read. Of course, we want them to read their assigned reading, but we also want them to read for fun, to make reading a hobby. How can we entice those children who do not read, and those children who do, to read more and even read "better"?

Schools and public libraries throughout the country are providing programs to encourage this leisure reading; many are scheduling time to read, planning reading campaigns, awarding prizes, and recognizing skillful readers, all as part of ongoing, year-long programs. In the following pages, some of these ideas are described. Some are old, some are new, but all are designed to bring books to children on a continuing basis.

Why do we feel it necessary to formalize these incentive programs? Can't we just assume that children will read when they have the time? The problem may be, in part, that they don't have the time. One gets the impression that children today are frequently overscheduled. From Little League to computer lessons, the demand on children's time increases every year. The importance of time for "just lounging around and reading" at home may not be understood and therefore not supported by busy, overworked parents. Also, children may not appreciate that reading can be for fun, because the formal reading lessons in school do not usually afford time to go beyond acquiring skills to foster real enjoyment.

But are we setting up still more competition and pressure for our children with some of these reading programs? The primary purpose of most of these incentive programs is promoting reading for pleasure. The competitive factor is lessened because the emphasis is on each individual choosing his or her own reading goal and gaining a sense of satisfaction when it is reached.

What we really want to accomplish is to have children introduced to reading in a pleasurable way. We all are sure that once a child reads one of the wonderful books published for children he or she will be hooked for life. You certainly don't lose anything by trying every way you can to get children into books.

Book Break

Everyday, at least once a day (twice if you can manage it), you will want to have a Book Break. You can carry a poster or banner from classroom to classroom or throughout the library announcing the BOOK BREAK. If you have a loudspeaker in your institution, you can utilize it for your Book Break.

Explain to the staff at your library or school that someone will come through the building unannounced and take a few minutes to promote a book. This plan really doesn't take more than a minute or two, so it won't be disruptive, and when done with energy and enthusiasm, this change of pace can send students back to their lessons with new interest. If a teacher or department head is doing something that she feels should not be interrupted, she can always put a sign on her door saying, "No Book Break today, please."

Everyone can take part in this project. Enlist the office staff, the administrators, custodians, parents, staff, and of course, the children. Anyone who wants to take part in the Book Break should be warmly encouraged to do so.

Here's how it works: Choose a book that you've read and want to tell people about. Write a sentence or two about the book and practice reading it aloud. When you have a few minutes free, pick up the BOOK BREAK sign and march around the school announcing the Book Break. After you have alerted everyone that you are the Book Break person for the day say, "Today's book is" and launch into your mini-booktalk.

I don't want anyone to say that they don't have time to make up the book talks themselves, so here are a month of Book Breaks, ready to go.

P.S.: If you haven't read the books mentioned here, you may want to borrow the books and read. . .

Sample Book Breaks

Today's Book Is:

Have you ever heard of a Sheep-Pig? Most folk haven't, but Babe is better than any dog at rounding up sheep. He just asks them nicely to go where he wants. Maybe, just maybe, he could win first prize at the fair.
Read: *Babe, the Gallant Pig* by Dick King-Smith; art by Mary Rayner (Crown, 1983).

Today's Book Is:

How come Herbie would rather go to the library than fishing with Ray? Could it be a girl? Could it be that Annabelle Louisa Hodgekiss? Herbie is even writing poetry.

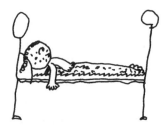

```
Annabelle, Annabelle,
   Sick in bed
spots on her nose
and spots on her head.
Think I will give her a
   bright red rose
then she nos
 I will tickle her toes
       with it.
```

Read: *What's the Matter with Herbie Jones* by Suzy Kline; art by Richard Williams (Putnam, 1986)

Today's Book Is:

The members of the team were doing one of four things: Standing around. Running the wrong way. Backing up, furiously. Falling down. Or, actually, five things, because some people did a combination of two of the above, like Macht, who backed up, and fell down. Yea team., Yea S.O.R. Losers.
Read: *S.O.R. Losers* by Avi (Bradbury, 1984).

Today's Book Is:

It was hungry. It had a voracious appetite. It gobbled up everything in its

path, and now it's coming to get Tommy Brown. Watch Out!
Read: *I'm Coming to Get You!* by Tony Ross; art by the author (Dial, 1984).

Today's Book Is:

This boy is always five minutes late. He never gets enough to eat, because he is always late for dinner. He is even late for his own wedding, but then he meets a princess who is always . . . five minutes late.
Read: *The Guy Who Was Five Minutes Late.* by Bill Grossman; art by the author (Harper, 1990).

Today's Book Is:

Milkshake with eggs:
my legs up on the table
as the screen shows
slow motion secrets
of my favorite pros. . . .
Do you want to be a famous tennis player? A baseball or basketball star? These poems will echo in your dreams.
Read: *Sports Pages* by Arnold Adoff; art by Steve Kuzma (Lippincott, 1986).

Today's Book Is:

The Mouse, aka Frederick Douglas, is looking for treasure, plays a quick game of basketball, and gets conned into dancing with girls. Dancing turns out to be hard work. After practice, The Mouse says, "When we finally finished, my sweat was so tired I had to throw it on the floor because it was too tired to roll down my arm and get there itself."
Read: *The Mouse Rap* by Walter Dean Myers (Harper, 1990).

Today's Book Is:

The Indians thought there were enough buffalo to last forever. They used every part of the buffalo for food, shelter and clothing. Then, the white hunters arrived, killing just for sport.

Bring your bow and arrow, jump on your horse, we're going buffalo hunting.
Read: *Buffalo Hunt* by Russell Freedman (Holiday, 1988).

Today's Book Is:
Launch plus eight and one-half minutes. Join us in space with Sally Ride, the first American woman to travel in space, and her fellow astronauts. We'll fly upside down and maybe even walk in space.
Read: *To Space and Back* by Sally Ride with Susan Okie (Lothrop, 1986).

Today's Book Is:
When did your father last cry? What are your mother's three biggest worries? Do you think your parents are fair? Why didn't your parents allow you to sleep-over at your friend's house? Find out who your parents really are while you . . .
Read: *How to Get Your Parents to Give you Everything You've Ever Wanted* by S. W. Harrington (Atheneum, 1982).

Today's Book Is:
Sam was terrified to sleep in his own room. Something went "Scrabble. Scrabble. Scrabble" every night. Could it be that Sam's room was just too, too messy?
Read: *In A Messy, Messy Room: And Other Strange Tales* by Judith Gorog; art by Kimberly Bulcken Root (Philomel, 1990).

Today's Book Is:
What are you planning for recess today? Are you free after school? Why not sharpen your pencil and grab a sketchbook and go for a nature walk. Draw from life and you will find yourself looking and seeing a lot more than you usually do. You will see water, land, plants, and animals in a new way and will want to draw them when you . . .
Read: *Drawings from Nature* by Jim Aronsky; art by author (Lothrop, 1982).

Today's Book Is:
Did your mother nag you about making your bed this morning, or practicing the piano, or brushing your teeth? Did you vow that when you grow up, you'll be a non-nagging mother or father? Victoria's mom calls her room a pigsty, and strongly suggests that she should "Put on your jacket. It's only May." Victoria has an adventure when she gets on a train for Philadelphia and somehow finds herself back in the 1940s, where she meets a thirteen-year-old girl who tells Victoria that, when she grows up, she's going to be the

perfect mom. Why does this new friend seem so familiar to Victoria?
Read: *Hangin' Out with Cici* by Francine Pascal (Viking, 1977).

Today's Book Is:

Are your parents divorced? Or, do you know someone who is living with just his mom or dad? If so, I bet you will think that Danny has a great idea. He lives in New York, just a short bus ride away from the Bronx zoo. He soon discovers that, especially on weekends, the zoo is filled with "zoodaddies!" These are dads that don't live with their children and see them only during the weekends. They take their kids to the zoo, but they don't seem to have too much to say to them, since they aren't involved in the kids on a daily basis. Danny figures that the dads and kids would be thrilled to have a third person along as a friend. So, suddenly Danny finds he has lots of daddies.
Read: *Son for a Day* by Corinne Gerson; art by Velma Isley (Atheneum, 1980).

Today's Book Is:

"Wanted! Dinosaur Bones. Will Pay Big Reward." After seeing that flier, Daniel hopes to find the remains of one of these gigantic reptiles. He'd use the money to help run the farm in Nebraska. It all took place a long time ago, when Julie was just a little girl—about your age.
Read: *My Daniel* by Pam Conrad (Harper, 1989).

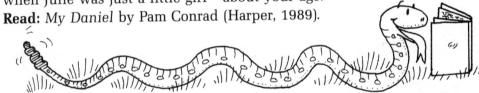

Today's Book Is:

Have you ever had a sleepover at your house? When you go to Elizabeth's house, her mom fixes a big platter of fruit. The apples are cut in rings and the orange slices are fixed with toothpicks. Grapes and cherries are artfully arranged around the edge of the plate. Alice isn't sure what her dad would fix if friends came to stay over at her house; a box of Ritz crackers and some cheese? Her brother Lester would probably walk by her room and toss in a sack of pretzels.
Read: *Alice in Rapture, Sort of* by Phyllis Reynolds Naylor (Atheneum, 1989).

Today's Book Is:

"'I have a surprise for you.'

'Oh, no,' I said. Mom's surprises are never ice cream or candy or a new video game. Her surprises are jobs or hard books or some kind of lessons."

Dan's right. This time the surprise is a camping trip with his Mom's boyfriend and his two kids.

Read: *I Hate Camping* by P. J. Petersen; art by Frank Remkiewicz (Dutton, 1991).

Today's Book Is:

When you lived with your mom, you didn't know anything about your dad, and then he turned out to be rich, handsome, a soap opera star, and . . . nice?

Read: *Worlds Apart* by Jill Murphy (Putnam, 1989).

Today's Book Is:

When Charlie Drummond drives the stage, you don't turn back and you don't stop—even if there is a rock slide—"Eeeyah!!!"—or an ambush, or Indians! "Holy Hannah!" Just hold on. Charlie Drummond will get you there on time. You bet she will!

Read: *Charlie Drives the Stage* by Eric Kimmel; art by Glen Rounds (Holiday, 1989).

Today's Book Is:

It looks like a big barbecue grill, but it's not. A flying saucer has landed in Moe's yard. A small hatch opens and out walk two visitors from outer space. "Greetings," they spoke in English. "We come in peace. Do you have a bathroom?"

Read: *Company's Coming* by Arthur Yorinks; art by David Small (Crown, 1988).

Today's Book Is:

Mooooo! The most beautiful singing you have ever heard came from Bluebell, Swensen's cow. She was a star. Crowds gathered around her. Reporters followed her endlessly. But Bluebell was homesick.

Read: *When Bluebell Sang* by Lisa Campbell Ernst (Bradbury, 1989).

Today's Book Is:

Stew Meat tried to tell Dan'l about Magda, the Witch, but Dan'l wasn't listenin'. Dan'l wasn't believin'. Now Dan'l has been turned into a donkey. Hee Haw. Hee Haw.

Read: *Devil's Donkey* by Bill Brittain; art by Andrew Glass (Harper, 1981).

Quiet! We're Reading

You arrive at school and are greeted by silence. The people in the office seem to be reading. Peeking in at the doors of the classrooms, you see the students and the teacher reading. The custodian is reading. The cafeteria

successful happening. At its best, it is a daily occurrence for a mandated twenty to thirty minutes. During this time all other activities stop and everyone reads. This period of recreational reading is called by various names such as Drop Everything and Read (DEAR), Be Enthusiastic About Reading (BEAR), or its more academic name: Sustained Silent Reading (SSR). Whatever it's called, it is a terrific idea. But to be successful, it needs the full endorsement of the entire school and some planning.

If you are unable to get a total commitment from your administrator (perhaps Mrs. Randolph, the teacher in Room 16, thinks it would be "too disruptive"), you can do it in your own classroom or library. This can work at home, too.

Why take time out from class "just to read"? Many school districts are so intent on teaching skills and scurrying to get their reading scores up from last year's level that they may have lost sight of the ultimate goal: We would like our children to naturally "think books" when they have graduated from formal schooling. We would like our students to mature into citizens who workers are reading. You sit down on the bench outside the office in the hall, pull out your book and read until the DEAR time is over.

In schools across the country, these scheduled quiet reading times are a turn to books when they have time to "play" and think of books as resources when they are in need of information.

To apply the skills that our students have mastered in language arts, let's give them time to find out what reading is all about. Unfortunately, many of our children do not have the available time or the supportive atmosphere at home to find out what the luxury of recreational reading is all about. Their homes may be dominated by a television set tuned to "on" all day and into the night. They may have parents who do not read themselves and think it odd to sit quietly with a book. Seeing a child who is not engaged in physical activity may actually be disturbing to some parents. They will suggest projects, such as taking out the garbage or cleaning. Some children spend much of their time in a home that has no adult guidance after school. Wouldn't you prefer to think that these children are reading rather than staring at a television screen? A quiet reading time at school can teach children what joys and comfort books and reading can offer.

If you do not already devote some time to leisure reading in your library or classroom, you may be surprised at how many children find twenty minutes of reading a long, long time. You may want to begin with a shorter period of time, say, ten minutes or even five minutes. There may be children who love to read, but who find reading in a classroom awkward, distracting, or uncomfortable. After all, if your favorite place to read is in the hayloft or the bathtub, then reading at a desk with thirty other children is not ideal. On the other hand, if you are a reader yourself, you'll understand the luxury of being able to bring your current leisure reading to work.

Whether you are implementing this reading habit in a single classroom, library, or the entire school system, you will want to explain the procedure to your children, confer with the administration, and describe the program to the parents.

It is always difficult for me to grasp the fact that not everyone will think it is a grand idea to read, but the truth is that many of our citizens never read anything they aren't required to read and are not at all sure that it is a worthwhile pursuit.

Just today I read an article in the *Los Angeles Times* about a new order given by General Gray, the Marine Commandant, who has ordered "sergeants and other noncommissioned officers below them to read two to four books a year and directed those ranked higher to read three to six a year." I thought this news was amusing and disturbing at the same time. All of the books on that reading list are titles related to the military, such as *All Quiet on the Western Front* and *The Red Badge of Courage*. It disturbs me that reading has to be mandated to adults. Didn't they find out that reading was satisfying in grade school? Three books a year? What do they do the other fifty weeks of the year? (This digression courtesy of my morning newspaper.)

Introducing a Reading Program

This is your chance to extoll the joys and wonders of reading. If you're not a reader yourself, I give you permission to fake it, or invite a friend in as a guest to rave about reading. Explain what a privilege it is to be given time to read. Tell the children about your own history as a reader. Did you read as a child? Where did you read? Where did you get the books and what kinds were your favorites? What are you reading now?

You need to give your rallying speech to the children, faculty and staff, the folks in the office, and you will want to meet with the parents or send home a letter telling about the program. Explain to parents that, if they visit their child's classroom (or library session) during the quiet reading time, they will want to bring a book so that they can join the reading group. You may want to have a sign to put up in the office and in the classroom alerting the public. In this way you can notify any guest to the program by simply pointing to the sign—and to a pile of paperback books.

Introducing Book Choices

By definition, any reading should be allowed during this leisure-reading time, but I also like to suggest books to those who welcome some direction. My hope is that a book will be begun during the reading period and there will be groans when it's time to stop. Children are then encouraged to continue reading during the lunch break, or after school.

I don't think it works to just say, "Read a book". Many children don't know how to find a book on their own; if directed to the library, they may not know what book to choose. We need to have a variety of good books available for free choice. Sue Alexander, a children's book author, gave her son, who was beginning his teaching career in a fourth-grade classroom, 150 paperbacks as his college graduation present.

I have long advocated that educators think in terms of a daily booktalk. If books were discussed every day, there would rarely be a "What should I read?" question. Children should be encouraged to recommend titles to each other. The oral book report serves a good purpose because it can get children excited about books that their peers have read. My husband always grades the books he reads when he finishes them. If you ever pick up one of these discarded titles at a garage sale, you'll see his grading system and marginal comments. You may want to post evaluation sheets on which your children can register their reactions to the books they read. This will help them to develop a critical judgment and form a better base of comparison when they choose and read new books.

Read a Book, Win a Prize

Our society is prize-oriented. We give awards to the best actress, and the fastest skier. We build multi-million dollar stadiums to house athletic contests. We build competition into almost every facet of our daily life.

Many educators and parents feel that this competition is over-emphasized in our children's lives. Some think that children should be taught to accomplish tasks because of an inner drive. It can be argued that to give awards simply for reading books is defeating this objective of teaching children to be inner-directed. Some children do seem to be born goal-oriented, but I think others often need some motivation to start a new course of action.

When I speak at Young Author conferences, summer reading programs, and school reading celebrations, I've seen the pleasure that an accomplishment in a language arts project can bring to both children and their parents. The children and parents arrive at one of these merit-recognition events dressed in their best and the parents' price is evident. Here are a few successful ideas that you might want to consider when planning an all-year reading program for your school, library or community center.

We Read Over a Million Pages

As the year-end speaker at the Rossmoor Elementary School in Alamitos, California, I was present for the award ceremony that was the culminating event of a year-long reading project. Its title is the Castle Rossmoor Reading Quest, and almost every child in the school received some sort of award. Each September, at the beginning of the school year, a letter is sent to the parents describing the program. It is explained that this is a year-long incentive program rather than a competition. Children are encouraged to read widely in all genres, fiction and non-fiction. Certificates are given three times a year at assemblies to encourage the reading habit and also to remind the children that the certificates are a goal to strive for. There are eight levels of awards. The first level is reached by reading just five books (or 150 pages) and the ultimate award—called the Castle—is awarded only in the final period. To achieve the Castle award a student must first attain two intermediate levels, the Knight of the Castle and the Knight of the Realm. The objective is to make sure that children who wish to obtain the highest award keep reading the entire school year and don't just go on a marathon read-in at the last minute. Yes, children do "count pages" as they read, but this is probably inevitable in a numbers-based program. You really must evaluate a program and its achievement of its goals as a whole. Are more children reading? If the answer is yes, then I don't think it's necessary to worry too much about a minor point.

Parents sign a simple form indicating that a child has indeed read an entire book and "understands the content." Obviously, some parents will take this commitment more seriously than others. Again, it really doesn't matter in the long run if you remember that the basic objective is to get children to read regularly.

The choice of books is important, and I suppose that it is possible for a child to confine her reading to inferior series books while gaining the endorsement of awards, but even that would be an accomplishment for a former nonreader. Most children will read books borrowed from the public or school library and they will be selected by professionals.

Award Basis

The Rossmoor School's goals are listed below, should you wish to use or adapt this plan as a model. You will have to assess whether the numbers that program used are realistic in your own situation. It is important that everyone gets a chance to achieve at least the first level of recognition, so that every student will have motivation to continue. The highest award, on the other hand, should be a challenge for which the most dedicated readers will strive.

Castle Rossmoor Reading Quest Awards:

5 books or 150 pages	Jester
10 books or 300 pages	Page
20 books or 600 pages	Squire
30 books or 900 pages	Blue Knight
50 books or 1,500 pages	White Knight
100 books or 3,000 pages	Knight of the Castle
+20 books or +1,000 pages	Knight of the Realm
+20 books or +1,000 pages	Castle award in June

The Castle award can be achieved only if a student has earned the Knight of the Castle in the first awards period, the Knight of the Realm in the second awards period, and continues to read in the final award period. Award assemblies are held in November, March and June. In its seventh year now, this program has gained in popularity since its inception. Over a million pages were read school-wide in the 1988–89 school year.

The proof of the success of the Castle Rossmoor Reading Quest? As guest speaker, I was asked to give out the awards at the last assembly of the year. Seven hundred fifty children were called up to the stage. As one little girl left clutching the ultimate reward, The Castle Award, "I did it," she said to a friend, "and I loved every book I read."

Book auction at the Monte Vista School in Monterey, California.

Book Bucks

Ann Ostenso at the Monte Vista School in Monterey, California, also runs a year-long reading-incentive program. The culminating event at this school is an auction. Children receive "Book Bucks" as they read throughout the year. This past year the rules were changed from granting the rewards on the basis of the number of pages read to focus on the time spent reading. If a child reads a minimum of twenty minutes a day, five days a week, he can earn up to $500 worth of Book Bucks during the school year. In the spring of 1990, the third, fourth, and fifth grades had read for 344,000 minutes, cumulatively, which translates into 239 days of reading. Once again, the program's emphasis is on building a lasting reading habit.

The prizes for the auction are displayed throughout the year as new ones are added to the storehouse. Prizes range from pencils and balloons to tape decks. The schools' parent-teacher organization is very supportive of the project and can be counted on to donate many of the prizes. The auction is an exciting event and the children learn that the more they read, the greater their chances for a coveted prize. Ann tells me that those children who were too cautious in their bidding one year to acquire many prizes become more savvy the next year. Although there are brief moments of regret as prizes are won by others, Ann reports that the day after the auction everyone seems to be quite satisfied with their loot. She also holds some things back for the raffle which takes place after the auction is held. So, through this approach, too, everyone ends up with a prize and a positive experience. Of course, the real prize is that the whole school is reading all year long and placing real value on the time spent reading. I've reprinted the "rules" of this project so that you can replicate the idea at your institution.

Book Auction Rules—A Year-long Reading Celebration
Sponsored by Monte Vista School, Monterey, California
Ann Ostenso, Librarian

1. In grades three to five, students can earn $500 worth of Book Bucks for each 100 minutes of validated reading (a minimum of 20 minutes a day, 5 days a week).

2. After reading the book, the student must fill in the Reading Record Card and have it signed by an adult. Reading Record Cards are supplied at the check out desk.

3. Books are to be on the student's reading level, and they cannot be read more than once for credit. Books can be selected from home, public, or school library. Each book must be read completely.

4. The Reading Record Card has spaces for: Author, Title, Number of pages read, Student's Name, Room Number, and Adult's Signature.

5. The library keeps each student's Reading Record Cards in a report card envelope filed by room number.

6. Students need $5000 in earned Book Bucks to qualify for the Book Bucks Auction, which is held in the late spring.

7. Prizes are put on display in February and are supported by PTA donations and a used-book sale. The range includes tape recorders, calculators, watches, games, model kits, jewelry, stationery goods, autographed paperback books, stuffed animals, T-shirts, and movie-and-popcorn tickets (for films to be shown in the library at a later date).

8. The Auction is held in late spring on a Friday afternoon. It starts at lunch recess and goes through till the end of the day.

9. Students can successfully bid on three (3) items. The denominations are: $500, $1000, and $2000; the bidding jumps in $500 increments.

10. When the Auction is over, students with money remaining receive one (1) raffle ticket for each $5000. On another day, a raffle drawing is held for those holding tickets. Prizes are given to whatever numbers are drawn.

The Fullerton (California) Public Library uses a variation of the Book Buck idea for their summer reading program. Children are given "money" after reading a prescribed number of books. They can then purchase prizes, many donated from local merchants, throughout the summer at the "store" set up in the children's room of the library. The most expensive item— restaurant gift certificates—cost $30 of bucks (called Dolphin Bucks the year that underwater treasure was the theme).

You might question whether children will become jaded and materialistic in their responses to reading programs that use prizes as incentives. My friend, a children's librarian in a high-income suburb, wrote to me recently about her library's highly successful summer reading club. For the past several years, the library had offered certificates and an impressive grand prize to young readers who attained their reading goals. This year, the children's room offers only small plastic carnival prizes, which are distributed throughout the summer, as the books are read. My friend is amazed at the success of this program.

The ABC unified school district in Cerritos, California, celebrates the language arts by giving their students an opportunity to perform orally. Children prepare presentations in various areas and genres, and then are given the opportunity to perform in front of an audience. No prizes are awarded, but the children have the satisfaction of appearing at the festival. All selections are from a published work, except the original-writing category. The range of choices affords everyone a chance to participate.

Fran Kammal, the co-ordinator of the three-year-old program, reports that about 600 children attend the three-hour Saturday festivities with their parents. Each child is pre-assigned a room and a time for their performance, each of which lasts ten minutes or less. The organizers try to provide variety in each forty-five-minute segment by having storytellers alternating with poetry presentations, and so on. Here is a description of the various categories:

ABC Unified School District
Language Arts Festival, 1988
Student Participation Category Descriptions

STORYTELLING—Student prepares a story to tell without the use of notes.

POETRY—Student memorizes a poem or reads a poem aloud.

PUPPETRY—Students make puppets and prepare a puppet show to give a booktalk, present a skit or a play.

DRAMA—Students act out a favorite scene from a selection, tell the entire story using creative dramatic techniques, or perform a skit or play.

READ-ALOUD—Student prepares a passage or an entire story to be read orally.

CHORAL READING—A group of students present a rhymed or metered poem speaking in unison as an interpretation of literature.

READERS THEATER—A group of students read aloud from scripts that are based on selections from stories.

ORAL HISTORY—Student prepares historical information about significant individuals in history and presents this material orally.

SPEECH—Student recites a speech that has been a public discourse (e.g., Preamble to the United States Constitution, Martin Luther King's speech, "I Have A Dream").

WRITING—Student(s) may submit an original written selection prepared on any topic. Suggested types of writing include language experience stories, plays, creative writing, nonfiction, etc.

As you can see the variety is such that almost everyone can have a chance to perform. Anyone is eligible to enter a maximum of two categories. There are no prizes, but everyone is given a certificate of participation. Teachers are encouraged to provide guidance for entrants with suggestions for materials and to help in preparation of the piece. Those children who would like to submit a sample of their writing to be exhibited at the festival are not limited in what they may submit. Anything from book reports to advertising samples are accepted.

A book sale is held on the morning of the festival and T-shirts and commemorative mugs are also on sale.

"When can we start preparing for next year?" asked a fourth grader after the festival this year.

Certificates, Bookmarks, Posters

Whether you choose to adapt or adopt one of these reading incentive approaches or create your own plan, duplicate and display or distribute the colorful posters, certificates, book marks, and medallions here and in the last chapter to stimulate excitement and encourage participation.

Badges

Use these as reading incentive awards.
They can be duplicated in the round and worn proudly around
the neck of a READER as a badge of honor.

Book Slogans

Use these on bulletin boards, bookmarks, posters. Mix and match with art.

THREE CHEERS FOR BOOKS

HOORAY FOR BOOKS

BRING ON THE BOOKS

READ READ READ

BOOKS ARE MAGIC

Chapter 3

Parents—We Need Their Support

My daughter called today. Yes, I'm a parent too. She is working in Japan and was surprised that we minded that she hadn't called this week.

"I'm a grownup now. You don't have to hear from me all the time," she snapped. "Of course we do," was my logical retort. "Dad calls Grandma every week and he's a grownup too."

When I hung up and opened this month's phone bill, I wondered if she might be right. Maybe grownups write letters instead of calling long distance across the world. One of Hilary's requests during that conversation was that "Mom (that's me) send some paperbacks for the flight to Bangkok."

"How wonderful", I thought, "I'm still useful when it comes to books." Then I thought, "but what should I send?" But *then* I thought, "What do you mean 'what should I send?' You're about to sit down and tell librarians and teachers what books to recommend to the parents of the children they work with and you don't even know what to get for your own daughter?" It's true. But Hilary, as she reminds me, is now a grownup. It was a lot easier when she was ten. Well, it wasn't all that easy then either. I'd say, "Here's a new Katherine Paterson" and she would say, "I'm reading fantasy this week."

In case you're wondering where these musings are leading, I just wanted to point out that no matter how old (or young) your children are, you still want to do something for them and you're sure that you still can influence their reading.

Because of these positive impulses, parents can be the perfect liason between you and the children you serve. They usually want to help, but often don't know how. You can reach them through floor work, special programs, and booklists.

Who are these parents? You will not be surprised to learn that these days parents can not be placed conveniently into a little demographic box marked "Mom and Dad". You will encounter traditional families, as well as single mothers and single fathers. You will meet the "blended family" which may consist of any combination of parents, stepparents, and assorted children, and you'll encounter caregivers ranging from a grandparent to a nanny or an au pair girl (who today may turn out to be an au pair boy.) These parents are busy. Both parents may work full time and may feel that they don't have the time to devote to frequent visits to the library, or even the time to share a book with their children. These are the same parents who somehow do find the time to become involved with all the activities surrounding their children's Little League games. Sharing literature takes a lot less time than playing a team sport and in my opinion, one gains a lifelong "thinking sport" in reading.

We need to make reading as fashionable as designer jeans and as much in demand as a popular rock group. I'd like to see people line up to hear Tomie De Paola in the same numbers as they queue for a rock concert. Actually, I'm not sure that I mean that. I dislike our current trend which counts everything to determine its value. You have public librarians boasting that they have 40,000 children or more involved in their summer reading program or 8,000 books checked out each week. But are all of those kids really reading those books and enjoying what they read? Numbers can give us some indication of how what we're achieving, but we have to remember to think of the children as individuals and not as "the pre-schoolers" or "the third graders." Reaching the parents will help you to reach the individual children, because most parents think in terms of "my child" first.

Where are these parents? To reach out and find them you have to think like a Madison Avenue advertising executive. One obvious place to find parents is through the school. Other venues are the supermarkets in your neighborhood, children's shops, commuter-bus stops and train stations, and fast food stores. You can also set up a booth at a local fair or shopping mall to inform parents and promote your reading programs.

The copy machine, computers, the washing machine, and the electric pencil sharpener all were designed to make our lives easier and to give us more time to enjoy our families and friends. Somehow, though, we all seem busier than ever. In general, it is increasingly difficult to attract an audience to hear a program. Of course, you don't need hoards of people attending to feel you have had a successful program. All you need are a few interested adults who will pass their new found enthusiasm for literature to their children. It helps if you already have an active Friends of the Library organization or Parent-Teacher Association group who will help get out their membership.

Consider taking your message to the workplace, too. Is there a factory in your town that employs a fair number of people? How about enlisting the aid of the local merchants' organization, whose members may allow you to place fliers and program schedules in their places of business? Perhaps there is a town square, office complex, or park where it would be feasible to set up a display or give a short noon-time program.

Now that you have located your audience, how will you actually reach them with your message? If you have decided to have a formal program, there are several factors to consider. Where will it be held? Your school library or public library meeting room are obvious places, but you may attract a better crowd if you hold your meeting in a place that is considered chic (the local hotel ballroom?) or interesting (the helicopter base?) that people enjoy visiting or are curious about. Some of these locations might cost money (unless you can cajole the manager into donating the space), so you'll have to determine the advantages of shifting the venue in terms of your budget, as well as appealing to your audience's interests and convenience.

The time you hold your meeting can be important, too. If you schedule it on a weekday during the midmorning, it's likely you will only attract those parents who are not working. Planning the program for a weekend may mean that you still lose the working parents, who must squeeze all of their chores, errands, and leisure pursuits into two short days. I've lectured at some very well-attended meetings held at the end of the workday in a convenient downtown location—before the parents can go home, change their clothes, have dinner, and get too comfortable to find it a bother to venture out again. You may have to try a few approaches before discovering what works well in your community.

Once you establish a time and location, you need to let people know that there will be a program. You may be able to reach families through a city mailing. Some public libraries even use the water bill or other community mailings, to enclose a program notice. Any time your library, school, or church mails *any* bulletins or newsletters, try to arrange to have book-promotion material included in the envelopes. Posters strategically placed around town can be effective, but it may be that your community has so many signs that no one reads them anymore. Or, maybe they have such a strict sign-posting policy that you can't put posters around town, so check into this, too.

The media has become the most effective way to reach large numbers of people. Your local newspaper is probably read by a fair amount of the public, but have you ever noticed how often you'll see the report of a community event that's already occurred, but never seem to see an announcement of it in advance, so that you can attend? Don't blame the papers; your best bet is to write a news release, so that it can be plugged right into the newspaper's community events column, or your own school or library newsletter. I know this works because when I did some consulting work for a large bookstore chain, their publicity people write a biography for me. I've been sending that ahead when I'm scheduled to speak, and I often find that it is reprinted in programs or local newspapers, exactly as written. My best advice, if you are serious about getting your programs into the local newspaper is to get to know the reporter assigned to cover local events. Ask her to lunch (this doesn't work as well if *The New York Times* is your local paper, I'll admit) to share your enthusiasm about the importance of reading programs for children, then keep her informed of your schedule of events with announcements sent well in advance of the date you want the notice published. Most radio and television stations also often have room for public service spots, so make an appointment with your local cable company and talk over your programming plans.

Putting the Program Together

The focus of your program should be that Books Are Fun. Most adults are totally unaware of the incredible wealth of reading material published for children. At the moment there are over 66,000 juveniles listed in *Books in Print*. For the last few years, there have been three to four thousand new books published each year. Unfortunately, in order to find a large selection of these books, parents often have to make a special trip to the children's bookstore or the children's room of a public library. Books are not as easy to pick as breakfast cereal. When a parent is confronted with a choice of unfamiliar titles, he or she may become anxious and confused. Not only are there so many books to choose from, but the schools have added to the confusion by talking so much about reading scores and reading levels. The average parent is likely to stand in the children's section of the library or book store wringing his or her hands and wondering what to buy or borrow. What if they choose a book that is too difficult for their child to read, or horrors, too easy? I'm sure you are familiar with the mother or father who comes into the library, looking for a book, and says, "My Helen is seven years old, but she tests on the level of a junior in college. Where do you keep James Joyce?" What if the book they select is not appropriate—too frightening, too sexy, a "boy's" book, a "girl's" book? We need to reassure the parents that, although there is a "right book, for the right child, at the right time," no dreadful consequences will result if they pick a less-than-perfect book this time. We want to encourage children to learn to make their own selections, as well, and books that aren't quite geared to their current interests can be both points of reference and—just possibly—windows on new worlds.

You will probably have your own ideas for a parents' program, but here are some suggestions to consider in planning your presentation. Incidentally, the Preschool Services and Parent Education Committee of the Children's Division of the American Library Association recently published a whole book of adult-programming ideas. I participated in that project, and we provided sample lectures directed to various audiences, such as pregnant mothers, church workers, and day care workers in *First Steps to Literacy: Library Programs for Parents, Teachers, and Caregivers*, by Nell Colburn and Maralita L. Freeny (American Library Association, 1990).

I like to open my own programs for parents with a story. This immediately entertains the audience and it's even more effective if the story's theme relates in some way to the objectives of your lecture. You will find several selections that relate to children and parenting in this chapter, ready for you to tell or read aloud. It is more personal for you to tell the story, but don't be ashamed to read aloud, *as long as you prepare the selection*. Read the story over several times so you are familiar with it (see tips in Read Aloud, pp. 3–31).

After you tell the story, you can take a few minutes to welcome the audience and explain your agenda. Recognize that the people in your audience have already made a commitment to the subject of reading by coming to the meeting. They need to be reassured that they are going in the right direction. Explain that their children are learning the skill of reading in school. They are learning or have learned to decode, sequence, recall, and interpret what they read. It is hard work. At home they need a reward: time to read "just for *fun*," so that they can establish reading as a habit, not a chore. Adults can help with this process by sharing books aloud with their children on a regular basis. They will be enjoying their children and also be giving them a Lesson in Literature—that books and reading are better than television and ice cream sundaes. Suggest that families find a time to "play with books" on a daily basis. They can share books after dinner, before bedtime, at the breakfast table, or the wake-up time could be ten minutes earlier to make time for books before getting involved with the obligations of the day.

Depending on the book background of your audience, you may want to demonstrate how to share a picture book and you certainly will want to show a number of titles to introduce your audience to the variety of children's books. Since I enjoy telling stories, particularly using visual props, I often tell a series of stories, while interspersing my thoughts on introducing literature in a family setting. You may want to try this technique using the visual stories in this book and providing your audience with copies of the story so that they can tell it to their children when they return home.

The paperback booklists at the end of this chapter can become your lasting message to your audience. They provide the parents with a guide to some of the wonderful titles in print for them to borrow from the library or purchase from the bookstore.

You may want to begin or end your talk with a poem, so I've included some short, book-oriented poems, as well as stories.

Guess What I Can Do?

I can read!
Not very good—
Not much speed,
But, I can READ.
Nonie Borba

Read

Do you remember
learning to read?
That book full of squiggles
like ants escaped,
the teacher's big thumb
on the page,
your heart beating inside,
afraid that all you'd ever see
was ants—

    Then a word popped out.
"See," and another, "Cat,"
and my finger on teacher's,
we read, "I see cat."
I ran around the room
so happy I saw words
instead of ants.
Ann Turner

Library

No need even
To take out
A book: only
Go inside
And savor
The heady
Dry breath of
Ink and paper,
Or stand and
Listen to the
Silent twitter
Of a billion
Tiny busy
Black words.
Valerie Worth

Life Savings

by Janet and Allen Ahlberg

There was once a woman who decided to save parts of her life till later, when she might have more need of them. She had the idea when she was quite young, and her parents encouraged her. The first part of her life she ever saved was half an hour from when she was four. Later, she saved a day from when she was five, another day from when she was five and a half, six days from when she was six . . . and so on, all the way through her life until she was seventy.

Well, she put all these life savings in a safe in her parents' office. (They had a fortune-telling business, with a little magic on the side.) Each one had its own special box with a label giving the duration—that means how long it was—and her age.

Eventually, as I said, the woman got to be seventy and decided to spend some of her savings. First she opened the box with a day in it from when she was eight. Her heart began to pound the moment the box was opened. She lost all interest in the office and the fortune-telling business, and rushed out into the park. Here she played on the swings and rolled on the grass and fished in the pond and ate ice-cream. By the end of the day she was worn out, but her cheeks were rosy and her eyes shone.

The next morning after breakfast the woman opened the box with a week in it from when she was ten. After that a great deal happened—and a great deal didn't happen. Dusting didn't happen, for instance, or washing-up or making an appointment at the hairdresser's. Not many bills were paid or weeds dug up. By the end of the week the woman needed another week to sort herself out. All the same her step was light as she walked about the town, and her friends said she was a changed woman.

Well, so it continued for some years with the woman spending her savings bit by bit. Not all her experiences were happy, of course; life is not like that. The two days from when she was fourteen, for instance, were dreadful. She felt terribly shy *all* the time and was desperately worried about an almost invisible spot on her chin.

Then, finally, when she had used up all her life savings, the woman took to her bed, read a book for a while and—presently—died.

Some days later when friends were clearing out the office one box of the woman's savings was discovered unopened. It was tucked away under a pile of old letters in the safe. The woman herself must not have noticed it. Its label (in her father's hand) said: Half an hour, age four.

Well, as soon as the box was opened, odd things began to happen. One of the friends went racing up and down the stairs—the office was on the third floor; another made a den under the desk, and a third played with the phone.

Of course, as you will realize, it was the last half-hour of the woman's life that was causing this. Now that the woman herself was dead, it had nowhere else to go and, apparently, reason to come to an end. In fact, as far as I know, it's still around . . . somewhere.

So, there we are. If ever you should feel the urge to act like a four-year-old (unless you *are* a four-year-old) you can blame it on the life savings of the woman in the fortune-telling business, with a little magic on the side. That's what I'd do.

Perfection

by Natalie Babbitt

There was a little girl once called Angela who always did everything right. In fact, she was perfect. She had better manners than anyone, and not only that, but she hung up her clothes and never forgot to feed the chickens. And not only *that*, but her hair was always combed and she never bit her fingernails.

A lot of people, all of them fair-to-middling, disliked her very much because of this, but Angela didn't care. She just went right on being perfect and let things go as they would.

Now, when the Devil heard about Angela, he was revolted. "Not," he explained to himself, "that I give a hang about children as a rule, but *this* one! Imagine what she'll be like when she grows up—a woman whose only fault is that she has no faults!" And the very thought of it made him cross as crabs. So he wrote up a list of things to do that he hoped would make Angela edgy and, if all went well, even make her lose her temper. "Once she loses her temper a few times," said the Devil, "she'll never be perfect again."

However, this proved harder to do than the Devil had expected. He sent her chicken pox, then poison ivy, and then a lot of mosquito bites, but she never scratched and didn't even seem to itch. He arranged for a cow to step on her favorite doll, but she never shed a tear. Instead, she forgave the cow at once, in public, and said it didn't matter. Next the Devil fixed it so that for weeks on end her cocoa was always too hot and her oatmeal too cold, but this, too, failed to make her angry. In fact, it seemed that the worse things were, the better Angela liked it, since it gave her a chance to show just how perfect she was.

Years went by. The Devil used up every idea on his list but one, and Angela still had her temper, and her manners were still better than anyone's. "Well, anyway," said the Devil to himself, "my last idea can't miss. That much is certain." And he waited patiently for the proper moment.

When that moment came, the Devil's last idea worked like anything. In fact, it was perfect. As soon as he made it happen, Angela lost her temper once a day at least, and sometimes oftener, and after a while she had lost it so often that she was never quite so perfect again.

And how did he do it? Simple. He merely saw that she got a perfect husband and a perfect house, and then—he sent her a fair-to-middling child.

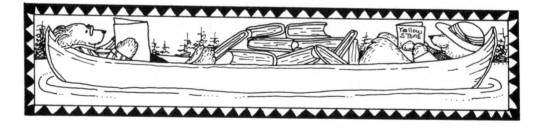

Slower Than the Rest

by Cynthia Rylant

Leo was the first one to spot the turtle, so he was the one who got to keep it. They had all been in the car, driving up Tyler Mountain to church, when Leo shouted, "There's a turtle!" and everyone's head jerked with the stop.

Leo's father grumbled something about turtle soup, but Leo's mother was sympathetic toward turtles, so Leo was allowed to pick it up off the highway and bring it home. Both his little sisters squealed when the animal stuck its ugly head out to look at them, and they thought its claws horrifying, but Leo loved it from the start. He named it Charlie.

The dogs at Leo's house had always belonged more to Leo's father than to anyone else, and the cat thought she belonged to no one but herself, so Leo was grateful for a pet of his own. He settled Charlie in a cardboard box, threw in some lettuce and radishes, and declared himself a happy boy.

Leo adored Charlie, and the turtle was hugged and kissed as if he were a baby. Leo liked to fit Charlie's shell on his shoulder under his left ear, just as one might carry a cat, and Charlie would poke his head into Leo's neck now and then to keep them both entertained.

Leo was ten years old the year he found Charlie. He hadn't many friends because he was slower than the rest. That was the way his father said it: "Slower than the rest." Leo was slow in reading, slow in numbers, slow in understanding nearly everything that passed before him in a classroom. As a result, in fourth grade Leo had been separated from the rest of his classmates and placed in a room with other children who were as slow as he. Leo thought he would never get over it. He saw no way to be happy after that.

But Charlie took care of Leo's happiness, and he did it by being con- genial. Charlie was the friendliest turtle anyone had ever seen. The turtle's head was always stretched out, moving left to right, trying to see what was in the world. His front and back legs moved as though he were swimming frantically in a deep sea to save himself, when all that was happening was that someone was holding him in midair. Put Charlie down and he would sniff at the air a moment, then take off as if no one had ever told him how slow he was supposed to be.

Every day, Leo came home from school, took Charlie to the backyard to let him explore and told him about the things that had happened in fifth grade. Leo wasn't sure how old Charlie was, and, though he guessed Charlie was probably a young turtle, the lines around Charlie's forehead and eyes and the clamp of his mouth made Leo think Charlie·was wise the way old people are wise. So Leo talked to him privately every day.

Then one day Leo decided to take Charlie to school.

It was Prevent Forest Fires week and the whole school was making posters, watching nature films, imitating Smokey the Bear. Each member of Leo's class was assigned to give a report on Friday dealing with forests. So Leo brought Charlie.

Leo was quiet about it on the bus to school. He held the covered box tightly on his lap, secretly relieved that turtles are quiet except for an occasional hiss. Charlie rarely hissed in the morning; he was a turtle who liked to sleep in.

Leo carried the box to his classroom and placed it on the wide windowsill near the radiator and beside the geraniums. His teacher called attendance and the day began.

In the middle of the morning, the forest reports began. One girl held up a poster board pasted with pictures of raccoons and squirrels, rabbits and deer, and she explained that animals died in forest fires. The pictures were too small for anyone to see from his desk. Leo was bored.

One boy stood up and mumbled something about burnt-up trees. Then another got up and said if there were no forests, then his dad couldn't go hunting, and Leo couldn't see the connection in that at all.

Finally it was his turn. He quietly walked over to the windowsill and picked up the box. He set it on the teacher's desk.

"When somebody throws a match into a forest," Leo began, "he is a murderer. He kills trees and birds and animals. Some animals, like deer, are fast runners and they might escape. But other animals"—he lifted the cover off the box—"have no hope. They are too slow. They will die." He lifted Charlie out of the box. "It isn't fair," he said, as the class gasped and giggled at what they saw. "It isn't fair for the slow ones."

Leo said much more. Mostly he talked about Charlie, explained what turtles were like, the things they enjoyed, what talents they possessed. He talked about Charlie the turtle and Charlie the friend, and what he said and how he said it made everyone in the class love turtles and hate forest fires. Leo's teacher had tears in her eyes.

That afternoon, the whole school assembled in the gymnasium to bring the special week to a close. A ranger in uniform made a speech, then someone dressed up like Smokey the Bear danced with two others dressed up like squirrels. Leo sat with his box and wondered if he should laugh at the dancers with everyone else. He didn't feel like it.

Finally, the school principal stood up and began a long talk. Leo's thoughts drifted off. He thought about being home, lying in his bed and drawing pictures, while Charlie hobbled all about the room.

He did not hear when someone whispered his name. Then he jumped when he heard, "Leo! It's you!" in his ear. The boy next to him was pushing him, making him get up.

"What?" Leo asked, looking around in confusion.

"You won!" they were all saying. "Go on!"

Leo was pushed onto the floor. He saw the principal smiling at him, beckoning to him across the room. Leo's legs moved like Charlie's—quickly and forward.

Leo carried the box tightly against his chest. He shook the principal's hand. He put down the box to accept the award plaque being handed to him. It was for his presentation with Charlie. Leo had won an award for the first time in his life, and as he shook the principal's hand and blushed and said his thank-you's, he thought his heart would explode with happiness.

That night, alone in his room, holding Charlie on his shoulder, Leo felt proud. And for the first time in a long time, Leo felt *fast*.

Ickle Bickle Robin
by Edna Mitchell Preston.

Little Bitty Robin fell out of the nest.

Big Mother Robin flew down beside him.
Big Mother Robin said,
"Are you all right?"
Itty Bitty Robin cried.

Big Father Robin flew down beside him.
Big Father Robin said,
"Did you get hurt?"
Itty Bitty Robin just cried.

Big Father Robin said,
"See here now, Son.
I have work to do.
I can't stand around here all day.
What is making you cry?"
Ickle Bickle Robin whispered,
"I wish I could fly."

Big Father Robin said,
"Hop on my back."
Big Father Robin flew
up to the next.

Big Father Robin said,
"Now hop off and fly."

Ickle Bickle Robin fell plunk.
Big Father Robin said,
"Hop on again, Son."
Big Father Robin flew up to the nest.

Big Father Robin said,
"Now fly."

Ickle Bickle Robin fell plunk.
Big Mother Robin said,
"Itty Bitty Robin Boo,
you can't fly yet.
You're only a baby."

Big Father Robin said,
"you stay out of this."
Itty Bitty Robin Boo cried.

Big Father Robin said,
"Hop."
Big Father Robin flew up to the nest.
Big Father Robin said,
"Fly."

Witty Bitty Wobin fell plunk.
Witty Bitty Wobin Baby cried.

Big Father Robin said,
"See here now, Son.
I'm a busy bird.
I can't stand around here all day
and watch you cry.
Make up your mind.
Do you want to fly?
Or cry?"

Ickle Bickle Robin whispered,
"Fly."

Big Father Robin said, "Hop."
Big Father Robin flew up to the nest.
Ickle Bickle Robin took a big brave hop.
Ickle Bickle Robin fell boom.

Big Mother Robin came and patted him all over.
Big Mother Robin said,
Wumpy Dump, don't cry.
You don't have to fly yet.
You're too wittle to fwy."

Big Father Robin said,
"Stop talking baby talk to that bird."
Wittle Wumpy Dump Wobin cwied.

Big Mother Robin flew at Big Father Robin.
Big Mother Robin said,

"He is a baby."
Big Father Robin said,
Does he have to be a baby ALL HIS LIFE?

Big Mother Robin said,
"It's cruel to make him try again.
All he can do is wump and dump and cry."

Big Father Robin said,
"Then Let him wump and dump and cry—
and try and try and try and cry."
Big Mother Robin said,
"He's too little to try and try.
He might get hurt."

Big Father Robin said,
"Maybe he will.
He's got to take his chances."

Big Mother Robin said,
"It's cruel to make him try and try."
Big Father Robin said,
"I didn't start this.
He did.

And I'm going to help him fly
if I have to stick around here
ALL DAY!
Now Son, Where are you?"

Ickle Bickle Robin stuck his head out of the nest.
Ickle Bickle Robin said, "Here."
Big Father Robin said,
"How in tarnation did you get
all the way up there?"

Big Mother Robin said,
"Wittle Bittle Dumpling Soup,
did you fly?"
Wittle Bittle Dumpling Soup said,
"I think I did."

Big Father Robin said,
"Come down from there at once.
You might fall."

Ickle Bickle Robin took a big brave hop.

Ickle Bickle Robin flew.

Paperback Home Library

Books are a wonderful investment for the whole family. Fortunately, we now have an abundance of choice in hard and soft covers. The five lists that follow may be given to parents and other interested adults who would like to build an at-home library for their children. Although these are paperback choices, they can be found in hardcover too and can be purchased at booksellers or borrowed from libraries.

There are five lists, each with approximately 25 titles for children from babies to 13 years. Since it can be overwhelming to recommend an enormous list of books at once, ideally, four of the lists should be distributed to the same audience over a year's time. Perhaps you will distribute a list at the beginning of each season. The fifth list can be handed out during any holiday season as a suggested list of gift books. I often suggest to parents that they make extra copies of this Gift List for Grandma and Aunt Bessie, both of whom always want to know, "What can I get Beth for her birthday?"

The idea for these lists came about when I spoke to parents and staff in International/American Schools around the world. The parents often move their families every three years to a new country. They don't want to carry heavy books from site to site but would like to provide their children with easy access to books. I've found that stateside parents are equally interested in providing their children with good books and buying books in paperback editions make them more affordable, as well as more portable.

The selection of books here tends to be rather classic. These are books that everyone should read at some time in their lives, preferably during childhood, so that they'll want to revisit them as old friends, later in life and in the context of other readings they've added. The date of publication has purposely been left off these lists, so that parents will not feel pressured to have only current bestsellers. Adults who primarily read bestsellers themselves may not be aware that classic children's books can stay in print for many years. Some of the very best children's books were written decades ago and are still easily available and as fresh as when they were first released. General age ranges are designated on the lists to indicate to parents the appropriateness of the readings for their children at various stages. The lists can be duplicated directly from this book for distribution and there is room for your own institution's logo and any note you wish to add on the lists, as well as a bookmark to accompany each list, which parents can cut out and give their children. In addition to these lists, the Children's Book Council (67 Irving Place, New York, N.Y. 10276) has developed lists of recent paperback and hardcover books for libraries to distribute to adults and these can be used to update and supplement your master lists as new titles become available.

Bookstores specializing in children's books are opening all over the country and you can track down such stores in your area through the yellow pages of your local telephone book or you can contact American Booksellers for Children, a division of the American Booksellers Association, 175 Ash Street, St. Paul, Minnesota 55126 for more information and for their book list.

A Paperback Home Library—List 1

Brenner, Barbara. *Wagon Wheels*. Art by Don Bolognese. Harper. Ages 6–8.
  A family travels to Kansas to settle on a homestead.

Bridwell, Norman. *Clifford, the Big Red Dog*. Art by author. Scholastic. Ages 0–5.
  First book in a series about a huge red dog.

Cole, Brock. *The Goats*. Farrar. Ages 12–13.
  A boy and a girl are left on an island as a practical joke and learn about themselves.

Cole, Joanna. *The Magic School Bus inside the Earth*. Art by Bruce Degen. Scholastic. Ages 7–12.
  Ms. Frizzle and her pupils travel inside the earth on a field trip.

Cole, William. *Oh, What Nonsense!* Art by Tomi Ungerer. Puffin. Ages 8–12.
  Funny poems and pictures.

Conford, Ellen. *A Job for Jenny Archer*. Art by Diane Palmisciano. Little. Ages 7–10.
  Jenny thinks of several money-making schemes.

Cooney, Barbara. *Miss Rumphius*. Art by author. Puffin. Ages 7–11.
  Miss Rumphius plants lupins and makes the world beautiful.

Day, Alexandra. *Frank and Ernest*. Art by the author. Scholastic. All ages.
  An elephant and a bear learn the special language needed to work in a diner.

DeJong, Meindert. *The House of Sixty Fathers*. Art by Maurice Sendak. Harper. Ages 12–13.
  Tien Pao searches for his family in Japanese occupied China.

Demuth, Patricia Brennan. *Max, the Bad-Talking Parrot*. Art by Bo Zaunders. Dutton. Ages 5–7.
  What is Max really saying?

duBois, William Pene. *The 21 Balloons*. Viking. Ages 8–11.
   Castaways on an island and each family takes turns in preparing meals.

Farber, Norma. *How Does It Feel to Be Old?* Art by Trina Schart Hyman. Dutton. Ages 8–12.
   A young girl and her grandmother talk about old age.

Flack, Marjorie. *Angus and the Cat*. Art by author. Doubleday. Ages 0–5.
   Angus, a Scotty, chases the new cat.

Galdone, Paul. *The Three Bears*. Art by author. Clarion. Ages 3–5.
   The classic story of the three bears and their visitor.

Gardiner, John Reynolds. *Stone Fox*. Art by Marcia Sewall. Harper. Ages 10–12.
   A memorable dog race between a staunch mountain man and ten-year-old Willy.

Hoban, Tana. *Is It Red? Is It Yellow? Is It Blue?* Photos by author. Mulberry. Ages 0–5.
   Photos help children identify the primary colors.

Howe, James and Deborah Howe. *Bunnicula: A Rabbit Tale of Mystery*. Art by Alan Daniel. Avon. Ages 8–12.
   Harold the dog and Chester the cat are sure the rabbit is a vampire bunny.

Hurwitz, Johanna. *Much Ado about Aldo*. Art by John Wallner. Puffin. Ages 7–11.
   Aldo observes the food chain at school and decides to become a vegetarian.

Kendall, Carol. *The Gammage Cup*. Art by Erik Blegvad. Harcourt. Ages 8–12.
   The Minnipins rise up against the Periods in an exciting fantasy.

Lofting, Hugh. *The Voyages of Doctor Doolittle*. Dell. Ages 7–12.
   Dr. Doolittle, who talks to animals, takes a trip with his animal friends.

McCloskey, Robert. *Blueberries for Sal*. Art by author. Viking. Ages 0–5.
   A little girl and a little bear enjoy a day of berry picking.

Mosel, Arlene. *Tikki Tikki Tembo*. Art by Blair Lent. Holt. Ages 5–9.
   A boy with a very long name falls into a well.

Myers, Walter Dean. *Scorpions*. Harper. Ages 12–13.
   Jamal reluctantly becomes the leader of a Harlem gang.

Naylor, Phyllis Reynolds. *Alice in Rapture, Sort of*. Dell. Ages 9–11.
   Alice's adventures with a "sort of" boyfriend in the summer before entering junior high school.

O'Dell, Scott. *Island of the Blue Dolphins*. Dell. Ages 12–13.
   Karona survives alone for 18 years on a deserted California island.

Paterson, Katherine. *Bridge to Terabithia*. Harper. Ages 10–13.
   Jess and Leslie make Terabithia their secret hiding place.

Pearson, Tracey Campbell. *We Wish You a Merry Christmas*. Art by collector. Dial. All ages.
   Exuberant art illustrates this Christmas song.

Sachs, Marilyn. *Dorrie's Book*. Avon. Ages 7–11.
   Dorrie is an only child . . . until the triplets arrive.

Simon, Seymour. *Stars*. Photos. Mulberry. Ages 6–9.
   Explore the night time sky with full color photographs.

Titherington, Jeanne. *Pumpkin Pumpkin*. Art by author. Mulberry. Ages 3–6.
Jamie watches a seed grow into a pumpkin.

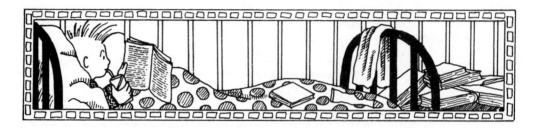

A Paperback Home Library—List 2

Babbitt, Natalie. *The Devil's Storybook*. Art by author. Farrar. Ages 8–12.
The Devil is outwitted in these short stories.

Banks, Lynne Reid. *The Indian in the Cupboard*. Art by Brock Cole. Avon. Ages 8–12.
A magic cupboard can turn toys into real live people.

Bemelmans, Ludwig. *Madeline*. Art by author. Viking. Ages 2–6.
A gritty orphan in Paris.

Blume, Judy. *Are You There, God? It's Me, Margaret*. Dell. Ages 11–13.
Margaret's story has become a classic story of a young girl's acceptance of puberty.

Brooks, Bruce. *The Moves Make the Man*. Harper. Ages 12–13.
Jerome tells the story of his white friend Bix's mental breakdown.

Cleary, Beverly. *Ramona the Brave*. Art by Alan Tiegreen. Dell. Ages 7–10.
Ramona's first weeks in first grade will have third graders laughing.

Clifton, Lucille. *The Lucky Stone*. Art by Dale Payson. Dell. Ages 7–11.
Three stories tell how a stone was lucky for three generations of girls.

dePaola, Tomie. *Hey Diddle Diddle*. Art by collector. Sandcastle. Ages 0–5.
Classic collection of nursery rhymes accompanied by Tomie dePaola's art.

Feelings, Muriel. *Jambo Means Hello*. Art by Tom Feelings. Dial. All ages.
A Swahili alphabet book.

Flack, Marjorie. *Angus Lost*. Art by author. Doubleday. Ages 0–5.
Angus, the Scotty, follows the milk man back home.

Gormley, Beatrice. *Mail-Order Wings*. Art by Emily Arnold McCully. Dutton. Ages 7–10.
The wings really work.

Griffith, Helen V. *Grandaddy's Place*. Art by James Stevenson. Mulberry. All ages.
Janetta makes friends with Grandaddy in his ramshackle house.

Haywood, Carolyn. *"B" Is for Betsy*. Harcourt. Ages 6–9.
  The first in a series of easy to read chapter books featuring Betsy in first grade.

Hurwitz, Johanna. *The Hot and Cold Summer*. Scholastic. Ages 8–12.
  Rory and Dick are confronted by a summer visitor, a girl named Bolivia.

Magorian, Michelle. *Good Night, Mr. Tom*. Harper. Ages 12–13.
  An abused evacuee from wartime London forms a bond of friendship with a crusty village man.

Marshall, James. *Yummers!* Art by author. Houghton. Ages 4–6.
  Eugene, a turtle, suggests a walk to overweight Emily, a pig.

Mayer, Mercer. *There's a Nightmare in My Closet*. Art by author. Dial. Ages 4–7.
  A little boy meets his nightmare.

Meltzer, Milton. *Starting from Home: A Writer's Beginnings*. Viking. Ages 12–14.
  A distinguished author tells his own story.

Morey, Walt. *Kavik, the Wolf Dog*. Scholastic. Ages 9–12.
  A dog journeys hundreds of miles to find the boy he loves.

Paulsen, Gary. *The Winter Room*. Dell. Ages 9–14.
  Uncle David tells stories through the long winter night.

Prelutsky, Jack. *It's Halloween*. Art by Marilyn Hafner. Scholastic. Ages 6–8.
  Happy Halloween in verse with a cassette to enjoy them.

Sachar, Louis. *Sideways Stories from Wayside School*. Avon. Ages 8–12.
  Thirty classrooms, one on top of the other. Zany stories and characters.

Sendak, Maurice. *Where the Wild Things Are*. Art by author. Ages 3–6.
  Max tames the wild things.

Smucker, Barbara. *Runaway to Freedom: The Story of the Underground Railway*. Art by Charles Lily. Harper. Ages 9–12.
  Two slaves struggle to reach Canada and freedom.

Steptoe, John. *The Story of Jumping Mouse*. Art by author. Mulberry. Ages 4–8.
  Magic frog gives courage to a valiant mouse with his advice.

Waber, Bernard. *Ira Sleeps Over*. Art by author. Houghton. Ages 4–6.
  Ira takes his teddy bear to Reggie's house.

Webster, Jean. *Daddy Long Legs*. Dell. Ages 11–13.
  This story of an orphan's college year is still charming. First published in 1912.

Ziefert, Harriet. *A New Coat for Anna*. Art by Anita Lobel. Knopf. Ages 7–12.
  Anna's mother manages to get a new coat for Anna after World War II.

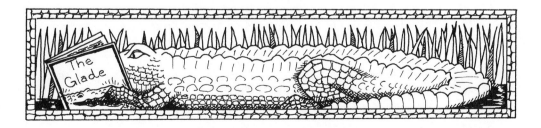

A Paperback Home Library—List 3

Aliki. *Dinosaur Bones*. Art by author. Harper. Ages 6–9.
How scientists study fossils and find out about dinosaurs.

Brown, Laurene Krasny and Marc Brown. *Visiting the Art Museum*. Art by Marc Brown. Dutton. Ages 6–9.
A family visits an art museum.

Campbell, Barbara. *Taking Care of Yoki*. Harper. Ages 9–11.
Two children rescue a horse destined for the glue factory in St. Louis during World War II.

Cleary, Beverly. *Ramona and Her Father*. Camelot. Ages 7–11.
Ramona supports her Dad when he loses his job.

Cole, William. *Oh, How Silly!* Art by Tomi Ungerer. Puffin. Ages 8–12.
A collection of funny poems.

Davis, Ossie. *Escape to Freedom: A Play About Young Frederick Douglas*. Puffin. Ages 9–12.
Frederick Douglas learns to read in this play about a former slave.

Flack, Marjorie. *Angus and the Ducks*. Art by author. Doubleday. Ages 0–5.
The Scotty, Angus, is chased by some ducks.

George, Jean Craigshead. *My Side of the Mountain*. Dutton. Ages 10–13.
Living alone in the Catskills. A survival adventure.

Goldstein, Bobbye S. *Bear in Mind: A Book of Bear Poems*. Art by William Pene deBois. Puffin. Ages 3–6.
Poems about bears in a picture-book format.

Holm, Anne. *North to Freedom*. Harcourt. Ages 8–12.
A 12-year-old boy tries to survive in a strange world.

Hush Little Baby. Art by Margot Zemach. Dutton. Ages 1–3.
An illustrated lullaby.

Kendall, Carol and Yao-wen Li. *Sweet and Sour: Tales from China*. Art by Shirley Felts. Clarion. Ages 9–12.
Short stories from the folklore of China.

Lewis, Thomas P. *Hill of Fire*. Art by Joan Sandin. Harper. Ages 6–8.
A volcano erupts in Mexico. For beginning readers.

Martin, Bill Jr. and John Archambault. *Here Are My Hands*. Art by Ted Rand. Holt. Ages 0–5.
The uses of various body parts accompanied by big bold art.

MacLachlan, Patricia. *The Facts and Fictions of Minna Pratt*. Harper. Ages 9–14.
Minna hopes to find a vibrato so she will be a better cellist. She gets some help from her new friend, Lucas.

McCloskey, Robert. *Make Way for Ducklings*. Art by author. Viking. Ages 1–6.
Mr. and Mrs. Mallard find the perfect place to bring up their family.

O'Brien, Robert C. *The Secret of Nimh*. Scholastic. Ages 8–12.
A group of highly intelligent rats search for a new home.

Prelutsky, Jack. *It's Valentine's Day*. Art by Yossi Abolafia. Scholastic. Ages 7–11.
Bouncy poems to read and a cassette for listening to them.

Sachs, Marilyn. *The Bear's House*. Avon. Ages 9–12.
Fran Ellen fantasizes about the family in the doll's house.

Shaw, Nancy. *Sheep in a Jeep*. Art by Margot Apple. Houghton. All ages.
Zany sheep travel by jeep. Short and funny.

Simon, Seymour. *Jupiter*. Illus. with photos. Mulberry. Ages 9–13.
Explore the planet Jupiter through color photos and a short text.

Singer, Isaac Bashevis. *Zlateh the Goat and Other Stories*. Art by Maurice Sendak. Harper. Ages 9–12.
Seven tales from Middle European folklore.

Slobodkina, Esphyr. *Caps for Sale*. Harper. Ages 0–5.
The classic story of a peddler who is imitated by monkeys.

Wells, Rosemary. *Through the Hidden Door*. Scholastic. Ages 9–14.
Barney makes friends with a younger boy at boarding school who leads him to a secret cave.

Westall, Robert. *Blitzcat*. Scholastic. Ages 12–13.
Follow the adventures of a cat through World War II Europe.

Williams, Vera B. *A Chair for My Mother*. Art by author. Mulberry. Ages 4–7.
A family saves pennies to replace mother's chair.

Yep, Lawrence. *Dragonwings*. Harper. Ages 12–13.
A Chinese boy and his father build an airplane.

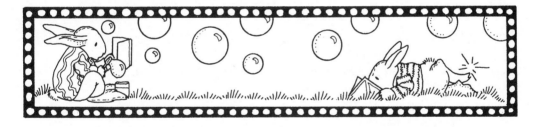

A Paperback Home Library—List 4

Adoff, Arnold. *Sports Pages*. Art by Steve Kuzma. Harper. Ages 10–13.
Poems about athletes.

Bond, Michael. *A Bear Called Paddington*. Art by Peggy Fortnum. Dell. Ages 8–12.
The first book in the series about an irrepressible bear.

Boston, Lucy. *A Stranger at Green Knowe*. Harcourt. Ages 8–12.
Ping and an escaped gorilla confront each other.

Cameron, Ann. *Stories Julian Tells*. Art by Ann Strugnell. Knopf. Ages 6–8.
Five stories about Julian, his friends and sensible father.

Cleary, Beverly. *The Mouse and the Motorcycle*. Camelot. Ages 7–10.
A mouse meets Keith and his toy motorcycle.

Conrad, Pam. *Prairie Songs.* Art by Darryll S. Zudeck. Harper. Ages 12–13.
   A stark look at pioneer life in Nebraska.

Dahl, Roald. *Matilda.* Art by Quentin Blake. Puffin. Ages 10–12.
   Matilda, a genius, leads her friends in a plan to get the better of some despicable adults. Children will love this.

Degen, Bruce. *Jamberry.* Art by author. Harper. Ages 3–6.
   A nonsense poem with exuberant art.

Dygard, Thomas J. *Winning Kicker.* Puffin. Ages 10–12.
   The place kicker is a girl.

Feelings, Muriel. *Moja Means One.* Art by Tom Feelings. Dial. All ages.
   A Swahili counting book.

Freedman, Russell. *Cowboys of the Wild West.* Photos. Clarion. Ages 8–14.
   What were cowboys really like?

George, Jean Craigshead. *Julie of the Wolves.* Art by John Schoenherr. Harper. Ages 12–13.
   Miyax, an eskimo, survives on the tundra on her way to San Francisco.

Griffith, Helen V. *Georgia Music.* Art by James Stevenson. Mulberry. Ages 6–9.
   A little girl finds a way to bring back Georgia music to her grandfather.

Hart, Jane. *Singing Bee.* Art by Anita Lobel. Lothrop. All ages.
   A collection of children's songs.

Holling, Holling Clancey. *Tree in the Trail.* Art by author. Houghton. Ages 7–12.
   A tree on the Santa Fe Trail watches history pass by for two hundred years.

Hurwitz, Johanna. *Hurray for Ali Baba Bernstein.* Scholastic. Ages 7–10.
   David Bernstein enters 4th grade and a world of fun.

King-Smith, Dick. *Pigs Might Fly.* Art by Mary Rayner. Scholastic. Ages 8–11.
   The runt of the litter can fly.

Lester, Julius. *This Strange New Feeling.* Scholastic. Ages 12–13.
   Three short stories about slavery and romance.

Miles, Betty. *The Real Me.* Avon. Ages 8–11.
   A girl fights sexism on her paper route.

Minarik, Else Holmelund. *A Kiss for Little Bear.* Art by Maurice Sendak. Harper. Ages 1–6.
   Easy-to-read stories featuring animals.

Noble, Trinka Hakes. *Apple Tree Christmas.* Art by author. Dial. Ages 7–11.
   A beloved apple tree is destroyed in a storm, but father saves pieces of it to make unique presents for his children.

Norton, Mary. *The Borrowers.* Art by Beth and Joe Krush. Harcourt. Ages 8–12.
   The first in a series about a miniature family who live under the kitchen floor.

Schwartz, Alvin. *All of Our Noses Are Here and Other Noodle Tales.* Art by Karen Ann Weinhaus. Harper. Ages 6–8.
   Five silly stories for the beginning reader.

_____. *Scary Stories to Tell in the Dark.* Art by Stephen Gammell. Ages 8–13.
   A traditional collection of scary stories.

Simon, Seymour. *Mars*. Photos. Mulberry. Ages 9–12.
  Explore the Red Planet through text and full color photographs.

Waber, Bernard. *An Anteater Named Arthur*. Art by author. Houghton. Ages 4–8.
  Short stories about a lovable anteater.

Walker, Barbara M. *The Little House Cookbook: Frontier Foods from Laura Ingalls Wilder's Classic Stories*. Art by Garth Williams. Harper. Ages 9–12.
  Food recipes from pioneer days.

A Paperback-Library Gift List

Atwater, Richard and Florence Atwater. *Mr. Popper's Penguins*. Dell. Ages 7–11.
  Mr. Popper is overjoyed to receive a penguin as a gift, but ends up with ten penguins.

Avi. *Romeo and Juliet Together (and Alive!) at Last*. Avon. Ages 12–13.
  A laugh-out-loud story of a 7th grade production of *Romeo and Juliet*.

Bang, Molly. *Ten, Nine, Eight*. Puffin. Ages 2–6.
  A counting book and a goodnight book.

Bauer, Marion Dane. *On My Honor*. Dell. Ages 9–11.
  Joel disobeys his father with tragic results. Excellent choice to share aloud.

Brittain, Bill. *Devil's Donkey*. Art by Andrew Glass. Harper. Ages 8–12.
  Dan'l is turned into a donkey.

Burnett, Frances Hodgson. *The Secret Garden*. Scholastic. Ages 9–12.
  A lonely disagreeable girl makes friends with a mysterious boy.

Byars, Betsy. *The Midnight Fox*. Art by Gail Owens. Puffin. Ages 8–12.
  A city boy adjusts to country life and saves a fox.

Cohen, Barbara. *Thank you, Jackie Robinson*. Atheneum. Ages 9–11.
  Sam and his elderly friend Davey love the Dodgers. Read aloud.

Crews, Donald. *Freight Train*. Art by author. Puffin. Ages 0–5.
  Follow a colorful freight train on its journey.

Eldin, Peter. *The Magic Handbook*. Wanderer. Ages 9–12.
  How to perform classic magic tricks.

Hautzig, Esther. *The Endless Steppe*. Harper. Ages 10–13.
  The Rudomir family spend five years in Siberia.

Haviland, Virginia, ed. *The Mother Goose Treasury*. Dell. Ages 1–3.
  Favorite nursery rhymes.

Hopkins, Lee Bennett. *Dinosaurs*. Art by Murray Tinkelman. Harcourt. Ages 7–12.
  Poems about dinosaurs.

———. *Surprises*. Art by Megan Lloyd. Harper. Ages 5–7.
  A selection of poems for the beginning reader.

Hurwitz, Johanna. *Aldo Applesauce*. Puffin. Ages 7–9.
  Aldo adjusts to a new school and makes a friend who wears a mustache.

Keats, Ezra Jack. *The Snowy Day*. Puffin. Ages 2–6.
  Peter plays in the first snow of the year.

King-Smith, Dick. *Babe, the Gallant Pig*. Dell. Ages 9–11.
  A pig becomes a sheep herder. A charming novel.

Leaf, Munro. *The Story of Ferdinand*. Art by author. Puffin. All ages.
  A gentle bull refuses to fight.

Lisle, Janet Taylor. *Afternoon of the Elves*. Scholastic. Ages 9–12.
  Who has made the tiny village in the backyard? Is it Sara-Kate—or elves?

Little, Jean. *Hey, World Here I Am!* Art by Sue Truesdell. Harper. Ages 8–11.
  Poems and vignettes on parents, cartwheels, clothes and war.

———. *Little by Little: A Writer's Education*. Penguin. Ages 9–12.
  From China to Canada—a writer for children tells her life story.

Lobel, Arnold. *Days with Frog and Toad*. Art by author. Harper. Ages 6–7.
  A classic early reader with five separate stories featuring two friends.

MacLachlan, Patricia. *Sarah, Plain and Tall*. Harper. Ages 8–12.
  A mail order bride is the new mother of two children of the prairie. A good read.

O'Neill, Mary. *Hailstones and Halibut Bones*. Art by John Wallner. Doubleday. Ages 7–11.
  Poems about colors.

Paulsen, Gary. *Hatchet*. Puffin. Ages 10–13.
  Brian learns to cope in the Canadian wilds when he survives a plane crash.

Perl, Lila. *The Great Ancestor Hunt: The Fun of Finding Out Who You Are.* Art by Erica Weihs. Illus. with photos. Clarion. Ages 8–14.
  Tracing family roots.

Potter, Beatrix. *The Tale of Peter Rabbit.* Art by author. Warne. Ages 0–5.
  The classic tale of a rabbit who disobeys.

Robinson, Barbara. *The Best Christmas Pageant Ever.* Art by Judith Gwyn Brown. Harper. Ages 8–12.
  The six Herdman children take over a school pageant.

Schwartz, David. *How Much Is a Million?* Art by Stephen Kellogg. Scholastic. Ages 8–11.
  Graphically and joyfully illustrates how much is a million.

Sendak, Maurice. *Chicken Soup with Rice.* Scholastic. Ages 3–6.
  An almanac of poems in a book-and-cassette set.

White, E. B. *Charlotte's Web.* Art by Garth Williams. Harper. Ages 8-11.
  A lovable pig is rescued by an intelligent spider.

Wilder, Laura Ingalls. *Little House in the Big Woods.* Art by Garth Williams. Harper. Ages 8–11.
  First in a series about the Ingalls pioneer family.

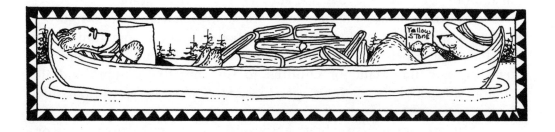

Chapter 4

Author Visits

Visit to Istanbul International Community School, Istanbul, Turkey

"An author is visiting today? A real author? A real, *live* author?"

How fortunate many of our students are today to have the opportunities to meet the people who write and illustrate books. There is something awe-inspiring about a person who writes a story and gets it published, and it's interesting and important for children to find out that authors and illustrators are people, sometimes very likeable, admirable, and fascinating people.

Some authors are also excellent, enthusiastic speakers; others are shy or uncomfortable about meeting students or are too busy to have time for school or library visits in their schedules. I've been lucky enough to be asked to give presentations to students in schools and groups of all sizes, ranging from a total of thirty-eight students with ages spanning kindergarten through eighth grade to giant Young Author Conferences with audiences numbering over one thousand.

Having just finished speaking at all twenty-three schools in a school district in California, the following are some suggestions for planning and carrying out an author visit. They are based on observations made during my own school visits and after discussions with author friends about their presentations in schools or public libraries.

Finding funds: Most authors will charge a fee for their visits, as they can only earn their livelihood when they are home writing books. Some may come at no cost (those are *very nice* people), but usually the only ones in a position to do this are those who live in the area and want to provide a service for their town, or brand-new authors who are thrilled to be asked to speak because for them it is an infrequent opportunity to meet and hear from their readers, or those who hope they will sell enough books at the presentation to cover the costs of lost time (but how do you put a price on delaying Chapter 3 of a novel-in-progress?). You can expect to pay anywhere from $50 to $5,000 with a large number of authors averaging between $100 and $1000, plus expenses. Sometimes, a popular author's publisher will pay a portion of the expenses involved, but usually only when the author is keynoting an important conference. Authors are often more generous with their time at regional, state, or national conferences, as in those situations they are getting more exposure to help promote their published works. When you can schedule an author's visit to your school for just before or after such a gathering that will be occurring in your city, and perhaps even publicize it in the conference program, your chances of receiving positive responses from "big name" authors increase.

You can raise money for the honorarium and author's expenses through the PTA, local business donations, school funds earmarked for special events, and, in some states, even state lottery money may be available for this use. Children take a valuable part in the author's visit when they work to raise the needed funds, and car washes, sales of popcorn or baked goods, and similar efforts are great ways to get everyone in the community involved. When an author must travel a great distance, the expenses may seem exorbitant. However, several schools in a district or an entire school system can partake in the event and share costs, or you can enlist the support and participation of other sponsors, such as the library, bookstores, parks and recreation department, private schools, and/or day care centers. Sharing the financial burden also makes it possible to share the excitement with other segments of the reading public and elicit support and involvement from the community at large.

Finding Authors: The Society of Children's Book Writers, Box 296 Mar Vista Station, Los Angeles, California 90066, can provide you with lists of authors in your area, and the state and local public library may also know of writers who live in the vicinity and who may be willing to participate in your program. Once you have some names of potential guests, it's natural to choose an author whose work you admire or who is widely renowned. I've discovered, though, that the most famous writers are frequently not affordable, or are not available for speaking engagements or—very often—are not appealing speakers. If possible, try to attend a meeting, conference, or talk where the author you are considering inviting to speak to your group will be presenting. If that isn't feasible, seek out opinions from those you trust who have heard that author speak to an audience. Because some authors write for a particular age group, keep your audience's interests and reading level in mind when choosing an appropriate speaker.

The most professional and efficient way to reach an author or his or her agent is through the author's last or most frequent publisher. You should write a letter inquiring about the author's availability for speaking engagements, clearly specifying the type of program you're planning and the fee and expenses you'd be able to pay. Follow up with a telephone call to confirm all arrangements. In many cases, you may only be able to deal with the author's agent and may not have direct contact with your speaker until the day of his or her talk. Whoever you speak with, though, be clear about the size of your group, the facilities you'll be offering, and the type of information you'd like your guest to cover.

Setting: Where you hold the author visit will set the tone of the talk. Keep the size of the audience, as well as the specific nature of the author or illustrator's presentation in mind when choosing a facility. If you know that the guest is coming armed with a slide show, video tape, or even a sketching pad in the case of an illustrator, be sure all in the room will have a clear view. Unless your group is extremely small, such as in a classroom setting, a microphone is almost always necessary. Check in advance that the sound system and any other required audio-visual equipment is in working order and that someone will be on hand throughout the program who is familiar with operating it.

Timing: Most speakers find thirty- to forty-minute talks, followed by brief (about fifteen minute) question-answer periods, the best length, but discuss this matter with the person you've asked to make a presentation. Most authors are willing to give two to four presentations during the day-long program, to accommodate different age groups, classes, or to keep the group size workable. Again, though, all such details should be negotiated at the time arrangements are made with the author or his or her agent.

Preparing the Audience: Talking to your students about what authors and illustrators do and reading aloud or suggesting individual readings of the books written by your upcoming guest will help build the children's anticipation and give them a better sense of what to expect. If there will be time for questions, discuss some of the things they'd like to know, so that you can field and gently discourage or rephrase inappropriate or inadvertently impolite queries (How old are you? How much money do you make?) and spark ideas, avoiding the awkward silences that can occur when questions are solicited. Decorating the classroom door, making placemats for a luncheon to honor the author, and creating book-centered mobiles or posters are all ways of building enthusiasm and helping the children participate in the event.

Depending on the age of your group and the frequency with which they encounter guests or assemblies, you may want to review some behavior guidelines, too, so that the excitement of a special day won't result in mayhem.

Getting Everyone Involved: Be sure to invite the Superintendant or Director, the school board members, parents, and any community members you know would be interested in attending the program. Be sure that the appropriate teachers are on hand to take charge, should discipline be necessary. Remember to designate a member of faculty, administration, or a student to come to the front and thank that speaker at the end of the presentation. Ask teachers to brief the children in advance on how to enter and leave the assembly in an orderly—quiet—fashion.

Introductions: How an author or illustrator is introduced will set the pace and tone for the presentation, so it's vital that whoever is handling the introduction be accurate and complete in researching the guest's background and accomplishments. Asking the principal or library director to make the introduction can add a note of formality and dignity. However, whether the whole task or just the preliminary research falls to you, ask for a brief biography of the author a few weeks before the visit. Then, send a draft of the planned remarks to the author or his publisher or agent in advance of the appearance, to be sure that you have all titles, dates, and chronologies straight and up to date. If you don't receive confirmation of accuracy, try to double-check with the speaker on the day of the presentation. It can be embarrassing for the author and for you if he needs to correct mistakes or mispronunciations before starting his talk. Some can cover such slip-ups with grace and humor; others will feel and seem uncomfortable, so do your best to be brief, welcoming—and right. It's important, too, to keep in mind when you introduce the guest. The second grade will be far more impressed that the author owns two llamas than they are concerned about where she earned her Ph.D.

Logistics: Some authors will bring copies of their books to sell on the spot, others will provide information for ordering the works. Be sure to contact the publisher of the books the author will be promoting to be sure that there are sufficient copies in inventory to cover orders and to find out about any discounts or other savings that are customary for group appearances. Some publishers also provide bookmarks, postcards, posters, shopping bags, or other giveaways to promote the author, the book, or the company itself. When available, such 'freebies' can heighten excitement, lend an air of festivity, and serve as momentos for those who attend, as well as advertising the author's books, so it's definitely worth checking.

Also, publishers sometimes will supply book plates for autographing books, and if you will be selling books after the talk, it's wise to allow time for signing. If special plates aren't available, consider reproducing your own with the school or library's logo or having the children design and make commemorative bookmarks that the author can sign. The book plates and bookmarks make nice souvenirs for all of those present, including those who may not be able to afford the cost of the book itself.

Details and Amenities: Remember that the speaker is your guest. A pleasant lunch at which administrators, faculty and/or staff, and perhaps a few of the older children, too, are present will help give the author a sense of the distinctive personality of your school or library. Don't forget to provide a glass of water on a table near the microphone, a pad and pencil for jotting last minute notes, and a floor plan of the building (with restrooms marked). If it's necessary to stay on a tight schedule, discuss the timing with your guest speaker before the presentation, letting her know the point at which you would like to open the program to questions from the audience. If an easy-to-read wall clock is not visible from where the guest will speak, place a small clock on a nearby table or lectern. Some speakers appreciate receiving a signal as a "time check" a few minutes before they're expected to conclude, so that they can be sure to make any remaining, important points and end their talk smoothly.

Publicity: Invite the local newspaper to do a story on the author's visit, and also have the school newspaper's reporter "cover" the event. Or, assign class reporters to take notes and write reviews of the talk for a class newsletter, the school newspaper, or even to submit to the local paper. Ask volunteers to take candid photos and display an assortment on the bulletin board or in the school scrapbook soon after the visit. Sending a few prints to the visiting author is a thoughtful gesture of appreciation.

This may seem like an awful lot of work, but good planning, well in advance, is essential for a large gathering or a formal assembly. For a small group, an impromptu invitation to an author who is an acquaintance or local resident, can lead to a relaxed, informal discussion and time for lots of questions. Whatever the size or schedule, be sure to follow up soon after the visit with a note of thanks. You might want to have students write a class thank you or individual notes, as well. Authors get lots and lots of these letters and, though compliments are wonderful, I always enjoy hearing the children's observations, or receiving a sample of *their* writing with the thank-you notes.

Something to Read Before the Author Arrives

Now that you have arranged for an author to visit, I'm sure you will want to share the author's books with the children, and the following short story about one author's school visit, told from the point of view of my dog, Robbie, might also help to set the mood.

In Portland, Oregon the children raised money for Beverly Cleary to come and visit the school. Each class chose one of Cleary's books to celebrate. The children made posters and banners. They wore costumes representing the

books and a parade was held in the neighborhood where the author had spent much of her childhood. She rode in a white Volkswagen convertible and wore a wide-brimmed hat and a pink suit. There were dogs in the parade, but none quite so charming and unpredictable as my dog Robbie. If he had been there, something like this probably would have happened.

The Day the Author Came to Town

I don't hate all cats. It's just Emily that I can't stand. She lives next door. Her very favorite activity is driving me crazy. She sits on my fence curled up into this innocent-looking ball with a sweet smile on her face. I hate it. It's *my* fence and I do everything I possibly can to get her off. I bark furiously and as loudly as I can. I jump up and down trying to reach her. I run around in circles and run in and out of the house (I have my own doggy door) hoping that someone will do something about Emily intruding on our property. Usually, what happens is that I get yelled at to come into the house and "stop that racket."

If the weather is bad, I don't mind sitting in the house at all. Even when The Mom and The Dad are at work, and The Kid is in school, they leave the television on so I won't get bored. I love television. The news programs are pretty boring—too much talk and not enough action—but the commercials are great. Lots of times, there are dog-food commercials that would make your mouth water. There's this really great one where the dog follows this little toy train to a gigantic bag of dog food. Sometimes, I bark to get the family's attention. They think I'm barking at the dog on the screen.

It's hard being a dog. No one understands what you're saying. The Mom is taking French lessons and she has these tapes going all the time. "Bonjour, Je ma'appelle Andre." I don't know when she's going to use her French. I wish she would take Dog. She'd be able to use it right away speaking to me. I'd tell her I think the television soap operas are dumb. I don't know why they're called opera—no one ever sings. I do like the TV cooking classes. Once they roasted a whole side of beef. Wish they'd have repeats of that one. It was great.

One day, I was curled up in The Dad's favorite chair when The Kid came home from school. Usually, he doesn't talk much with The Mom. She says, "How was school?" and he says, "Fine" in this bright, cheery voice, and then goes out to play. I get to come along a lot. I love going out into the real world. I have to wear a leash because the family thinks I'll run away. Just because I ran away that one time when I was a puppy doesn't mean I'll ever do it again.

So, this one day The Kid comes home and says that he needs a costume.

"What for?" asks The Mom.

"Well, this author is coming to town and she's going to come to our school and we're going to have this big parade and everyone is going to wear costumes representing books. I don't know who or what to be," said The Kid.

"Don't worry about it," said The Mom. "We'll go to the library and read lots of books. We'll find a book character that just suits you."

So, that's how I got to be this big expert on children's books. Just ask me anything. I know all about Winnie the Pooh, Peter Rabit, and that spider, Charlotte. Every night, and sometimes after school, The Mom and Dad read to The Kid. The Kid reads aloud to them, too. They usually remember to show me the pictures.

The books I like best are the ones about dogs. There was one about a dog named Poofy that always jumps on people when they come visiting. Very true to life; I do that all the time. And there was one about this dog Harry that doesn't want to take a bath. I hate baths, too. There were books about cats, too, but those usually made me mad. One was about a cat that stows away on a balloon and I thought, "A dog could do that." The next day, The Kid brought home a book about a dog who gets to ride in a balloon.

Pretty soon, The Kid told us that Katherine, who lives next door, was going to be Ramona in the parade and she was going to take Emily along as a book character called Socks. Wow, was I jealous. I've seen lots of parades on television. They look like fun. I was furious, too. Emily doesn't look at all like Socks the cat. She just looks like Emily the pest.

And then one day, The Kid brought home the best book of all: a story about a dog who gets lost and who has a great adventure trying to find his kid. Right away, I realized that I'd be a perfect Ribsy. I mean I even look like him . . . well, sort of. I tried to tell the family that I wanted to be in the parade. I barked and chased my tail. I even spoke French. "Moi, voyez moi." The Mom didn't understand and no one else did either.

The very next day, The Kid comes home with this idea.

"I'm going to be Henry in the author parade and bring Andy along as Ribsy."

"What a splendid idea," said The Dad.

"It was actually Miss Burman's idea. There are going to be about five dogs and five cats in the parade.

"What if they fight?" asked The Mom.

"Why would they fight?" said The Kid. "Andy's great on a leash."

Finally, the day of the parade arrived. I had to have a bath, and as I said, I hate baths almost as much as I hate Emily. I got soap in my eyes and bubbles up my nose, and I had to get dried with a hair dryer. Dreadful! I went out to bark at Emily and was called back in immediately, so I wouldn't get dirty.

The Dad drove us to the school—and was it ever exciting. There was a band playing stuff like you hear on television on the Fourth of July and The Author was there, too. I didn't get to see her very well. She was too far away, sitting in an open car, dressed in pink and wearing a big white hat. She was surrounded by kids, all dressed in costumes. There was a witch, a robot, a lot of mice, a rabbit, a monkey, and a lot of princesses. Some of the adults were in costume, too. I recognized a Pinocchio, a Pippi Longstocking, and a Mary Poppins.

A giant pickle came over and told us where to stand for the parade. We had to stay with the other dogs. I know I looked exactly like my book character and so did The Kid, but some of the dogs and their kids didn't fit at all. I mean, no way could a Bedlington Terrier look like the Airedale in *What-a-Mess-the-Good* and that prissy little poodle-thing was supposed to be Josephine. I've never heard of a kid's book with a character named Josephine. I was polite, though. I sniffed everybody, and I jumped up on a few kids. I really tried not to bark, but it was all so exciting that I'm afraid I forgot myself until The Kid yelled at me.

Standing right there in front of the school was when I smelled Cat—a whole lot of Cat. I got into my point position. I look great that way: head held high, tail waving. I strained against the leash to see if I could see Cat, but all I saw was a huge house on wheels and the backs of four girls trying to hold the house without tipping it over.

The parade started. We walked slowly past a bunch of parents and kids. I got into a pretty good conversation with the poodle-thing who was pulling at her leash, too.

It happened just as we turned the corner. The girls stopped paying attention to the house, and it tipped over. Then I saw the Cats. Two groups ahead of us, there were at least six of them, and sitting in Katherine's arms like a princess on a throne was Emily. The Kid was pulling me to the left to help the girls, but I tugged straight ahead and found myself free.

I didn't stop to think. I just ran toward the Cats. It wasn't very polite to race through legs and around a bicycle and across a wagon, but I did.

It was mighty smart of Emily to see me coming. Cats scattered to the right and left, while Emily jumped down and sped straight ahead. She raced right past the honor guard and leapt up and into The Author's car.

Now, I've had lots of practice leaping against our fence, but I'm not really very tall. My first lunge at Emily failed; so did the second. I'm certain that I would have made that third try, but I didn't get the chance. At least five people (two cowboys, one bear, one Wild Thing, and The Kid) grabbed for my leash and I was back in captivity.

I was so disappointed that I stopped dead and sort of hung my head. I used my best "please take me with you" expression. That one often works if the family is going somewhere in the car and hadn't planned to take me. After I give them that look, I sit a little crookedly, open my mouth and sort of tilt my head. I'm sure that I look very appealing, because it works a lot, particularly if The Dad is standing around.

The Author must have been impressed with my superb acting, because in the midst of a lot of screaming and yelling she turned to one of the guppies standing near her and said, "Oh, I just love dogs." She leaned over the car door to pat me and her hat fell off. My Kid picked it up to hand to her and, before you could say "dog biscuit," The Kid and I were invited into The Author's open convertible. The truth is I didn't know what happened to Emily, but I was proud to be riding in the car, and I behaved pretty well. I sort of stood on The Author and leaned out of the car a few times, but mostly I just sat and enjoyed the ride, putting on my "best little doggie in America" expression.

Moms and dads waved from the street and little kids pointed at me. I was really excited and licked The Author's face. Got a direct hit, too! She pretended that she didn't mind, but she did. I can always tell the people who really enjoy being kissed. There aren't many of them. They tilt their heads back for more and sometimes put their arms around you. The "pretend-to-like-it" folks sort of gently ward you off with a straight arm while they wipe their faces.

We had wound around the neighborhood and when we got back to The Kid's school, The Mom was waiting to take me back home. There was lots of talk and The Author was surrounded again. I tried to go into the school but I was forced into our car instead.

Just before dinner, I was curled up on The Dad's lap, dozing. The television news was on—no good dog food commercials that night, just toothpaste—when suddenly The Dad called The Mom and The Kid. I was on television. They were showing the book parade and there I was inside the box with The Author beaming and The Kid waving.

Emily was there, too. How could I have been so dumb? She was sitting in her "drive Andy crazy" position on the trunk of the author's car. I barked and barked and jumped toward the television set.

"Look," said The Mom. "Andy sees himself and Emily on television. He's proud to be on the news, but he's furious that Emily is, too."

Good old The Mom. She is finally picking up a little Dog.

That was some day, the day The Author came to town.

PART II

Stories and Books to Show and Tell, to Read and Write

Chapter 5

Visual Storytelling

Visual storytelling refers to any visuals that you may use while telling a story. Although, applied broadly, this concept might include live animals or slides, our discussion here will be limited to reproducible pictures that can be used in a variety of ways to present a story. Hopefully, this short selection of visual stories will stir your creativity and inspire you and your student storytellers to develop your own visual stories.

Although, personally, I enjoy working with visuals, this concept should not be overused and may not fit everyone's temperament. If you begin to feel that every time you tell a story there must be visual media involved, you may soon find that you are competing with yourself for more and better visual ideas. There is also a danger that the visuals will overwhelm the narrative.

Beginning storytellers, including children, sometimes find that having something to do with their hands makes performing easier. If the pictures are put in order before the telling, the visuals can also give tellers a visual reminder of what happens next in the story. On the other hand, some people find that having to worry about manipulating pictures makes the telling more complicated. Try telling the same story with and without visuals to discover which approach seems most natural and comfortable for you. The stories included here are, for the most part, simple tales that can also be used with a more traditional style of telling. If you choose to tell the story without pictures, your listeners can imagine their own images (I find that many children who have been brought up watching television can no longer visualize a story, so they may need some practice in imagining the scenes and characters). Another time, you can use the pictures while telling the story. And, for yet a third rendition, let the children take the text and pictures home to tell that story to their families.

You might want to experiment with various visual techniques, using the pictures as stick puppets, pieces to be used on boards or aprons made of felt or Velcro, or as flip-card drawings. The drawings may be reproduced directly from the book. Many copy machines now have enlarging features, if you wish to make larger copies that the audience can see more easily. If the machine available to you does not, check a nearby professional copy service.

Use your choice of medium to color the pictures: watercolor, poster paint, puff paint, crayons, felt tip pens or a combination of media are all viable options. You will probably want to mount the pictures onto poster-board to make them more rigid, and so, easier to display. Rubber cement works well for this job, especially if you spread the fixative on both sides of the piece, wait one minute until the pictures are tacky, and then press them together. The pictures will be more durable and easier to handle if they are laminated. If you don't have access to a laminating machine, the telephone directory yellow pages can help you find a facility near you. The pictures can also be reproduced onto fabric if you prefer the flexibility of felt figures.

One approach I like in using pictures is to duplicate all of the drawings for children to take home as souvenirs. Then, they can tell the story themselves, arranging the pictures on the kitchen table or with the addition of craft magnets on the refrigerator or on a cookie sheet.

Using the Pictures as Stick Puppets

First, duplicate the pictures from the book. Then, you can color them, mount them on posterboard, and cut around the outlines of the pictures to create your puppet characters. In this case, too, laminating the pictures will give them longer wear and a more professional look. Turn a business envelope sideways (with a short side at the top), seal it, and slit the bottom short side; use glue or strapping tape to attach the envelope to the back of the picture. This will serve as a holder for the handle of the puppet. Paint sticks make good handles and are usually offered free at hardware stores or wherever paint is sold. If you are going to need more than two or three, you might find that a generous supply is provided more graciously if you confess that they will be used with children to create puppets. The sticks can be painted to give the puppets a finished look, and the envelope-holders on your puppets allow the handles to be removed for easy storage and to be used with other characters.

Using the Pictures on a Board

These reproducible pictures also make perfect figures to use on a felt board, magnetic board, Velcro board, or Velcro apron. Prepare the pictures by reproducing them, coloring them, and mounting them onto posterboard as explained above. Affix sand paper (rough cut), craft magnets, or Velcro to the back of the figures depending on the surface of the board you are using.

The Hook n' Loop Apron

Although I enjoy using these figures on boards, I now use a Hook N' Loop apron almost exclusively. This fabric was developed by the Charles Mayer

Studios (168 E. Market Street, Akron, Ohio. 44308–2095). It is surprisingly soft, comes in a large selection of colors, and can be purchased in yardage, boards, or as a one-size-fits-all apron (which I first asked them to make up for me several years ago). Write to the company for a catalog and color chart. The fabric acts as the loop part of the velcro. The hook part is available in notions departments of department stores, variety stores, and some hardware stores and comes in rolls with a peel away back that reveals a very strong glue. A small piece of the hook material can easily be adhered to the back of the pictures. I've discovered several advantages in using the apron, rather than a board. One is the fact that it is easier to store than the boards: You can just roll up the apron and put it away until you need it the next time. Also, since you are now wearing the fabric, your hands are free to gesture and manipulate the figures. You are more mobile and can walk right up to the children to show the pictures. In addition, you never need to turn your back on the audience to put something on a board behind you.

Using the Pictures as Flip Cards

If you duplicate and color the pictures and then glue them onto rectangular pieces of posterboard, you'll have the "pages" of a book. You can tell the story by holding up the cards one by one or perch them onto the tray of a chalkboard, or easel as you tell the story.

The Adventure

This is my retelling of a Swedish folk story that has all the appeal of a traditional fairy tale: there is a Princess, trolls, a magic incantation, and a plain, ordinary young adventurer.

The Adventure

It was a frightening time in the country. The princess had been captured by a troll family and been hidden somewhere in the deep dark forest.

The king's soldiers had tried to find the princess. The king's wizard had tried to find her using magic spells. A search committee appointed by the Queen had gotten as far as the forest. Of course, no one wanted to look for the princess in the forest . . . it was much too frightening.

The king sent out a proclamation: "Hear Ye, Hear Ye. Anyone who can find the princess and bring her back to the palace will win a prize." No one needed to know what the prize was to be, the king always awarded good prizes.

Several men made elaborate plans to look for the princess. Several women made lists of ideas to try, but most people just stood around and cried a lot.

One young boy who hadn't even heard about the missing princess decided when he woke up in the morning that it would be a good day to Have an Adventure. Since he didn't want to waste too much time looking for an Adventure, he went directly to the forest. He hadn't gone very far into the forest when he found a nice smooth rock that looked like a good place to lie down and look at the sky through the trees that grew all around the rock. Of course, he had brought a book to read, and he had just gotten to page two when he heard a "Ka-lump, Ka-lump, Ka-lump." He sat up and peered through the gloom. Coming towards him was a large, ugly troll with a big, bulbous nose. He was carrying a sack. . . .

"Greetings," said the boy.

"Who are you?" said the troll. "You have the smallest nose I've ever seen. Are you a dwarf?"

"I'm a boy. What have you in the sack?"

"It's a snake for our guest to eat. I'm sure she'll love it and love me for giving it to her."

"Who is your guest?" asked the boy.

'It's the king's daughter, the princess Katrine, but it's a secret."

The troll went off to the west and the boy went back to his book, but not for long. "Ka-lump, Ka-lump, Ka-lump" pounded through the forest. Along came another troll. This one had a chin that hung down to his knees, and he too carried a sack.

"Hello," said the boy.

The troll squinted at the boy. "Who are you? You're so little, are you an elf?"

"No. I'm a boy. What have you in the sack?"

"It's a surprise for the princess. I mean . . . for someone. I know she'll find it divine and she'll choose me to marry instead of one of my brothers. I have a toad for her."

The troll carried his sack off to the west.

The boy continued reading. A loud eerie sound, "Ka-lump, Ka-lump, Ka-lump" echoed through the trees.

The boy looked up to see a troll with enormous ears.

"Hello," said the boy.

"Who or what are you?" said the troll. "How can you hear with such small ears?"

"I'm a boy and I'm pretty sure I'm right in the middle of an Adventure. What's in the sack?"

"Oh, we are very excited . . . one of us will marry the princess. Don't tell anyone, but she's staying at our house. I've brought her a fat juicy spider to eat for dinner."

The troll started down the path, but this time the boy followed the troll right to an enormous, gloomy castle. He peeked in the window just in time to see Troll Mother greet her three sons. She had enormous ears, a large bulbous nose, a long chin that reached to her knees. She was very proud of her ugly looks and proud that her sons had inherited her best features.

"Hello, sons. Did you bring presents for the princess?"

"Yes. I have a snake and I saw a boy," said the troll with the big nose.

"I have a toad and I saw a boy," said the troll with the long chin.

"I have a spider and I saw a boy," said the troll with the large ears.

"What!" said the Troll Mother. "Don't you know that boys are dangerous? They can get rid of us by chanting . . .

> Come West Wind
> Come West Wind
> Blow on ears, nose, and chin
> Come West Wind
> Blow the trolls away."

"Never mind," said the first troll brother. "He'll never find us."

"Never mind," said the second troll brother. "He doesn't know the chant."

"Never mind," said the third troll brother. "Bring in the princess and let us see who she chooses to marry."

Troll Mother brought in the princess. She was usually a cheerful young lady, but not today. She missed her parents and fervently wished that she was home.

The trolls gave the princess her presents.

"Look. A tasty snake."

"Look what I brought, a nice fat toad."

"Look. I chose a spider just for you."

"Thank you," said the princess. She was always a polite young woman.

"It was thoughtful of you to think of me, but please, I would like to go home now."

"What an ungrateful girl you are," said the Troll Mother. "My handsome sons have brought you fine delicacies and you reject them and their gifts. You'll be sorry, we will have to punish you now."

Just then the boy called through the window:

"Come West Wind
Come West Wind
Blow on ears, nose and chin
Come West Wind
Blow the trolls away."

The trolls disappeared.
The boy introduced himself to the princess.
She was overjoyed to see the trolls disappear and thanked the boy.
When they got back to the king's castle the boy was awarded a prize of three bags of gold. He married the princess and kept the snake, the frog and the spider as pets.
What a delightful Adventure.

When Rabbit Fooled Tiger

Children, as well as adults, will appreciate the irony of this concise story in which a small rabbit outwits a fierce tiger. The figures I use, shown in the photograph have been painted on silk with a fabric dye. When they are used on a board or apron, they have a strong visual impact and are easily seen by everyone in a large group. Simpler drawings, such as the patterns here, would work as well, and the story can also be just as effective when told without visuals.

When Rabbit Fooled Tiger

Rabbit was frightened. It was her turn to provide food for the Tiger; king of the jungle.

Each morning a different animal was chosen to bring the tiger something to eat for his breakfast. Rabbit had nothing to bring but herself.

However, she did have an idea.

Tiger looked out of his house. "What is it, Rabbit?"

"You are the mighty king of the jungle. You must save us from the other tiger," said the rabbit.

"The other tiger? What other tiger?" said the tiger.

"The one by the river. Hurry, you must run him out of the jungle. He's as big as you are and he also has black and orange stripes."

The tiger followed the rabbit to the river.

"He was right here. Look! There he is," said the rabbit, and she pointed to the river.

Tiger peered into the river. He saw his own reflection staring up at him; a big fierce tiger.

"Ah ha," cried the tiger. "This is my territory. I'm coming to get you."

Tiger sprang into the river. Imagine how silly Tiger felt as he sputtered back up to the surface.

He put his wet tail between his legs, hung his head, and slunk off into the jungle.

The Seven Camels

This will be a familiar story type to anyone who has ever heard a story in which the hero forgets to count himself when he counts his horses, donkeys, or friends. You'll have to duplicate the camel figure six times to make this the seven-camel story of the title. If you have a lot of time, you can make it the ten-camel story or any number you wish. The story can be told using any other animal. I chose camels because I wanted to tell the story to children who were attending international schools while living in the Middle East. And . . . I like camels.

You might start this story by placing the seven camels on the storyboard or apron. Then, place Abdullah on one camel. As you count the camels, point to each one, skipping the camel Abdullah is riding. When it is appropriate to the story, remove Abdullah from the camel and then replace him, being sure to count the camel Abdullah rides only when he has dismounted. Another time that you tell the story, you might choose a child from the audience to act out Abdullah's part.

The Seven Camels

Abdullah was proud. Of all the boys in the village it was he who had been chosen to bring the seven camels to the Sultan's palace.

"Be careful," said his father. "Remember, the village is counting on you. Make sure that the camels don't stray off into the desert."

Abdullah assured his father that he would be careful. He climbed up onto one of the camels, waved goodbye and started off into the desert on the way to the Sultan's palace.

After a few minutes he started to worry. What if he lost one of the camels. "I better count and see if they are all here. 1-2-3-4-5-6."

Abdullah began to weep.

He got off the camel and looked to the left and the right, ahead and behind. Where was the seventh camel?

He counted again, 1-2-3-4-5-6-7. "Allah be praised," shouted Abdullah, and happily he remounted his camel.

After a few miles Abdullah called a halt and counted again: 1-2-3-4-5-6. Oh no! He lost one of the camels again.

He dismounted and raced here and there looking for the stray camel. Sadly he counted once again: 1-2-3-4-5-6-7.

Oh wonderful! The missing camel had reappeared.

He re-mounted and continued his journey. Abdullah and the camels arrived at the Sultan's gate. He was proud that he had safely brought all the camels to the palace. He counted one last time, 1-2-3-4-5-6.

Oh woe! At the last moment he had lost one of the camels.

Abdullah began to weep. "Why are you crying?" asked a little boy.

"I started from my village with seven camels and I've arrived with only six."

"Why do you say that?" asked the boy. "You have seven camels with you. 1-2-3-4-5-6-7."

"But no," protested the weeping Abdullah. "1-2-3-4-5-6."

"Silly man, you have not been counting the camel you are riding!"

"Thank you," said Abdullah. "Won't the Sultan be pleased that I arrived with all seven."

(Remove camels as you count: 1-2-3-4-5-6-7, ending with Abdullah's camel.)

Dessine-Moi Une Maison/Draw Me a House
By Helene Ray

Here is a draw-your-own story to use on a chalkboard. The text is provided in French and in English. The story is simple and repetitious, so even if a child doesn't understand a word of French (or another language that you may choose to use), she will be able to understand this story and will come to recognize the foreign words.

Draw the parts of the house as you tell the story. If you draw fairly well, you can add the figures for people, the cat, and the dog. If not, use the patterns provided, coloring and mounting them on posterboard. After you draw the house, you can set the characters on the chalkboard tray.

Dessine-Moi Une Maison
Draw Me a House

By Helene Ray

—c'est une maison.
—non, ce n'est pas une maison,
elle n'a pas de port.

This is a house.
No, this is not a house,
it has no door.

—voilà la porte,
c'est une maison.
—non, ce n'est pas une maison,
elle n'a pas de fenetres.

Here is the door,
this is a house.
No, it's not a house,
it has no windows.

—voilà les fenêtres,
c'est une maison.
—non, ce n'est pas une maison,
elle n'a pas de toit.

Here are the windows,
this is a house.
No, this is not a house,
it has no roof.

—voilà le toit.
c'est une maison.
—non, ce n'est pas une maison,
elle n'a pas de cheminée.

Here is the roof.
This is a house.
No, it's not a house,
It has no chimney.

—voilà la cheminée,
c'est une maison.
—non, ce n'est pas une maison,
il faut des volets
pour proteger du froid
pendant les nuits d'hiver,
et du soleil
pendant les jours d'été.

Here is the chimney,
this is a house.
No, this is not a house,
it needs shutters
to keep out the cold
winter nights,
and the sun
during the summer days.

—voilà des volets aux fenêtres,
c'est une maison.
—non, ce n'est pas une maison,
elle est vide,
personne n'y habite.

Here are the shutters,
this is a house.
No, this is not a house,
it is empty.
No one lives there.

—voilà des personnes aux fenêtres,
c'est une maison.
—non, ce n'est pas une maison,
il n'y a pas de chat,
une maison sans chat,
ce n'est pas une vraie maison.

Here are the people,
this is a house.
No, this is not a house,
there is no cat.
A house without a cat
is not a real house.

—voilà un chat
qui dort devant la porte.

Here is a cat
that sleeps in front of the door.

c'est une maison.
—non, ce n'est pas une maison,
une maison sans jardin,
ce n'est pas une vraie maison.

—violà le jardin
devant la maison.
es-tu contente?
—non, ce n'est pas une jardin,
il n'y a ni fleurs,
ni arbres,
ni oiseaux.

—voilà des fleurs,
des arbres

This is a house.
No, this is not a house,
a house without a garden
is not a real house.

Here's a garden
in front of the house.
Are you happy?
No, this is not a garden,
there aren't any flowers,
no trees,
no birds.

Here are flowers,
trees

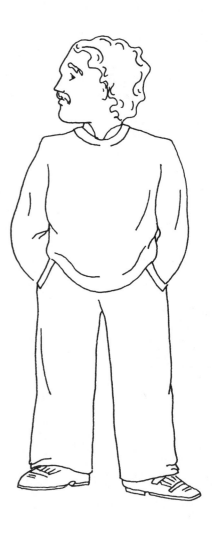

et des oiseaux,
c'est un jardin.
—je veux aussi un chien
pour garder la maison
et jouer avec moi.

—voilà le chien,
un gros toutou
tres doux.
est-ce tout?
oui, mais une chose encore.
le maison doit moi.
me voilà.

Maintenant c'est une vraie maison.

and birds,
this is a garden.
I also want a dog
to guard the house
and play with me.

Here's the dog,
a nice big
gentle dog.
Is that all?
Yes . . . but one last thing.
The house needs me.
Here I am.

Now it's a Real House.

Using Animals to Tell Visual Stories

The animals shown here can be used with several stories, including the three that follow. Animal masks also work very well with these stories, and you might want to explore variety stores during the pre-Halloween season for the best prices and selection. Or you can use the reproducible paper masks in the following books:

Anno, Matsumasa. *Anno's Masks.* Art by author. Crown, 1990.
Asch, Frank. *I Can Roar and I Can Blink.* Art by author. Crown, 1986.
Valat, Pierre-Marie. *Animal Faces.* Art by author. Dutton, 1987.

Say Cat

This is really just a joke, but when told with visuals, it becomes a full fledged story. A picture-book version of this story, *Who's A Clever Baby?* by David McKee (Lothrop, 1989), is based on city sights, instead of the country setting of this version, and will be fun to share with your students, as well.

You can involve the audience in your telling by enlarging the pictures of the animals, making them into stick puppets, as described above, and handing them out to different members of the audience as you tell the story.

Say Cat

Aunt Agatha came to visit. Baby was just learning to talk. Agatha took a walk around the farm with the baby.

"Look, Baby, look. See the Cat.
Say Cat, Baby."

"DOG," said Baby.

"Look, Baby, look. See the Goat.
Say Goat, Baby."

"DOG," said Baby.

"Look, Baby, look. See the Donkey.
Say Donkey, Baby."

"DOG," said Baby.

"Look, Baby, look. See the Cow.
Say Cow, Baby."

"DOG," said Baby.

"Look, Baby, look. See the Rooster.
Say Rooster, Baby."

"DOG," said Baby.

"Look, Baby, look. See the Chicken.
Say Chicken, Baby."

"DOG," said Baby.

"Look, Baby, look. See the Pig.
Say Pig, Baby."

"DOG," said Baby.

"Look, Baby, look. See the Dog.
Say Dog, Baby."

"CAT," said Baby.

Hello, Cat

This story is perfect for telling to young children or to children whose English is poor. The text is minimal and follows a simple pattern. The children will quickly catch onto the pattern, and spontaneously join into the telling of the story by imitating the animal sounds. Almost every child—around the world—enjoys making animal sounds. As you tell the simple story, select children and give them the animal puppets to hold up in front of the audience. If some of the children speak languages other than English, you will find out that domestic animals do not make the same sounds in foreign languages. This story is also effective without the pictures. Assign each child the part of a different animal to act out. Have a large group? Several children can be assigned the same animal.

Hello, Cat

One spring day a little boy took a walk.
He met a cat. "Hello, Cat."
The cat said, "Meow."
He met a dog. "Hello, Dog."
The dog said, "Woof, Woof."
He met a cow. "Hello, Cow."
The cow said, "Moo, Moo."
He met a pig. "Hello, Pig."
The pig said, "Oink, Oink."
He met a rooster, "Hello, Rooster."
The rooster said, "Cock-a-doodle-do."
The boy met a girl. "Hello."
The girl said, "Hello."

We Love Books

Any tag line (Happy Birthday, Happy New Year, Congratulations) can end this short story. Use the names of the animals for which the patterns are provided for the story, or use the names of each of the children. Alert the audience that they will shout out the last line of the story and have them rehearse the last line before you begin.

The cat told the dog.
The dog told the cow.
The cow told the pig.
The pig told the rooster.
The rooster told you.
And you told them:
WE LOVE BOOKS

Chapter 6

Teaching Children to Tell Stories

When I was a child, our home in Washington, D.C., had a fenced back yard with a porch that made a perfect stage. This was where the neighborhood kids gathered to "perform" in fairy-tale plays directed by me. I took over the role of director because not all of my friends could imagine what happened next as easily as I could. The only reason that I knew what the princess said to the witch is that I had had hundreds of stories read aloud to me. I liberally borrowed from these tales as we acted in plays on my back porch.

In order to retell these stories and make up new ones, I felt I had to have a cast of players to help me. It never occurred to me then that I didn't have to write every event as a scene in a play, but could just simply tell a story. Now that I've discovered storytelling, I'd like to encourage the whole world to tell stories. If I were really an evangelist, I would want to begin my National Storytelling Campaign by educating the youth—and, in fact, that's exactly what I'd like to see happen.

Introduce your children to the art of storytelling and they will surely keep telling into adulthood. Telling stories familiarizes children with the world of literature and teaches listening and speaking skills. Another wonderful by-product of storytelling is an increase in a child's self esteem. It's difficult not to feel good about yourself when your peers are praising you for telling a great story.

126

At the moment, I'm living in California, where schools tend to have large classes. Therefore, I think in terms of teaching thirty-five children at once; when I conduct school storytelling sessions, I often tell stories to four hundred to five hundred children in an assembly setting. Neither situation is ideal for teaching children the mechanics of telling stories. If you are planning a storytelling class, you might find it more workable to design it as an elective or after-school activity, so that you attract a smaller, highly motivated group.

The storytelling class can be held in one day, as an intensive seminar, or it can be extended for an entire school term or summer program. Obviously, the longer the period of time that you devote to the class, the more proficient your students will be at telling—and the more they'll enjoy their confidence in new expertise.

Choosing Your Students

We tend to think that the better students will excel in everything they try, and they often do. However, excellent storytellers are not necessarily academically oriented. I find that children who are not particularly good students are often extroverts. These youngsters are eager to be guided into an activity where they will win praise for their performance skills. Therefore, I'd suggest that anyone who thinks that they might be interested in this activity should be encouraged to attend the class.

I'm calling it a class, but learning to tell stories can be considered an "extracurricular" activity, just as learning to play a musical instrument or learning a sport. Since many of your potential students may not be sure what storytelling is, your first class is apt to be small. Once your first students graduate, become full-fledged storytellers, and start showing off their talents, you will probably end up with standing room only.

Although I constantly stress that book activities should be *fun*, I also believe children should have the same high standards of performance as adults who perform professionally. This means that the class and its work must be taken seriously by you and your students.

Getting Started

Each semester, I ask my college-age daughter whether her professors began the term by having the class introduce themselves. Because our sup-

posedly relaxed society really has a very formal structure, we need to emphasize poise and social skills throughout children's development, not just when they are very young. Although almost everyone in an elementary school class will raise their hands when I ask for volunteers, there is still a good deal of shyness about performing in front of a group of strangers.

Even if your students do know each other, you should take the time to have everyone in the room introduce themselves. If your class is large, let them break up into smaller groups of about five students, introduce themselves, and then rotate your groups. You can't just say, "Let's all get acquainted, introduce yourselves." To dispel any awkwardness, present the introductions as a warm-up exercise. Begin by telling the group exactly what is expected in their introductions. You might suggest that they give their names, what class they are in, what their favorite food is, and depending on how much time you have, you can ask students to tell what kind of animal they would choose to be and why or what color personality they think they would be if they were a color crayon. In this way, the introductions can be a brief lesson in developing a natural manner when speaking in front of a group.

To reassure your new recruits that this is a storytelling class, after the introductions, start them in telling stories right away. This is a good opportunity to expand the group's concept of what a story really is. You might want to have each child team up with a partner, so they can exchange jokes or riddles. Provide a collection of jokes and riddles on a sheet of paper, or if possible, bring in a collection of books. Let the children browse through the material and ask each to choose a joke to tell to his or her partner. When they are comfortable telling their selection to one person, they can tell the same joke to the whole group. The younger the children are, the more at ease they will be with this exercise. Almost any second or third grader has a repertoire of jokes and riddles.

Finding the Stories

The next step is to show children what the process of storytelling is all about. It feels good to go away with a story that you can tell when you get home. You can take a look at some of the visual stories in this book that might serve as good take-home stories. Or you can tell one of the stories in this chapter and let the children retell the story to each other until they feel comfortable with it. Usually, if you tell a "short and easy" story, the children will be able to learn it in one session and will go home with a story. Of course, that is your story; you selected it and told it for them to learn. During the next session, start working to help the children find the just-right-story for each of them.

For me, finding the story I want to tell can be the most difficult part of the whole storytelling process. While many people prefer to make up stories based on personal experience, as a librarian, I've made it a rule to tell almost exclusively from printed sources. Eventually, the story becomes tailored to your personality and may be considered "retold," but my theory is that, if you hear a good story well-told, you will want to rush to the library to borrow the book from which it came or on which it is based.

I really enjoy reading through stacks of books and stories in search of the perfect one, but because time and access to a good variety of story sources may often be limited, I've included some selections in this chapter that range

Bob Rubenstein's storytelling troupe in training are middle-school tellers from Eugene, Oregon.

from easy-to-tell to some slightly more advanced tales that I have been using with pleasure and success during the past thirty years. Of course, you don't have to limit yourself to just the stories I've collected for you in this book. In fact, story-finding is a perfect opportunity to introduce your students to the library's resources. Borrow as many books as you can find that contain stories your students may want to learn: folktales, fairy tales, short stories, myths, legends, and picture books are all possible choices. If you have enough time available during your class, let the students browse through the selection of books and take home those they'd like to read through more carefully. If your class is large, each student might informally offer an oral summary of the stories he or she read to help other students in choosing.

Kim Beri
(Viet Nam)

Nura Maznavi
(Sri Lanka)

JeeSoo Park (Korea)

Leslie Lin (China)

Adela Smith (America)

These girls have been telling stories since third grade and are now in seventh grade at Whittman Elementary School in the ABC Unified School District in Cerritos, California. They tell tales reflecting their own and many other cultures.

Of course, not everyone in the class needs to tell a different story. If you and they prefer, the whole group can work on the same one, comparing notes and contrasting individual storytelling styles. I still find it fascinating to hear how different a story becomes when another person tells it.

Story-Learning Techniques

Whether you provide the story or help the students find those they want to tell, do lead the class through the process of learning a story from print.

When I first entered storytelling, we didn't teach children to tell stories. No one *learned* to tell stories. An expressive person simply grew up following the lead of a family member, friend, or teacher who had told them the stories. And, when I first began teaching storytelling classes, my philosophy was "learn by doing"—sort of a whole-language approach to telling a story. I've noticed, though, that although whole language has become a popular educational trend, many storytelling instructors have students dissect a story in order to learn it. They outline the story, map the story, use memory cards, and do voice exercises. These tactics may work for some and are probably useful, but I find that children tend to be impatient with process; they want to see the results as quickly as possible while they're still learning. I also feel that making a big production of learning the story makes the whole enterprise feel like work, not fun. I find it easier and more rewarding for all to just plunge right into the telling.

Once a student has found a story, the first question usually posed is, "Do I have to memorize the story?" The answer really depends on the story. If you have chosen the story because of the wonderful writing, why would you not want to preserve the effect of the words as they were written? On the other hand, some stories, such as traditional folktales like The Three Bears or Little Red Riding Hood, are available in many different renditions, so it isn't the writing style that makes them memorable, but the familiar, amusing, or touching nature of the tale itself. In such instances, memorizing the story isn't necessary, as long as you know the events, characters, and important details and the order in which the plot unfolds. My technique is to start out by memorizing the story, letting it evolve through repeated tellings. Usually, the beginning and the end stay pretty much intact. However, somewhere in the middle, I start relating the tale in my own words. I've noticed that, when working with children, the tounger they are, the faster they learn the story. Often, after you read or tell a simple story to them once, they will be able to tell it back to you. Our educational system has taught children strong memo-

Leslie Lin

Adela Smith

JeeSoo Park

ry skills; why shouldn't we let them be used for something more enjoyable than tests?

Each person will find her own story-learning method, but my technique is to read the story once or twice and then start telling it to myself. My learning process accelerates if I can find someone to listen to me tell the story. I've joked in my seminars about telling stories to my dog, but I really do find animals to be good listeners, and they never say, "NO!" when you ask if they'd like to hear a story. It's the feeling of an audience I need, not a critique oof a half-learned story. So, if you try my method or learning by telling, look for a very patient friend. . .or a faithful dog.

The real challenge in storytelling is not in remembering the story, but in refining it and making it one's own. Like many storytellers, I refine while telling the story to successive audiences. That's why storytelling classes and clubs are so valuable and popular with professional storytellers, as well as with those new to the field. By trying it out and honing it in a group, you won't insult your formal audiences with a stumbling, unpolished presentation, and you'll receive informed criticism—and offer it to others.

The actual process of refining the story is a little tricky to define. Children, in particular, may not realize that knowing the words of a story is really only the beginning of learning to tell that story well to an audience. Often, like mini-computers, they will store the story in their memories, and then when the appropriate button is pushed, they reel it off in a monotone, word for word. The best way to encourage your students to incorporate expression, gestures, and timing and emotion into their performances is not to have them copy your inflections and mannerisms, but to help them visualize the charac-

Kim Beri   Nura Maznavi

ters and events of the story. Urge the children to take a minute or two to see the stories unfold in their heads. As their imaginations play out the scenes, your students will develop more personal interpretations of their stories. For instance, I often tell Jill Murphy's *Peace at Last,* in which Papa Bear is looking for a quiet place to sleep. He goes into the kitchen and lays down on the kitchen counter. Sometimes, I'm tempted to burst out laughing during my telling, as I'm envisioning my own kitchen counter—piled high with the books and papers that constantly cover it. I've noticed some of my students laughing during this part, as well. Are they seeing leftovers, dirty dishes, and homework books on their counters? I hope so. In another section of that story, Papa bear goes outside and lies down under a tree. When I'm telling this story in southern California, I picture a palm tree, when I'm telling it in Oregon, it's a fir. The more frequently you tell a story, the less you need to worry about the words and the more easily you can slip into the mood and spirit of the story.

It's good practice to urge your new storytellers to tell their stories out loud several times before they perform their story for the group. A practical way to accomplish this is to pair your students, letting them tell the stories to each other. Then, rematch the pair and have them tell the stories again to a new partner.

Once again, I find that children often learn the words of a story quickly and you may not find this step necessary at all, but it is usually a help in building confidence in telling the story to others. If your group of children becomes a bit bored with listening to each other, an alternative method is for each student to tell only the first part of the story to one partner and then tell the last half of the story to another student. Before resorting to this technique, though, try pointing out that developing listening skills is an important part of the art of storytelling.

Polishing the Story

Once your students know their stories and have improved their delivery, you can begin working on the fine points of interpretation and personal style. Although I truly believe that anyone can be taught to tell a story, it is here at the beginning that you will discover the truly gifted storyteller. This is the individual who, by instinct and talent, is able to put feeling into the telling and make the experience of the tale happen for the audience.

Voice

The voice is the instrument with which one "plays" the story. Some children's high voices are not suited to a particular story they may choose to tell. But, just as adults can concentrate on lowering and modulating their voices, so can children. The voice can be selectively lowered or raised for dramatic effect in the course of telling a particular story. Pausing between phrases or sentences can also increase the impact and help make the story come alive.

Using Dialects and Accents

Many of the folktales that will attract your young students will be recorded in dialect. I have mixed feelings about using accents. Done well, there is no doubt that an authentic ethnic or regional accent can improve the story and give it a measure of authenticity. On the other hand, if they are not done

with elan, they can actually be offensive and even seem derisive to the listeners. Another problem is that unless you are really confident with your telling of the story, you might find yourself changing dialects or losing it altogether in the middle of the tale.

I suggest that you encourage your beginning tellers to let the descriptions in the story give the listener the flavor of an accent. A well-written story should recreate the atmosphere and characters without the necessity of adding an accent that might seem artificial.

I once asked Virginia Hamilton, the noted children's author who has retold many black folktales in a literary style, incorporating dialect, for her opinion. I expressed my fear at telling these stories using the dialect inaccurately. She suggested that I just tell the stories in a way that makes me feel comfortable. This advice is probably wiser than any dictum on the subject could be; if the storyteller is natural and sincere, any effect she uses (or chooses not to use) is more likely to add to the telling.

Projection

One of the pitfalls into which adults and children alike often stumble is a poor vocal projection. Beginning tellers (and, often, seasoned performers, as well) are sometimes not aware that they cannot be heard. You'll need to alert your young performers to this danger. Simply tell them to speak up and look to the back of the room. They need to pretend that the President of the World is sitting in the back of the room and that they must speak up in order to be heard clearly and make a favorable impression. As important as developing good projection is, though, since microphones are available and used routinely in almost every school and library today, it's also important to teach children how to use the microphone without awkwardness.

Finding an Audience

Now that your students have their stories perfected, to whom can they tell them? I often start my students out by suggesting that they have ready-made audiences in their own families. Casual after-dinner tellings and more formal performances at family celebrations, such as birthday parties and holiday dinners, will give new tellers the confidence that only frequent presentations can provide—and may also prompt other family members to share stories.

Staff meetings at your school or library, PTA meetings, school assemblies, community fairs, fund-raisers, and block parties are all other chances for your students to demonstrate their skills. Offering their time and talents to tell stories to other classes in school, for day care centers, senior citizens centers, hospitals, and nursing homes will furnish the new storytellers opportunities to share the love of story with appreciative listeners. You and your group may be surprised how many eager audiences you'll find, once you let your community know of your availability for all kinds of events. And, as with any other talent, each appearance will give your storytellers added confidence and self-assurance.

Accessing Story Collections

This is the perfect time to encourage children to read with pleasure for a purpose of their own choosing. They can borrow books from the school or public library and just start reading until they find a story that they find appealing and want to learn. The obvious starting points in the search are folktales and fairy tales, myths, legends, picture books, and short stories. With such a treasure trove from which to pick, how can your students not become more familiar with good literature and develop a growing appreciation for story as an art form?

Part of learning to tell stories is gaining an understanding of the craft of storytelling and the issues and controversies that affect it. In aiding your students in making their story selections, it's useful to be aware of the ongoing dispute among some groups of librarians and folklorists over what constitutes a valid story. Many librarians tend to favor stories that are well-written over those that may have greater claims to authenticity as folklore. Despite my background in folklore and respect for the field, I tend to share that literary bias. I'm usually most concerned with whether I'm presenting a good story, well told. As important as it is that our folktales provide accurate reflections of various cultures, the genre of Paul Bunyan stories (one of which you'll find in Chapter 14 of this book) offer a good case in point for the argument that authenticity can be overly stressed. Many Americans who grew up with the tall tales about this giant logger, whose purported feats include the creation of the Grand Canyon and the Great Lakes, are somewhat shocked to learn that he is the creation of journalists and fiction writers, not the bona fide product of the regional folk imagination. As the stories of Paul were told to school children over the generations, however, and were embroidered and made more and more elaborate, I feel he's become a part of our national mythology, earning his status as a folk hero, regardless of his origins.

Members of storytelling troupe tell at fairs and to younger children

And, in cases of this kind, I prefer to table the argument over authenticity and get on with the good stories.

I think it's important that you have a story or two that you tell well ready when you introduce your students to storytelling, as well as several selections on hand from which they can choose, in case your library doesn't have an extensive selection of storytelling sources, or alternatively, if your students are, initially, overwhelmed by the vast assortment of story types that is available in many libraries.

In this chapter, you'll find a small collection of stories to get you and your students started. I've always wanted to have easy access to some of my favorite selections—sort of one-stop-shopping for stories. In assembling that dreamed-of grouping of "I promise they are wonderful" stories here, I found it very difficult to choose from a thirty-year collection of tried-and-told stories, and so I decided to eliminate the obvious: nursery tales and the more familiar, traditional tales. All of the stories in this batch are fairly easy to learn because the "plot" is so structured. I suggest that you just read through the stories and see if you think you would enjoy taking the time to learn one or more—or all of the stories. If you have not heard these stories told, you may want to read them aloud or find someone to read them aloud to you. Hearing the stories orally will give you a much better idea of how to evaluate them for your own telling.

I have told all of these stories a number of times to audiences of all ages and all levels of sophistication. Based on my experiences an audience responses, I have added brief introductory notes and tips on telling for each selection, as you may want to incorporate some of these suggestions into your own tellings. I know that these stories have "worked" reliably for me, and I think that you'll enjoy them, too.

These very short stories are really closer to jokes or anecdotes than to folktales, but they are easy to learn for beginners and always entertaining to audiences. The first, "Mario the Beggar," appears in several cultures; this version is Italian. When telling this short short story, the teller can puff himself up to look big and menacing. At the punch line, he should change demeanor and tone to appear and sound meek.

Mario the Beggar

a story from Italy

Mario was a great huge man. He had a bushy beard and piercing brown eyes. He made his living by begging. Mario would get close to someone, bend down, and say very softly, "Give me some money, or else. . . . "

This system worked very well. One day a frightened old woman went to her husband and said, "You must do something. I'm frightened of Mario."

The next day Antonio, the old woman's husband, walked close to Mario.

The beggar bent over Antonio and said in his hoarse whisper, "Give me some money, or else. . . . "

Antonio straightened himself up and looked as tough as he could and said in a loud voice, *"Or else what?"*

"Or else?" said the beggar—"or else? I will go away." And he crept meekly away!

"The Lost Donkey" is a story about Goha, and although he is at home in Saudi Arabia, the stories about him are similar to the Hodja stories told in Turkey. I suspect that Hodja and Goha stories are cousins. Joke-like in length and tone, the stories about this foolish trickster are useful for beginners to use for pacing between longer, more difficult stories to learn.

The Lost Donkey

a Goha story from Saudi Arabia

Goha's friend came to see him. "I am so sorry, Goha. The donkey you lent me ran away. He is lost."

Goha was sad. The donkey was his only possession. His shoulders slumped and he hung his head.

Suddenly he jumped up and danced for joy.

His friend was astonished. "Why are you laughing? Why are you dancing? Your donkey is gone."

"Well," said the Goha. "I'm happy because if I had been on the donkey I would be lost too."

"Three Rolls and Chocolate Eclair" is a very short joke that I heard in France. It won't take you long at all to learn, but when your audience chuckles after you tell it, you'll feel like a genuine storyteller.

Three Rolls and a Chocolate Eclair

One spring day a young student passed by a bakery in a small town in France. He was poor and hungry. Staring in the window, he counted his money and decided to step into the shop.

He bought a *petit pain*, a small tasty roll, and devoured it as soon as he left the shop. He was still hungry and, so, he reentered the bakery and purchased a second *petit pain*. It tasted good, but since he was still famished, he returned and bought a third roll. He ate it quickly. He still had enough money to buy yet another roll.

"No," thought the student. "This time I shall try one of those divine-looking chocolate eclairs." It was delicious.

"The eclair tasted better than the rolls," said the student. "And I am no longer at all hungry. What a fool I was not to buy the eclair first. Now I have wasted my money on three rolls when one eclair would have satisfied my hunger."

I think that everyone should try to have at least one Hans Christian Andersen story in his or her repertoire. The Princess and the Pea is a logical first choice because of its length. Nevertheless, it is a literary tale, that is, an authored piece and not one that was handed down from storyteller to storyteller, changing with each retelling. Andersen's stories were told in a spare, witty style and, indeed, should be told in a manner as close to the printed version as possible. Keep in mind, though, that you are not really telling the original story anyway, as the story has been translated from the Danish and retold in English by many writers.

This is one of the first stories I learned and, of course, I told it whenever I had a chance. How exhilarating it was for this new storyteller to hear that a child had come into the Children's Room of the main building of the New York Public Library at 42nd Street in New York City looking for the pea. (Frankly, I'm still puzzled at the poor manners of the princess. Why in the world does she complain about the pea in her bed when she was lucky to be offered a bed after arriving dripping wet at the palace?)

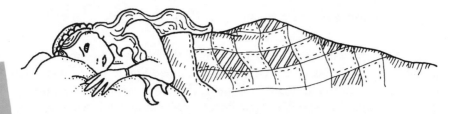

The Princess and the Pea

There was once a prince who wanted to marry a princess—but she must be a real princess. So, he traveled all around the world in order to find one. Princesses he found aplenty, but whether or not they were real he could never quite tell. There was always a little something the matter. And so, he came home and was so very sad because he could not find a real princess.

One night there was a dreadful storm. The rain came down in torrents and the wind blew. All at once there was a knock on the palace door. The old king himself went down to open it. Standing there in the wind and the rain was a princess. At least, she said that she was a princess. She certainly didn't look like one. Her hair was stringy and plastered against her face. Her clothes were sodden. The water had come in the toes of her shoes and out again at the heels. She was a dreadful mess. And yet, she declared that she was a real princess.

"We'll see about that," said the old queen. She went up to the spare bedroom and took all the bedclothes off the bed. On the bare boards she put one little pea. On top of the pea she put twenty mattresses. On top of the mattresses she put twenty feather beds. That was to be princess' bed for the night, and that's where she slept.

The next morning, they all asked, "How did you sleep?" "Just dreadfully," said the princess. "There was something round and hard in my bed. I'm black and blue all over."

Well, then the royal family knew that she was a real princess, for only a real princess could feel one little pea under twenty mattresses and twenty feather beds.

And so the prince married his princess and they lived happily ever after. As for the pea, they put it in a museum and it's probably still there—unless someone has stolen it.

And that's a true story.

The following is a silly ghost story that was told to me by Pat Gay, a children's librarian in LaGrange, Georgia. Learning this story should prove easy for your students, both because they'll be delighted to have a scary story to tell and because the surprise bit of nonsensical business at the end will show them the fun of storytelling. You may soon hear everyone in your town telling this story!

Long Red Fingernails and Red, Red Lips

Our house is the big white Victorian at the top of the hill. It's the one with the porch and lots of old oak trees with long branches. Sometimes, when the wind is blowing, those branches scrape against the windows making a "scratch . . . scratch . . . scratch" noise that scares you to death when you're alone.

Once, on a dark and stormy night, our daughter was upstairs in her room watching TV. The wind was howling and the rain beat down on the roof. Suddenly, she heard a "scratch . . . scratch . . . scratch" on her window. At first, she didn't pay much attention. But, something kept making that noise. She went to the window and opened the shutters. There, looking in, was an old, old woman. Water was dripping down her face and her hair was all wet and stringy.

"Do you want to know what I do with these LONG RED FINGERNAILS AND THESE RED, RED LIPS?" she moaned.

"No!" shouted Alejandra, and slammed the shutters.

Alejandra didn't tell anyone about this; perhaps she thought no one would believe her. Several weeks went by, but on the next stormy night, Alejandra was alone in her room doing homework. Again, she heard that "scratch . . . scratch . . . scratch" on her window. She really did not want to know what it was, but she went to the window and slowly opened the shutters. There, looking in the window, was that old, old woman. Water was pouring down her face and her hair was all wet and stringy.

"Do you want to know what I do with these LONG RED FINGERNAILS AND THESE RED, RED LIPS?" she groaned.

"No!" shouted Alejandra, and she slammed the shutters.

Months later, it was pouring down rain and the wind howled outside. Alejandra was in her room alone, reading. She heard that noise again at the windows: "scratch . . . scratch . . . scratch." This time, she went right to that window and threw open the shutters. There, staring back at her, was that same old, old woman. Water dripped down her face and her hair was all wet and stringy.

"Do you want to know what I do with these LONG RED FINGERNAILS AND RED, RED LIPS?" she moaned.

"What?" screamed Alejandra.

And she went "Blip—blip—blip!" (Put finger on bottom lip and flip lip up and down.)

As you start to search library shelves for good stories to tell, you will, no doubt, come across the collections of folklore by Harold Courlander. These compilations are a treasure trove for any storyteller. This story features the antics of the trickster Anansi the Spider. As you read, you will encounter Anansi in many tales and in all genres from picture books to scholarly works.

"Anansi's Hat-Shaking Dance" can be considered a *porquoi* story, that is, a tale that explains a fact of creation, for it does tell why the spider has a bald head. But, like other Anansi tales, it also gives insights into human nature and behavior. Although it is a bit longer than the preceding tales, this is still well within the easy-to-learn-and-tell category.

Many beginning storytellers wonder how to use their hands while telling. Anansi's frenetic dance with the hot beans on his head gives a textual clue for the appropriate movements: Start dancing!

Anansi's Hat-Shaking Dance

retold by Harold Courlander

If you look closely, you will see that Kwaku Anansi, the spider, has a bald head: It is said that in the old days he had hair, but that he lost it through vanity.

It happened that Anansi's mother-in-law died. When word came to Anansi's house, Aso, his wife, prepared to go at once to her own village for the funeral. But Anansi said to Aso: "You go ahead; I will follow."

When Aso had gone, Anansi said to himself: "When I go to my dead mother-in-law's house, I will have to show great grief over her death. I will have to refuse to eat. Therefore, I shall eat now." And so he sat in his own house and ate a huge meal. Then he put on his mourning clothes and went to Aso's village.

First there was the funeral. Afterwards there was a large feast. But Anansi refused to eat, out of respect for his wife's dead mother. He said: "What kind of man would I be to eat when I am mourning for my mother-in-law? I will eat only after the eighth day has passed."

Now this was not expected of him, because a man isn't required to starve himself simply because someone has died. But Anansi was the kind of person that when he ate, he ate twice as much as others, and when he danced, he danced more vigorously than others, and when he mourned, he had to mourn more loudly than anybody else. Whatever he did, he didn't want to be outdone by anyone else. And although he was very hungry, he couldn't bear to have people think he wasn't the greatest mourner at his own mother-in-law's funeral.

So he said: "Feed my friends, but as for me, I shall do without." So everyone ate—the porcupine, the rabbit, the snake, the guinea fowl, and the others. All except Anansi.

On the second day after the funeral they said to him again: "Eat, there is no need to starve."

But Anansi replied: "Oh no, not until the eighth day, when the mourning is over. What kind of man do you think I am?"

So the others ate. Anansi's stomach was empty, and he was unhappy.

On the third day they said again: "Eat, Kwaku Anansi, there is no need to go hungry."

But Anansi was stubborn. He said: "How can I eat when my wife's mother has been buried only three days?" And so the others ate, while Anansi smelled the food hungrily and suffered.

On the fourth day, Anansi was alone where a pot of beans was cooking over the fire. He smelled the beans and looked in the pot. At last he couldn't stand it any longer. He took a large spoon and dipped up a large portion of the beans, thinking to take it to a quiet place and eat it without anyone's knowing. But just then the dog, the guinea fowl, the rabbit, and the others returned to the place where the food was cooking.

To hide the beans, Anansi quickly poured them in his hat and put it on his head. The other people came to the pot and ate, saying again: "Anansi, you must eat."

He said: "No, what kind of man would I be?"

But the hot beans were burning his head. He jiggled his hat around with his hands. When he saw the others looking at him, he said: "Just at this very moment in my village the hat-shaking festival is taking place. I shake my hat in honor of the occasion."

The beans felt hotter than ever, and he jiggled his hat some more. He began to jump with pain, and he said: "Like this in my village they are doing the hat-shaking dance."

He danced about, jiggling his hat because of the heat. He yearned to take off his hat, but he could not because his friends would see the beans. So he shouted: "They are shaking and jiggling the hats in my village, like this! It is a great festival! I must go!

They said to him: "Kwaku Anansi, eat something before you go."

But now Anansi was jumping and writhing with the heat of the beans on his head. He shouted: "Oh no, they are shaking hats, they are wriggling hats and jumping like this! I must go to my village! They need me!"

He rushed out of the house, jumping and pushing his hat back and forth. His friends followed after him saying: "Eat before you go on your journey!"

But Anansi shouted: "What kind of man do you think I am, with my mother-in-law just buried?"

Even though they all followed right after him, he couldn't wait any longer, because the pain was too much, and he tore the hat from his head. When the dog saw, and the guinea fowl saw, and the rabbit saw, and all the others saw what was in the hat, and saw the hot beans sticking to Anansi's head, they stopped chasing him. They began to laugh and jeer.

Anansi was overcome with shame. He leaped into the tall grass, saying: "Hide me." And the grass hid him.

That is why Anansi is often found in the tall grass, where he was driven by shame. And you will see that his head is bald, for the hot beans he put in his hat burned off his hair.

All this happened because he tried to impress people at his mother-in-law's funeral.

The following story appeals to all ages and is particularly nice for new tellers to tell to family and community groups, as the theme of what we really do need in life and the old woman's creative solution of shooting the diamonds skyward to become stars in the heavens cut across all age barriers. This story is even more charming and memorable when used with an evening program, so that the audience can look up at the sky as they leave, searching for and counting the old woman's diamonds. And, of course, I do love the dog. . . .

I envy your fun in introducing this story to beginning tellers, and if you are tempted to save it for yourself, remember that wouldn't be fair to the story. Enjoy.

The Sack of Diamonds

by Helen Kronberg Olson

One day many years ago—so long ago in fact that the sky did not have stars as it does now—a little old woman, who lived alone except for her dog, had her one hundredth birthday.

The townspeople rejoiced with her and there was much feasting and dancing in the streets. Then, to the surprise of everyone, the king himself appeared and gave the little old woman a sack of diamonds for her birthday.

"Oh, me! Oh, my!" said the little old woman. "What a rare gift, a sack of diamonds!"

"Yes, indeed," exclaimed the people. "What a rare and valuable gift!"

Then the sun began to set and, after bidding the others good-by, the little old woman hurried home with her sack of diamonds and her dog. She did not want to be out late as, unless the moon was out, the starless nights were very dark indeed.

The next morning the little old woman sat in her little chair in her little house and considered what to do with the sack of diamonds.

"It is a rare gift, indeed," she said to her dog. "But I already have everything I need. I have my little house, my garden, and my warm cloak which will last for many a year."

Suddenly she jumped up from her chair. "Here I am sitting," she said, "when I should be up and about hiding this valuable treasure so it will be safe from robbers."

No sooner had she said this, than she dug a hole in her garden and buried the sack of diamonds.

But the dog immediately dug them up and brought them back to the old woman.

"Oh, me! Oh, my!" said the little old woman. "This will never do."

Next she hid them in the well. But when she took a drink of water she had to spit it out because it tasted of the sack.

"Oh, me! Oh, my!" said the little old woman. "I will hide the sack of diamonds in the chimney."

However, when she started a fire, all the smoke came into the house because the diamonds had stopped up the chimney.

"I cannot stand this," said the little old woman. "I will have to think of something else."

She strapped the sack on her back. But her back ached so from the weight that she soon had to take the sack off.

"Oh, me! Oh, my!" she said. "What to do? What to do?" And so saying, she sat on the sack of diamonds, but it was so uncomfortable that she soon had to get up.

"I wish I were rid of these diamonds," she said to her dog. "They have caused me nothing but trouble."

Early the next morning, the little old woman loaded the sack into her wheelbarrow. She pushed the wheelbarrow to the town square, and there she left her burdensome treasure.

Then she returned home with the empty wheelbarrow.

"Oh, me! Oh, my!" she told the dog. "How glad I am to be rid of those troublesome diamonds!"

Just then there was a knock on the door. Some townspeople were standing on the doorstep. They set down the sack of diamonds.

"We have found the sack of diamonds the king gave you," they said. "It was in the town square."

"Imagine that!" said the little old woman.

After the townspeople had left the little old woman shook her head.

"Oh, me! Oh, my!" she said. Then she opened the sack and looked at the diamonds. They sparkled and sparkled.

"The diamonds are pretty," she said to the dog, "but they are of no use to me."

Then she sat down in her chair, put her chin in her hand, and thought and thought.

Suddenly she jumped up. "Oh, me! Oh, my!" she said. "Now I know what to do. Why didn't I think of it sooner?"

She set to work immediately. Soon she had finished making a fine strong slingshot.

That night she went outside with the sack of diamonds and the slingshot. It was pitch black outside as it was most nights.

Then with her slingshot the little old woman shot one diamond after another into the black sky. There the diamonds stayed, making the night sky bright.

By the time she had gotten rid of the whole sack of diamonds the sky was filled with twinkling lights, where they still twinkle away to this very day.

"Now the diamonds are of use to everyone," she said to her dog. "And now I can enjoy my old age in peace without that sack of diamonds cluttering up my house."

This story appears in several different versions, most notably the Japanese folktale featuring a Mouse King looking for the perfect groom for his daughter. It can be useful for those readers who are looking for something that can be used to help children with sequencing as the story must be told in a logical order or it won't make sense.

The Wonderful Cat

There was once an Emperor who was exceedingly fond of his cat. He thought it was the most wonderful cat in the world. He wanted to give his cat a worthy name, something that would be fitting for this the most wonderful cat in the world.

Looking out of the palace one day, he observed that the sky covered the entire earth. "There is nothing so powerful as the all-encompassing sky. I will call my cat Sky." Everyone in the Emperor's court called the cat Sky for two whole weeks.

One morning the Emperor's wife looked up at the sky and said to her husband, "Look at the clouds up in the sky."

"Ah," said the Emperor. "There are clouds covering the mighty sky. Clouds must surely be more powerful than the sky. Attention, everyone. My wonderful cat will henceforth be called Cloud."

Everyone at court called the cat Cloud for the next two weeks.

One morning the Emperor's eldest son looked out and saw the clouds rolling across the sky.

"Look, father, the wind is moving the clouds."

"You are right, my son. The wind seems to be more powerful than the clouds. Attention, everyone. From now on my cat will be called Wind."

For two weeks everyone in court called the cat Wind.

One morning the Emperor's daughter was sitting in the sun with her back against the garden wall.

"Look, Father," she said. "The wind is stopped by the wall."

"You're right," said the Emperor. "The wall is surely more powerful than the wind. Attention, everyone. My wonderful cat will henceforth be called Wall." For two weeks everyone at court called the Emperor's cat Wall.

One morning the Emperor's youngest son was playing in the garden when he observed a mouse gnawing a hole in the garden wall.

"Look, Father" said youngest son. "This little mouse is making a hole in the wall."

"You're right" said the Emperor. "The mouse is surely more powerful than the wall. From now on we will call my wonderful cat Mouse."

For the next two weeks everyone in court called the Emperor's cat Mouse.

One morning the Emperor's mother was strolling in the garden when she chanced to observe the Emperor's cat at his work.

"Look, the cat is chasing the mouse. Look, the Emperor's cat has caught the mouse."

"Ah," exclaimed the Emperor. "My wonderful cat is more powerful than the sky. He is mightier than the wind. He is stronger than a wall. He is faster than a mouse. My wonderful cat is the most wonderful cat in the entire world. Attention, everyone. Henceforth the cat will be called . . . CAT."

And from then until now the Emperor's wonderful cat is called *Cat*.

Although I've told this story to children in grades four through six and they have all been astonished by the surprise ending, this is an especially great story to tell to young adults and adults. Your teenage storytellers will enjoy building the suspense throughout the tale.

I've frequently used this story to open a daylong workshop, a keynote address or any activity for which I want my audience's undivided attention, as it is usually received with stunned, thoughtful silence. Similarly, young storytellers might choose this selection to focus the scattered attention of a large or raucous group and to convince their peers that stories aren't just "kid stuff."

I haven't met Judith Gorog, the author of this short story, but we've maintained a correspondence since the publication of the collection in which this piece appears, *A Taste for Quiet and Other Disquieting Tales* (Philomel, 1982). She is delighted that her story is a popular choice for telling. If you and your storytellers like the somewhat eerie tone of this selection, look for some of Judith Gorog's other short story collections, including *Three Dreams and a Nightmare and Other Tales of the Dark* (Philomel, 1988), *In a Messy, Messy Room and Other Strange Stories* (Philomel, 1990), and *Winning Scheherazade* (Atheneum, 1991).

I consider this a slightly more advanced story to tackle because, although it is not difficult to learn, it is longer and requires some finesse in the timing of the telling to create the appropriate jolt of shock for the listener at the end of the story. One tip for creating that impact when you tell this: Make sure that you pause before the final wish to create the proper tension for the audience.

Those Three Wishes

by Judith Gorog

No one ever said that Melinda Alice was nice. That wasn't the word used. No, she was clever, even witty. She was called—never to her face, however—Melinda Malice. Melinda Alice was clever and cruel. Her mother, when she thought about it at all, hoped Melinda would grow out of it. To her father, Melinda's very good grades mattered.

It was Melinda Alice, back in the eighth grade, who had labeled the shy, myopic new girl "Contamination" and was the first to pretend that anything or anyone touched by the new girl had to be cleaned, inoculated, or avoided. High school had merely given Melinda Alice greater scope for her talents.

The surprising thing about Melinda Alice was her power; no one trusted her, but no one avoided her either. She was always included, always in the middle. If you had seen her, pretty and witty, in the center of a group of students walking past your house, you'd have thought, "There goes a natural leader."

Melinda Alice had left for school early. She wanted to study alone in a quiet spot she had because there was going to be a big math test, and Melinda Alice was not prepared. That A mattered; so Melinda Alice walked to school alone, planning her studies. She didn't usually notice nature much, so she nearly stepped on a beautiful snail that was making its way across the sidewalk.

"Ugh. Yucky thing," thought Melinda Alice, then stopped. Not wanting to step on the snail accidentally was one thing, but now she lifted her shoe to crush it.

"Please don't," said the snail.

"Why not?" retorted Melinda Alice.

"I'll give you three wishes," replied the snail evenly.

"Agreed," said Melinda Alice. "My first wish is that my next," she paused a split second, "my next thousand wishes come true." She smiled triumphantly and opened her bag to take out a small notebook and pencil to keep track.

Melinda Alice was sure she heard the snail say, "What a clever girl," as it made it to the safety of an ivy bed beside the sidewalk.

During the rest of the walk to school, Melinda was occupied with wonderful ideas. She would have beautiful clothes. "Wish number two, that I will always be perfectly dressed," and she was just that. True, her new outfit was not a lot different from the one she had worn leaving the house, but that only meant Melinda Alice liked her own taste.

After thinking awhile, she wrote, "Wish number three. I wish for pierced ears and small gold earrings." Her father had not allowed Melinda to have pierced ears, but now she had them anyway. She felt her new earrings and shook her beautiful hair in delight. "I can have anything: stereo, tapes, TV videodisc, moped, car, anything! All my life!" She hugged her books to herself in delight.

By the time she reached school, Melinda was almost an altruist; she could wish for peace. Then she wondered, "Is the snail that powerful?" She felt her ears, looked at her perfect blouse, skirt, jacket, shoes. "I could make ugly people beautiful, cure cripples . . . " She stopped. The wave of altruism had washed past. "I could pay people back who deserve it!" Melinda Alice looked at the school, at all the kids. She had an enormous sense of power. "They all have to do what *I* want now." She walked down the crowded halls to her locker. Melinda Alice could be sweet; she could be witty. She could— The bell rang for homeroom. Melinda Alice stashed her books, slammed the locker shut, and just made it to her seat.

"Hey, Melinda Alice," whispered Fred. "You know that big math test next period?"

"Oh, no," grimaced Melinda Alice. Her thoughts raced; "That damned snail made me late, and I forgot to study."

"I'll blow it," she groaned aloud. "I wish I were dead."

I've long been a fan of Charlotte MacLeod's mysteries, so I bought *Grab Bag*, a collection of her short stories, to read during a long airplane flight. When I finished this selection, I was so excited that I turned to the dour man in the seat beside me and asked, "Want to hear a good story?"

This piece is quite short and easy to learn, but it takes some practice to master the several voices and to maintain the suspense that makes the ending a surprise, not merely a shock for the audience. Tell this one with a twinkle, so that your students will want to create the same sense of irony.

The High Price of Cat Food

by Charlotte MacLeod

"Puss, puss, puss."

"There she goes," said Miss Johnson. "That old cat of hers must have slipped his lead again. You might think she'd have more sense than to go looking for him at this time of night."

"Don't tell me," sighed Miss McGuffy. "I've begged and pleaded with her a hundred times. "Mrs. Quinter, I tell her, no cat's worth getting yourself killed for. There've been five stranglings so far this year already. You stay off the roads after dark, I tell her, or you'll be the sixth. But will she listen?"

"You can't tell her a thing," said Miss Johnson. "I said the same thing to her myself only last Thursday. If you think so much of that precious cat of yours, I said, why don't you keep him indoors? But she only simpered in that featherheaded way of hers and said oh no, she couldn't do that. Tommy would be so unhappy if he didn't have his little run. Then let him run in the daytime, I said. But you might as well talk to a stone wall."

"She ought to be locked up, if you ask me," said Miss McGuffy. "Living on bread and tea herself and feeding that smelly old thing chicken and tinned salmon, if you please. It's a disgrace."

"Well, she'll get herself strangled one of these foggy nights while she's out there hunting for him," said Miss Johnson, tugging the tea cosy sharply down over the pot. "And then where will she be?"

Where was she now? Mrs. Quinter thought she knew, but she wasn't quite sure. She pulled her old black coat tighter around her bent body. There was a bone-chilling dampness coming up from the slimy cobblestones.

"Puss, puss, puss!"

She'd put a long way between herself and her tiny basement flat by now. Still no lithe, shadowy form had bounded out of the blackness behind the dust bins. She slapped Tommy's thin nylon lead anxiously against the palm of her free hand. The empty collar dangled at one end. Miss Johnson had suggested that she buy the cat a smaller size, but Mrs. Quinter wouldn't hear of it.

"Oh no, I couldn't do that. What if the collar got caught on something and Tommy wasn't able to squirm loose from it? A cat could strangle that way."

"Better a cat than a human," Miss Johnson had sniffed. She'd meant well, of course.

"Puss, puss, puss!"

It would be warm at home. She'd set the teapot on the back of the stove and fixed Tommy's chicken on a blue willow plate. She'd been careful to remove all the bones. A cat might choke on a chicken bone. They knew how to make themselves cosy, she and Tommy.

She did wish they were both there right now, she in her comfortable chair by the fire and Tommy purring on her lap. It was no night for an old woman and a middle-aged cat to be prowling the streets.

"Puss, puss—oh!"

A figure loomed out of the mist, directly beside her. She had not heard footsteps.

"You'd best be getting home, Ma," boomed a not unfriendly male voice. "This is no place for a woman alone. Not with a mad strangler about."

"I know," she quavered, "but my cat slipped his collar and ran off. I daren't leave him out, in this neighborhood. There's no telling what might happen to him."

"A cat's got nine lives. You've only one. He'll find his way back all right, don't you fret. They always do. Get on with you, now. You're not safe here. Nobody is."

There was an edge of panic in the man's gruff voice as he tramped on past her over the cobblestones. He was much taller than she. Mrs. Quinter had to stand on tiptoe to fling the lead around his neck.

It was too bad he had to be the one this time. He had seemed a pleasant sort of man. But it cost so much to keep a cat properly fed these day. Her mended gloves fumbled awkwardly at his wallet. Twelve pounds. Excellent. That would take care of her and Tommy for weeks to come. She tucked the money inside her glove and replaced the wallet neatly in the dead man's pocket.

"Puss, puss, puss!"

She was almost home before the familiar, sinuous form pounced out of nowhere to wind its purring length around her weary legs.

"Tommy, you naughty cat," she cried. "I've been looking everywhere for you. Come home this instant and get your supper."

She snapped the collar under his jowls and took a turn of the lead around her glove. Miss Johnson, peering out from behind her curtain, saw the light go up in the entry across the way.

"Well, she's found him at last."

"And lucky she didn't find more than him," said Miss McGuffy. "A night like this, it isn't safe to be out."

Storytelling Resources—A Selected List

The best way to find a story to learn is to READ READ READ. Your beginning storytellers will need to find their own favorites that fit their particular personalities. A good story doesn't date or go out of style. This means that once you have taken the time to learn a story you will be able to tell it for years. This also means that the storytelling collections will be useful even after they have long gone out of print. The books listed in this bibliography are meant to give you a starting place in your search for the perfect story for you. Some of the collections are scholarly in tone, some will seem simpler, more like nursery stories. Several of the storytelling manuals have their own bibliographies of stories to tell and manuals to help you.

A good place to start hunting is at your public library. Browse through the folklore section, the short stories and the picture books. If you are interested in video or audio tapes write to the National Directory of Storytelling (NAPPS), PO Box 309, Jonesborough, Tn. 37659 for their catalog of storytelling materials.

Storytelling Manuals and Resources

Baker, Augusta and Ellin Greene. *Storytelling: Art and Technique.* Bowker, 1977.
    Selecting, preparing and presenting stories.

Bauer, Caroline Feller. *Handbook for Storytellers.* American Library Association, 1977.
    Finding, learning and telling stories, plus magic, puppets, music, and board stories.

Bettelheim, Bruno. *The Uses of Enchantment: The Meaning and Importance of Fairy Tales.* Knopf, 1976.
    The role of fairy tales in the lives of children—an academic discussion.

Blumberg, Rhoda. *The Truth About Dragons.* Art by Murray Tinkelman. Four Winds, 1980.

Dragon lore that can be used to introduce dragons stories or to create a dragon program.

Colwell, Eileen. *Storytelling*. Bodley Head, 1980.
A famous British storyteller and anthropologist tells "how to."

Gryski, Camilla. *Super String Games*. Art by Tom Sankey. Morrow, 1987.
Directions for creating string figures. Consider for transitional or introductory material in story programs.

Hamilton, Martha, and Mitch Weiss. *Children Tell Stories: A Teaching Guide*. Richard C. Owen, 1990.
Teaching children to tell stories including personal stories and tying into the curriculum. Sample stories appended.

Irving, Jan, and Robin Currie. *Glad Rags: Stories and Activities Featuring Clothes for Preschool Children*. Art by Tom Henrichsen. Libraries Unlimited, 1987.
Stories, poems, activities: a treasure chest of material. The authors have also written a similar book on another subject, *Full Speed Ahead: Stories and Activities for Children on Transportation* with art by Karen Wolf (Libraries Unlimited, 1988).

Lieberman, Jan. *Once Upon a Tradition: The Art of Storytelling*. Self-published, available by writing to: 121 Buckingham Dr. #57, Santa Clara, CA 95051.
A personal look at the art of storytelling.

Livo, Norma, and Sandra A. Rietz. *Storytelling: Process and Practice*. Libraries Unlimited, 1986.
Storytelling as an art. Another book by this author is *Storytelling Activities*. Libraries Unlimited, 1987.

Lyons, Mary E. *Sorrow's Kitchen: The Life and Folklore of Zora Neale Hurston*. Scribner's, 1990.
A biography and some of the tales told by a prolific African-American author.

MacDonald, Margaret Read. *The Storyteller's Sourcebook*. Gale, 1982.
Indexes folktale collections and picture books by motif, tale type and subject.

Maguire, Jack. *Creative Storytelling: Choosing, Inventing, and Sharing Tales for Children*. McGraw, 1985.
Overview of storytelling.

McHargue, Georgess. *The Beasts of Never: A History Natural and Unnatural of Monsters Mythical and Magical*. Art by Frank Bozzo. Delacorte, 1988, revised.
Dragons, sea monsters, unicorns and more examined and described.

Pellowski, Anne. *The Family Storytelling Handbook*. Art by Lynn Sweat. Macmillan, 1987.
Includes storytelling using paper, handkerchiefs and objects.

_____. *Hidden Stories in Plants*. Art by Lynn Sweat. Macmillan, 1990.
Plant-centered stories, folklore and activities.

_____. *The World of Storytelling: Expanded and Revised Edition*. H. W. Wilson, 1990.
History and styles of storytelling around the world.

Ross, Ramon. *The Storyteller.* Merrill, 1980.
    Practical handbook covers traditional storytelling, flannel boards, and puppets.

Schimmel, Nancy. *Just Enough to Make a Story: A Sourcebook for Storytelling.*
    Sister's Choice Press, 1982.
    Hints for the beginner, stories too.

Sierra, Judy. *The Flannel Board Storytelling Book.* H. W. Wilson, 1987.
    Text and patterns for traditional stories to use on a flannel board.

A Storytelling Calendar. Stotter Press, P.O. Box 726, Stinson Beach Ca. 94970.
    Yearly offering features full-color reproductions of art objects relating to storytelling.

Organizations

National Association for the Preservation and Perpetuation of Storytelling (NAPPS),
    P.O. Box 309, Jonesborough, TN 37659
    NAPPS publishes a journal and newsletter and puts on the largest storytelling festival
    in the U.S. A catalog of storytelling resources is available.

National Story League, 3509 Russell, #6, St. Louis, MO 63104
    The League has state and local groups that offer storytelling sessions in public institu-
    tions and it also publishes a magazine.

Newsletters

These publications are usually four to eight pages in length and publish regional
news and storytelling ideas and voice common concerns.

Association of Black Storytellers Newsletter
Box 11484
Baltimore, MD 21239

Jewish Storytelling Newsletter
Penninah Schram
Jewish Storytelling Center
92nd Street YM/YWHA Library
1395 Lexington Avenue, NY 10128

New York City Storytelling Newsletter
c/o Shelley Brenner
112 President Street
Brooklyn, NY 11231

Stories
Katy Rydell
12600 Woodbome Street
Los Angeles, CA 90066

The Story Bag Newsletter
c/o Harlynne Geisler
5361 Javier Street
San Diego, CA 92117-3215

Storyline
c/o Kate Frankel
1 Rochdale Way
Berkeley, CA 94708

Taleteller
Word Works Society of Alberta
10523-100 Avenue
Edmonton, Alberta
T5J 0A8 Canada

Tennessee Storytelling Journal/TAPPS (Tennessee Association for the Preservation and Perpetuation of Storytelling) Newsletter
Flora Joy
Eastern Tennessee State University, Box 21910A
Johnson City, TN 37614

Texas Teller
Texas Storytelling Association
c/o Stacy Schoolfield
Box 2806
Denton, TX 72602

Collections

Andersen, Hans Christian. *Tales and Stories by Hans Christian Andersen.* Translated by Patricia L. Conroy and Sven H. Rossel. University of Washington Press, 1980.
   The classic stories authentically translated from the Danish. Since there are no illustrations, the storyteller interprets from his own experience. The obvious choices of The Tinderbox and The Nightingale are here, as well as little-known tales.

Anderson, Lorrie, Irene Aubrey, and Louise McDiarmid. *Storytellers Rendezvous: Canadian Stories to Tell to Children.* Canadian Library Association, 1979.
   Notes and stories from both folk- and contemporary tales from Canada. *Storyteller's Encore: More Canadian Stories to Tell to Children* (Canadian Library Association, 1984) by the same authors is also of interest.

Babbit, Natalie. *The Devil's Storybook.* Art by author. Farrar, 1974.
   Delightfully witty. The devil is outwitted by a variety of memorable characters. The follow-up volume is *The Devil's Other Storybook* (Farrar, 1987).

Bach, Alice and J. Cheryl Exum. *Moses's Ark: Stories from the Bible*. Art by Leo and Diane Dillon. Delacorte, 1989.
Bible stories in narrative.

Bierhorst, John. *Doctor Coyote: A Native American Aesop's Fables*. Art by Wendy Watson. Macmillan, 1987.
Short fables that are easy to tell—with delightful pictures.

_____. *The Monkey's Haircut and Other Stories Told by the Maya*. Art by Robert Andrew Parker. Morrow, 1986.
These are short tales suitable for beginning storytellers.

Bryan, Ashley. *Beat the Story-Drum, Pum-Pum*. Art by the author. Atheneum, 1980.
Lots of rhythm in these Nigerian tales.

Cecil, Laura. *Boo! Stories to Make You Jump*. Art by Emma Chicester Clark. Greenwillow, 1990.
Short, easy-to-tell, slightly scary stories.

_____. *Stuff and Nonsense*. Art by Emma Chichester Clark. Greenwillow, 1989.
Folktales and literary contemporary tales, some humorous poems. Children will enjoy looking through this collection. Another worthwhile book by the same author and illustrator is *Listen to This* (Greenwillow, 1988).

Christian, Peggy. *The Old Coot*. Art by Eileen Christelow. Atheneum, 1991.
These amusing tales feature an old prospector and his mule.

Climo, Shirley. *Someone Saw a Spider: Spider Facts and Folktales*. Art by Dirk Zimmer. Crowell, 1985.
Create a spider program using the stories in this collection.

Cole, Joanna, and Stephanie Calmenson. *The Laugh Book: A New Treasury of Humor for Children*. Art by Marilyn Hafner. Doubleday, 1986.
Short stories from contemporary books, jokes, poems give this collection great child appeal.

Corrin, Sara, and Stephen Corrin. *The Faber Book of Modern Fairy Tales*. Art by Ann Strugnell. Faber, 1981.
Short stories authored by such famous British writers as Eleanor Farjeon, Philippa Pearce, and A. A. Milne.

Coville, Bruce. *Herds of Thunder, Manes of Gold: A Collection of Horse Stories and Poems*. Art by Ted Lewin. Doubleday, 1989.
Mostly excerpted from novels, these stories are introduced with the author's notes. Another book to look for by the same author is *The Unicorn Treasury: Stories, Poems, and Unicorn Lore* with art by Tim Hildebrandt (Doubleday, 1988).

Garner, Alan. *A Bag of Moonshine*. Art by Patrick James Lynch. Delacorte, 1986.
This collection of stories from Britain are suitable for young children to tell and hear. Some dialect is woven into the stories.

Gellman, Marc. *Does God Have a Big Toe? Stories about Stories in the Bible*. Harper, 1989.
The Old Testament seen with a twinkle of humor.

Gorog, Judith. *Three Dreams and a Nightmare and Other Tales of the Dark*. Philomel, 1988.

Just one of Gorog's slightly sinister stories collections. A good choice for younger children is *In A Messy Room* (Philomel, 1990).

Grindley, Sally. *The Read-to-Me Treasury.* Art by Toni Goffe. Doubleday, 1989.
Short stories, colorfully illustrated for younger children.

Hamilton, Virginia. *The People Could Fly: American Black Folktales.* Art by Leo and Diane Dillon. Knopf, 1985.
Authentic folktales with some dialect used. Another excellent book by the same author is *In the Beginning: Creation Stories from Around the World* with art by Barry Moser (Harcourt, 1988), a collection of twenty-five myths from various cultures with often-similar accounts of the origins of the universe.

Harris, Joel Chandler. *Jump on Over! The Adventures of Brer Rabbit and His Family.* Adapted by Van Dyke Parks. Art by Barry Moser. Harcourt, 1989.
These Brer Rabbit stories are lengthier than those in the collection by Julius Lester.

Hoke, Helen and Franklin Hoke. *Horrifying and Hideous Hauntings.* Dutton, 1986.
This is just one of several collections by Helen Hokes; all are excellent sources of telltale short stories.

Joseph, Lynn. *A Wave in Her Pocket: Stories from Trinidad.* Art by Brian Pinkney. Clarion, 1991.
Six short stories from Trinidad.

Kennedy, Richard. *Richard Kennedy: Collected Stories.* Art by Marcia Sewall. Harper, 1987.
Sophisticated and fairly long, these short stories are also original and intriguing.

Kimmel, Eric A. *Herschel of Ostropol.* Art by Arthur Friedman. Jewish Publication Society, 1981.
Short funny stories feature a Jewish folk hero.

Kipling, Rudyard. *Just So Stories.* Art by Michael Foreman. Viking, 1987.
The 1902 edition illustrated with paintings. Original how-and-why stories.

Jaffrey, Madhur. *Seasons of Splendor: Tales, Myths, and Legends of India.* Art by Michael Foreman. Atheneum, 1985.
Excellent background material accompany these tales.

Jennings, Paul. *Quirky Tales.* Viking, 1987.
Short stories frightening and original from Australia. Another book to look for by the same author is *Unbelievable!* (Viking, 1986).

Lester, Julius. *The Tales of Uncle Remus: The Adventures of Brer Rabbit.* Art by Jerry Pinkney. Dial, 1987.
These Brer Rabbit stories retain the spirit of the original version. An excellent source, and you'll find the further adventures of Brer and his friends in *More Tales of Uncle Remus* (Dial, 1988).

Low, Alice. *The Macmillan Book of Greek Gods and Heroes.* Art by Arvis Stewart. Macmillan, 1985.
The myths of Greece including Pandora, and the Golden Fleece.

MacDonald, Margaret Read. *Twenty Tellable Tales: Audience Participation Folktales for the Beginning Storyteller.* Art by Roxane Murphy. Wilson, 1986.
These are short and easy to tell. Notes and a useful bibliography are included. A

collection of spooky tales from the same author and illustrator is *When the Lights Go Out: Twenty Scary Tales to Tell* (Wilson, 1988).

Miller, Teresa, and Anne Pellowski. *Joining In: An Anthology of Audience Participation Stories and How to Tell Them.* Edited by Norma Livo. Yellow Moon, 1988.
Stories and tips from master tellers and teachers.

Monroe, Jean Guard, and Ray A. Williamson. *They Dance in the Sky: Native American Star Myths.* Houghton, 1987.
Sky lore of native American storytellers.

Nhuong, Nuynh Quang. *The Land I Lost: Adventures of a Boy in Vietnam.* Art by Vo-Dinh Mai. Harper, 1982.
Village stories feature water buffalo, and stories of character.

Peretz, I. L. *The Seven Good Years and Other Stories of I. L. Peretz.* Translated and adapted by Ester Hautzig. Art by Deborah Kogan Ray. Jewish Publication Society, 1984.
Yiddish stories adapted for telling.

Perrault, Charles. *The Glass Slipper: Charles Perrault's Tales of Times Past.* Translated by John Bierhorst. Art by Mitchell Miller. Four Winds, 1971.
Cinderella, Puss in Boots, Little Red Riding Hood and other familiar tales. These tales first appeared in 1697.

Philip, Neil, Ed. *The Spring of Butterflies: And Other Folktales of China's Minority People.* Translated by He Liyi. Art by Pan Aiqing and Li Zhao. Lothrop, 1983.
Tales of trickery and intrigue from Thai, Tibetan, and Yunnan people.

Pollack, Pamela. *The Random House Book of Humor for Children.* Art by Paul O. Zelinsky. Random House, 1988.
Short stories and excerpts from children's literature.

Porte, Barbara Ann. *Jesse's Ghost and Other Stories.* Greenwillow, 1983.
These original short stories will be popular with new and experienced storytellers.

Quayle, Eric. *The Shining Princess and other Japanese Legends.* Art by Michael Foreman. Arcade, 1989.
My Lord, Bag-O'-Rice, The Tongue-cut Sparrow and other traditional Japanese tales.

Rylant, Cynthia. *Every Living Thing.* Art by S. P. Schindler. Bradbury, 1985.
Short stories that feature animals and their relationships with children and adults. All of the stories are excellent.

Sandburg, Carl. *Rootabaga Stories.* Art by Michael Hague. Harcourt, 1989.
Lively nonsense in both Part I and Part II.

Sanfield, Steve. *The Adventures of High John the Conqueror.* Art by John Ward. Orchard, 1989.
A black American folk hero is featured in these short, amusing stories.

Schram, Peninnah. *Jewish Stories One Generation Tells Another.* Jason Aronson, 1987.
A lengthy collection of traditional Jewish stories.

Schwartz, Alvin. *Tales of Trickery from the Land of Spoof.* Art by David Christiana. Farrar, 1985.
Hoaxes and urban tricks.

Shannon, George. *Stories to Solve: Folktales from Around the World.* Art by Peter Sis. Greenwillow, 1985.
   Short puzzle stories. The audience can guess the ending before the storyteller reveals it.

Sierra, Judy and Robert Kaminski. *Twice Upon a Time: Stories to Tell, Retell, Act Out, and Write About.* Wilson, 1989.
   Twenty traditional stories and ideas to use for telling, creative drama, and as springboards to writing exercises.

Singer, Isaac Bashevis. *Zlateh the Goat and Other Stories.* Art by Maurice Sendak. Harper, 1966.
   A Nobel Prize-winner retells traditional Jewish tales.

Smith, Jimmy Neil. *Homespun: Tales from America's Favorite Storytellers.* Crown, 1988.
   American storytellers share their favorite stories.

Sonntag, Linda. *The Ghost Story Treasury.* Art by Annabel Spenceby. Putnam, 1987.
   Children will enjoy searching for stories here. There is color art on every page.

Timpanelli, Gioia. *Tales from the Roof of the World: Folktales of Tibet.* Art by Elizabeth Kelly Lockwood. Viking, 1984.
   These four stories have mystical quality. You'll want to introduce the culture of Tibet before you tell them.

Walker, Barbara K. *A Treasury of Turkish Folktales for Children.* Linett, 1988.
   These are short easy to tell folktales.

Wolkstein, Diane. *The Magic Orange Tree and Other Haitian Folktales.* Art by Elsa Henriguez. Knopf, 1978.
   Truly tellable tales from Haiti.

Yee, Paul. *Tales from Gold Mountain.* Art by Simon Ng. Macmillan, 1989.
   Short stories featuring the Chinese who came to North America.

Yep, Laurence. *The Rainbow People.* Art by David Wiesner. Harper, 1987.
   Authentic collection of Chinese tales told by Chinese Americans.

Yolen, Jane. *The Faery Flag: Stories and Poems of Fantasy and the Supernatural.* Orchard, 1989.
   Yolen is an excellent source for the storyteller in search of wonderful literary tales. She is also the author of *Dream Weaver* (Collins, 1979) and *Neptune Rising* (Philomel, 1982).

_____, ed. *Favorite Folktales from Around the World.* Pantheon, 1986.
   One of the many lengthy and worthwhile collections in the Pantheon fairy tale and folklore library. Browse around the world.

_____, Martin H. Greenberg, and Charles G. Waugh. *Dragons and Dreams: A Collection of New Fantasy and Science Fiction Stories.* Harper, 1986.
   Short stories scary and fun. Try "The Box," and "The Thing That Goes Bump in the Night."

Picture Books

Folktales

There are numerous attractively illustrated picture-book versions of original stories and folktales. Start with some of these and then browse through the library for others. Tell the story, and share the pictures.

Aardema, Verna. *Bringing the Rain to Kapiti Plain.* Art by Beatriz Vidal. Dial, 1981.
  Rhythmic story tells how Ki-put brought rain.

———. *Traveling to Tondo: A Tale of the Nkundo of Zaire.* Art by Will Hildebrand. Random House, 1991.
  Bowane, the civet cat, invites his friends to his wedding.

———. *Why Mosquitos Buzz in People's Ears: A West African Tale.* Art by Leo and Diane Dillon. Dial, 1975.
  An action story with magnificent pictures to share after or during the story.

Ada, Alma Flor. *The Gold Coin.* Art by Neil Waldman. Trans. from Spanish by Bernice Randall. Atheneum, 1991.
  Juan learns that a gold coin does not bring real happiness.

Alexander, Sue. *Nadia the Willful.* Art by Lloyd Bloom. Pantheon, 1983.
  A family comes to grips with the death of Hamed.

Carrick, Carol. *Alladin and the Wonderful Lamp.* Art by Donald Carrick. Scholastic, 1989.
  One of the classic stories from the Arabian Nights adapted for children. The art helps tell the story.

Cole, Judith. *The Moon, the Sun, and the Coyote.* Art by Cecile Schoberle. Simon, 1991.
  In folktale style, the coyote is granted wishes by the moon.

Kellogg, Steven. *Paul Bunyan.* Art by the author. Morrow, 1984. Paul and his blue ox adventure across America.

McKissack, Patricia. *Flossie and the Fox.* Art by Rachel Isadora. Dial, 1986.
  A spunky girl outwits a fox. Both the fox and Flossie are well-characterized. A long story.

———. *Mirandy and Brother Wind.* Art by Jerry Pinkney. Knopf, 1988.
  How do you catch the wind?

Steptoe, John. *Mufaro's Beautiful Daughters: An African Tale.* Art by the author. Lothrop, 1987.
  A modern fable features a kind and considerate daughter and a selfish bad-tempered daughter.

Tompert, Ann. *Grandfather Tony's Story: A Tale Told with Tangrams.* Art by Robert Andrew Parker. Crown, 1990.
  This story can be told traditionally or visually using tangrams.

Wright, Jill. *The Old Woman and the Willy Nilly Man.* Art by Glen Rounds. Putnam, 1987.

This is a long story, but worth the time to learn. The old woman bribes the Willy Nilly man to help her with her troublesome dancin' shoes. Dialect.

Zelinsky, Paul O. *Rumplestiltskin.* Art by reteller. Dutton, 1986.
Zelinsky's art illuminates this traditional Grimm tale.

Zemach, Margot. *The Three Wishes: An Old Story.* Art by author. Farrar, 1986.
Share the art after or during the telling of this well-known, easy-to-tell tale.

Easy to Share

Here are some picture books with short, easy-to-read text and great pictures that beginning storytellers can share with their young audiences.

Allen, Pamela. *Who Sank the Boat?* Art by author. Coward-McCann, 1983.
A group of amusing animals all crowd into a small boat.

Brandenberg, Franz. *Cock-a-Doodle-Doo.* Art by Aliki. Greenwillow, 1986.
The audience can imitate the sounds of the animals on the farm.

Degen, Bruce. *Jamberry.* Art by author. Harper, 1983.
This nonsense verse is rhythmic and predictable.

Dunbar, Fiona. *You'll Never Guess.* Art by author. Dial, 1991.
Silhouettes are on one page and actual images on the next making this a wonderful audience-participation book, as everyone guesses the objects from the shadows.

Ehlert, Lois. *Color Farm.* Art by author. Lippincott, 1990.
Big, bold color shapes indicate a farm of animals. Look at the pictures and say their names.

Florian, Douglas. *A Carpenter.* Art by author. Greenwillow, 1991.
Minimal text and bright art show a carpenter at work. Similar in approach by the same author is *A Potter* (Greenwillow, 1991).

Hellen, Nancy. *The Bus Stop.* Art by author. Orchard, 1988.
Cutout pages show a group of people waiting for bus and then on the bus.

Hennessy, B. G. *School Days.* Art by Tracey Campbell Pearson. Viking, 1990.
Text and art show a typical school day in a lively classroom.

Kitchen, Bert. *Animal Numbers.* Art by author. Dial, 1987.
Oversized format depicts animals crawling over numbers from one to one hundred.

Lawson, Carol. *Teddy Bear, Teddy Bear.* Art by author. Dial 1991.
A picture-book rendition of the traditional rhyme.

Lobel, Anita. *Alison's Zinnia.* Art by author. Greenwillow, 1990.
Glorious full-color paintings of flowers in a rhyming alphabet book.

Morris, Ann. *Bread, Bread, Bread.* Photos by Ken Heyman. Lothrop, 1989.
Photos and short, rhyming text depict bread around the world.

Miller, Margaret. *Who Uses This?* Photos by author. Greenwillow, 1990.
Alternate pages show an object, then a child and an adult using it.

Rounds, Glen. *Cowboys.* Art by author. Holiday, 1991.
Round's lively art and text show cowboys at work.

Sawicki, Norma Jean. *The Little Red House*. Art by Toni Goffe. Lothrop, 1989.
A child is shown playing with colorful toy houses-within-houses. There is minimal text.

Sefozo, Mary. *Who Said Red?* Art by Keiko Narahashi. McElderry, 1988.
A look at colors done in watercolors and with a rhythmic response story.

Shaw, Nancy. *Sheep in a Jeep*. Art by Margot Apple. Houghton, 1986.
Join some silly sheep in a rollicking picture-adventure.

Sis, Peter. *Waving: A Counting Book*. Art by author. Greenwillow, 1988.
Everyone is waving, and so can those who listen to this happy story.

Williams, Sue. *I Went Walking*. Art by Julie Vivas. Harcourt, 1989.
Animals follow a boy as he takes a walk in this large-format book with colorful pictures.

To Ponder

These are picture books to share and to think about.

Bang, Molly. *The Grey Lady and the Strawberry Snatcher*. Art by the author. Four Winds, 1980.
The Grey Lady escapes from the Strawberry Snatcher in this wordless picture book.

Blyer, Allison. *Finding Foxes*. Art by Robert J. Blake. Philomel, 1991.
Explore a day and a night with a fox.

Browne, Anthony. *Piggybook*. Art by author. Knopf, 1986.
Mr. Piggott and his two sons learn to appreciate Mom in a most interesting picture book.

Johnston, Tony. *Yonder*. Art by Lloyd Bloom. Dial, 1988.
Johnston explores the endurance of a farm family.

Lobel, Anita. *Potatoes, Potatoes*. Art by the author. Harper, 1967.
Two brothers on opposides during a war meet at their mother's farm.

Luttrell, Ida. *Three Good Blankets*. Art by Michael McDermott. Atheneum, 1990.
How an old woman finds a way to stay warm.

Macauley, David. *Black and White*. Art by author. Houghton, 1990.
Four stories in one book—or just one story?

McDonald, Megan. *The Potato Man*. Art by Ted Lewin. Orchard, 1991.
The peddler was an object of scorn until . . . the day before Christmas.

Mollel, Tolowa M. *The Orphan Boy*. Art by Paul Morin. Clarion, 1990.
Kileken brings happiness to an old man in this Maasai legend.

Polacco, Patricia. *Thunder Cake*. Art by the author. Philomel, 1990.
A little girl learns how to keep from being scared when it thunders.

Schwartz, David M. *How Much Is a Million?* Art by Steven Kellogg. Lothrop, 1985.
Visually explores the mathematical concept of a "million."

Spier, Peter. *We the People: The Story of the U.S. Constitution*. Art by author. Double-day, 1987.
Pictorially presents the U.S. Constitution.

Tsuchiya, Yukio. *Faithful Elephants: A True Story of Animals, People and War.* Art by Ted Lewin. Trans. from Japanese by Tomoko Tsuchiya Dykes. Houghton, 1988.
> The elephants in the Tokyo zoo starved to death during World War II.

Vagin, Valdimir and Frank Asch. *Here Comes the Cat.* Art by authors. Scholastic, 1989.
> A Russian artist and an American artist help us ponder the meaning of groundless fears.

Wisniewski, David. *Elwyn's Saga.* Art by author. Lothrop, 1990.
> An Icelandic tale of good and evil illustrated with paper cutouts.

Yenawine, Philip. *Stories.* Illus. with fine art prints. Museum of Modern Art/Delacorte, 1991.
> Simple text and reproductions of fine art show young readers the basics of art. Also in this series are *Colors, Lines,* and *Shapes* (all Museum of Modern Art/Delacorte, 1991).

Yolen, Jane. *All Those Secrets of the World.* Art by Leslie Baker. Little, 1991.
> A little girl tells about her father's World War II absence.

Chapter 7

Read to Write or Tell

"Where do you get your ideas?" This is one of the first questions asked an author by children and adults alike. The specific answer can vary from "my trip to Italy" to "observing my little brother." One broad way to spark writing is to "get" ideas from what you read. Periodicals, picture books, novels can all be sources of inspiration. Because my major mission in life is to encourage children to read, I think that using literature as a springboard to writing is wonderful, as it almost always leads back to books.

Recently, I visited one of the schools I attended as a child. What do you remember forty years later? Sorry, teachers. You do not remember that you learned fractions in that school—or at least I didn't. I remembered that I lost my ring in the girl's room (*never take off your ring when washing your hands*). In the playground, I looked for the flight of steps down to the lower yard. I attended that school during World War II and representatives from the army came to demonstrate the versatility of a jeep. It was driven down that flight of steps to the amazement of all of us children. Actually, when I returned, I was a bit disappointed in the steps. There were only three of them. That feat also seemed paltry to me now, in light of an incident several years ago. I had volunteered to pick up a friend at church. Instead of following the driveway from the church to the road, I blithely turned the car and absent-mindedly started down the steps leading down from the church. My car was not a jeep, however, and it had to be towed away in full view of the entire town. In addition to the obvious embarrassment of the situation, I had dashed out with my hair uncombed and in my most disreputable warm-up suit. After that experience, when I once again saw the steps in my old school playground, I was no longer impressed.

There was another memory that surfaced on my visit. Our fourth-grade teacher read aloud to us every day. I loved that time of the day. She read us all the books in the P. L. Travers' Mary Poppins series. She obviously had a premonition about the contents of the book you're reading now, because one of our writing assignments was to write a story showing how Mary Poppins might arrive in the next book. I wrote simply, "She will come on a horse." I reprint my masterpiece in its entirety to show that these ideas don't always work just as planned. No matter, Think of it this way: You are now reading hundreds of pages written by that same reluctant writer.

The book-based writing ideas in this section offer a sampling of print items that you might want to use with children to develop their writing skills. Rather than exercises, consider them writing games to use in conjunction with your more formal writing lessons to make the whole process of reading and writing more creative and enjoyable. The concern of teachers to "teach" writing sometimes overwhelms the fun of it all. These writing ideas are "just for fun," without the pressure of graded assignments. They can be used in a classroom before or after a lesson, and they can be implemented in the school or public library whenever there are children present who are interested in reading . . . and writing. You may also want to focus on developing the children's oral skills; these ideas can be used interchangeably as "telling" ideas for your storytellers.

It's exciting to visit schools and discover that many classrooms are "literature-based." While the meaning of this term varies from classroom to classroom, at least more teachers are thinking about *books* in relation to all kinds of curriculum material. Thinking of "books and writing" at the same time is a natural, useful extension of the concept.

Picture books make fine catalysts for writing. It is refreshing to see that picture books are being read and enjoyed in the middle grades as well as with the younger children. Access to a collection of picture books can sometimes be hampered when the school system chooses to separate the grades in different buildings or areas. It is difficult to justify the purchase of picture books if a school only serves fourth- to sixth-graders. The public library often has the best picture-book collection in town, though, so take advantage of it often.

Almost any picture book can be used as a story starter. Asking questions such as "What happens after the story is finished?" will stimulate imaginations and fuel writing and telling projects. When I discussed some of these writing ideas with a friend of mine who really *is* a "famous author," she replied, "The question I find distasteful is 'If you could write a new ending what would you write?' I already wrote the perfect ending." My own least-favorite writing assignment is 'compare and contrast. . . .' I'm glad I don't have to do that anymore.

To spur some ideas for using picture books to initiate writing projects, the picture books listed here are accompanied by brief annotations and include suggestions for writing or telling activities to give you the option to work on oral as well as written skills. An effective procedure, I've found, is to present the picture book orally, and then suggest a writing idea. Using these picture-book ideas as guidelines, you will find it easy to formulate your own activity-starters when you read a picture book aloud.

Periodicals can yield writing ideas as well. In fact, I've noticed how many writers say that their idea for a novel or short story was "generated by a news item." A few short pieces excerpted from newspapers are collected here to give you and your writing group samples of this genre.

Novels are also good sources for writing ideas. Excerpts, like those I've included are helpful, but hopefully the children will be eager to read the books in their entirety. As they read some of the books, young writers will begin thinking about their own families and peer groups, and they may want to write or tell about a relative or friend.

Poetry can also be used for entertaining writing exercises. Reading a poem out loud will not take much time. You may just find that poetry is the perfect story starter. But the assignments needn't be full-blown stories. Sometimes just writing down a reaction or two can help in the creative process. For instance, you can allocate just a few minutes to write fortunes to go with the fortune cookie poem.

Hopefully, you will have easy access to the books that are excerpted in the following "games" and will be able to display them and make them available for the children to take home and read at their leisure. Try these ideas along with your children—you'll enjoy them too and will probably come up with new ones of your own.

Newspapers and Magazines

Periodicals can be excellent sources for writing ideas. Americans seem to be captivated by human interest stories, and these can often be the foundation of a story idea. As your young writers read newspapers, magazines, and journals for ideas, they might also end up with a daily newspaper habit—a good habit to encourage. Here are some examples of articles that could be intriguing to budding writers. Look for story starters in your local or school newspaper, library newsletter, and other familiar publications.

On April 14, 1990, *The San Diego Union* reported that a family of ducks had taken over the swimming pool in an El Cajon backyard. Twelve chicks had hatched and were now learning to swim in the backyard pool. Although the family was delighted with the idea of the ducks, the children miss being able to swim in the pool.

from *The Los Angeles Times*, June 18, 1990

Harrods of London Orders 'Cover-Up'

From Reuters
LONDON—The ritzy Harrod department store has banned shoppers in skimpy shorts from its opulent aisles, telling those flashing flesh at the doors to come back after they cover up.

A spokesman said scores of customers have been turned away, "politely, but firmly," during the current hot spell because they did not meet the dress code of Egyptian owner Mohammed Fayed.

"What we do not want to see are shorts so skimpy as to be potentially offensive, tops that reveal too much naked flesh, be it male or female . . . ," the store's spokesman told reporters.

from *Time Magazine* July 10, 1989
TEXAS
"Please Don't Die, Tree"
Visibly ailing since Memorial Day, Austin's historic Treaty Oak—alleged site of a treaty signing by Native Americans and Father of Texas Stephen F. Austin—has been receiving the kind of diligent attention usually given a gravely ill head of state. A team of eleven has meticulously removed the contaminated soil from around its huge root network, and last week billionaire H. Ross Perot flew in 18 technical specialists from around the nation to assist in a bedside diagnosis.

About 600 years old and 50 ft. high, the great tree, with its 52½ inch girth and 127-ft. limb spread, has inspired an outpouring of sympathy. Well-wishers stand vigil, send get-well cards, flowers, candles, even cans of chicken soup with anguished messages: "Please don't die!"

It seems that someone poured the potent herbicide Velpar in a circle around the tree early this year, committing a "malicious act against an innocent creature," said city forester John Giedraitis. When the tree shed beads of sap, he said, "it's weeping. This tree is under a tremendous amount of stress."

excerpts from *San Diego Union* August 28, 1990

Yellowstone Grizzly Joins Cookout: 180 Abandoned Steaks

New York Times News Service

YELLOWSTONE NATIONAL PARK, Wyo.—Every visitor to this mountainous park is warned not to approach or feed the grizzly bears.

But the other night 180 paying customers at the daily Western cookout at Yancey's Hole got a rare close-up glimpse of a grizzly, and promptly abandoned their meals to him.

The grizzly, a 170-pound yearling, ambled into the campground, scattering humans just by reputation.

He calmly lumbered from table to table, devouring the remains of 12-ounce steaks—rare, medium and well-done—along with coleslaw, baked beans and watermelon. The visitors had paid $29.87 each, which included a horseback ride into the camp.

With that meal, the grizzly, Ursus horribilis No. 181, rekindled the debate over commercial activities in the park, where the giant bear, an endangered species, has been staging a slow comeback from the brink of extinction.

And so No. 181, which had bedded down last Wednesday waiting for more steaks to arrive, was quickly relocated to a remote part of the park by the rangers.

Park officials do this to eliminate the threat to people, and to prevent the bears from becoming dependent on humans for their food. . . .

. . . It is said that bears never forget where they found a good meal, and the one that the yearling grizzly had last week was certainly one of his best.

Books and Short Stories

List Your Likes—and Dislikes

Novels can be great sources of ideas for writing. This passage from Suzy Kline's *Orp* (Putnam, 1989) can be read out loud as a book talk to introduce *Orp*, or copies can be given to the students to read as a prompt for them as writers in drawing up their own lists.

from *Orp* by Suzy Kline

I was working on a list of things I hate.

Mrs. Lewis, who runs an enrichment activity room at school, asked me to do some brainstorming over the summer. She wants me to come to school in the fall with a good idea for a project.

She suggested I make a list of things I love to do. I said I didn't feel like it. That's when she got miffed. "Make a list of things you hate, then. THAT might help."

So that's what I was doing in my think tank. I looked over my last nine entries:

30. hot, muggy weather
31. no milk in the fridge
32. making my bed
33. poverty

Mom said I didn't need to get a regular allowance this summer. She said I could earn money by doing chores.

34. chores

I knew I was going to be poor all summer.

35. when Ralph throws up.

Ralph is my dog, I've had him for ten years. Mom and Dad gave him to me for my first birthday. Nowadays he loves to eat desserts—Mom's brownies, lemon meringue pie, butterscotch pudding, anything that's sweet! And then he throws up all over the place. Once he threw up all over my bumblebee collection. If you've ever seen bumblebees coated with barf, it's a real gross out.

36. pimentoes

Mom always puts those red slimy things in her potato salad. I tell her not to, but she says they are packed with flavor and add zest to a salad. I usually manage to pick the pimentoes out but every now and then I miss one. Swallowing one of those things is a killer.

37. drying the dishes

It's not that I mind drying the dishes so much, it's just that every time I do, Mom gives me a lecture on how to use wrist movements with the dish towel so that I can add extra sparkle to the glasses.

38. Derrick's stinginess

Derrick is my best friend. Sort of. He's just so tight with his money. He never loans me a dime. And when we play Monopoly, he always gets to be the banker. He's probably the only guy in the world who knows how much money is in a Monopoly set—$15,140.00.

Right now I was on the thirty-ninth thing hated. Mrs. Lewis said when you're brainstorming, the best idea is usually the last one.

"ORVIE! GET OUT OF THAT BATHROOM!"

That was my sister, Chloe, banging on the door. I put the breadboard that I was balancing over the edges of the tub on the bathroom floor. "All right! All right, I'm getting out," I said, adding my sister's name to the list.

Writing Suggestion: Make a list of things *you* love, as well as things you hate. Explain why each item appears on the list.

Other books by Suzy Kline to read and enjoy: *Herbie Jones* (Putnam, 1985), *What's the Matter with Herbie Jones?* (Putnam, 1986), *Herbie Jones and the Class Gift* (Putnam, 1987), *Herbie Jones and the Monster Ball* (Putnam, 1988).

Another listmaker can be discovered in the pages of *Anastasia Krupnik* by Lois Lowry. (Houghton, 1979)

A Bedtime Story for Your Pet

Beverly Conrad's *Doggy Tales* is a collection of rewritten fairy tales meant to be read aloud to a dog. But you can read this selection from it to your students to prime their literary pumps before trying their own switch-arounds on classic stories.

Little Red Riding Dog

by Beverley Conrad

Once upon a time in a faraway wooded land, there lived a little doggy named Little Red Riding Dog. She was named this because one year for Christmas a well-meaning friend gave her a hooded red cape so that her ears wouldn't freeze.

One day Little Red Riding Dog's mother said, "Fetch the basket and fetch the bone and take them to your grandma's house."

Little Red Riding Dog leaped into the air. She was so happy that she was being let out of the house without her leash. Fetching the basket in her teeth, she took off down the wooded trail.

Soon she spied a little boy playing in the woods.

"You had better watch out Little Red Riding Dog," the little boy said. "You don't have your leash on and the dogcatcher is out today."

Little Red Riding Dog whined, then she hurried down the trail so that if the dogcatcher were around, he would not see her and certainly would not catch her.

Before long she was at her grandma's house, and when she scratched on the door, she heard a voice say, "Come in, Little Red Riding Dog, so she went in.

"Hello, Grandma, Little Red Riding Dog barked."

"Fetch it here, my little granddog."

"I fetched a bone for you from mother." But Little Red Riding Dog's fur went up because it did not sound like her grandma anymore.

"Arf!" barked Little Red Riding Dog. "Grandma, what strange eyes you have!"

"The better to see you with."

"Grandma, what strange ears you have!"

"The better to hear you with."

"Grandma, what strange *paws* you have!"

"The better to catch you with!" And all of a sudden her grandma leaped from the bed, and all of a sudden it wasn't her grandma at all. It was the dogcatcher!

Little Red Riding Dog quickly leaped out of the window, and who should be standing there but the little boy. He promptly snapped a leash on her and was calmly walking her home by the time the dogcatcher saw her.

Before long she was safely inside her house and living happily ever after. And to this day, although she likes going for walks without her leash, she certainly knows why it is better to wear one.

Writing Suggestion: Write a story that's appropriate to real aloud to your pet—or stuffed animal. Other classic tales rewritten in a contemporary style to share aloud:

Brooke, William J. *A Telling of the Tales: Five Stories* Art by Richard Egielski. Harper, 1990.
  Classic tales (Cinderella, Jack and the Beanstalk, Sleeping Beauty) retold with interesting twists.

Calmenson, Stephanie. *The Principal's New Clothes.* Art by Denise Brunkus. Scholastic, 1989.
  Hans Christian Andersen's The Emperor's New Clothes in a contemporary school setting.

Dahl, Roald. *Roald Dahl's Revolting Rhymes.* Art by Quentin Blake. Bantam, 1986.
  Updated fairy tales in rhyme.

Scieszka, Jon. *The True Story of the Three Little Pigs.* Art by Lane Smith, Viking, 1989.
  The 3 little pigs told from the point of view of the wolf. The same author has also written *The Frog Prince, Continued* with art by Steve Johnson (Viking, 1991), adding a quirky update to that tale of enchantment.

Strauss, Gwen. *Trail of Stones.* Art by Anthony Browne. Knopf, 1990.
  A collection of poems featuring the inner feelings of famous fairy tale characters.

Tear-Jerker Story

"Tear-Water Tea" is one of the stories in Arnold Lobel's *Owl at Home* and it is both fun to tell and wonderful to have your group read and use as a story starter. Bring your favorite tea pot to cry into when you tell this story, or you can use the pattern here to make a paper teapot as a prop. If you choose to work from the pattern, duplicate it twice. After you've decorated both teapots (one with the handle toward your left, the other with the handle on the right), staple or glue them, right side out, leaving an opening at the top of the pot into which you can slip your tears.

Tear-Water Tea

by Arnold Lobel

Owl took the kettle out of the cupboard.

"Tonight I will make tear-water tea," he said.

"Now," said Owl, "I will begin."

Owl sat very still. He began to think of things that were sad.

"Chairs with broken legs," said Owl.

His eyes began to water.

"Songs that cannot be sung," said Owl, "because the words have been forgotten." Owl began to cry.

A large tear rolled down and dropped into the kettle.

"Spoons that have fallen behind the stove and are never seen again," said Owl.

More tears dropped down into the kettle.

"Books that cannot be read," said Owl, "because some of the pages have been torn out."

"Clocks that have stopped," said Owl, "with no one near to wind them up."

Owl was crying.

Many large tears dropped into the kettle.

"Mornings nobody saw because everybody was sleeping," sobbed Owl.

"Mashed potatoes left on a plate," he cried, "because no one wanted to eat them. And pencils that are too short to use."

Owl thought about many other sad things.

He cried and cried.

Soon the kettle was filled up with tears.

"There," said Owl. "That does it!" Owl stopped crying.

He put the kettle on the stove to boil for tea.

Owl felt happy as he filled his cup. "It tastes a little bit salty," he said, "but tear-water tea is always very good."

Writing Suggestion: Write a story using a recipe for "smile-water tea." Display the smile suggestions on smile-shaped slips of paper on the bulletin board.

Pourquoi Stories

Stories appear in many myths, as well as folk and cultural traditions to explain natural events and animal traits and they are great prompters for children's original "why nots." Read this one to your group to get them thinking.

Why Dogs Have Cold Noses

If you touch a dog's nose it will feel cold. Have you ever wondered why?

A long time ago, when Noah built the ark, the dog was enlisted as Noah's helper. It was Dog's job to help herd the animals into the ark. Although the ark was quite large, it was a very tight squeeze for two of every species of animal to board the ark.

Since Dog was the shepherd herding the animals into the ark, he was the last one to walk up the gangplank. By then, all the other animals, from the huge elephants to the tiny ants, had already found a place in the large chamber of the ark. At first, there seemed to be no place left for Dog at all, but Noah commanded that all of the people and animals on the ark take a deep breath at the same time. One, two, three. . . . Everyone held their breath, making a little bit of space. The dog squeezed himself into the ark and Noah shut the door.

When the people and animals exhaled, the dog's nose was thrust outside through the planks into the cold sea air. For forty days and forty nights the dog's nose was exposed to the cold air.

Today, if you touch the dog's nose it will still feel cool and wet as a reminder of this animal's sacrifice and sense of duty.

Writing Suggestion: Write a story demonstrating the "real" reason for a distinctive animal trait.

Journals

Writing in a journal can provide writing practice, but more than that, and especially important for young people, a journal can also be a good friend. It listens, but never talks back. It is sometimes difficult to convince children that descriptions of encounters with ordinary people, everyday events, thoughts, and memorable quotes make good journal entries. The various kinds of journal entries below can show children that you don't have to win a million dollars or meet a being from Mars to have something to write in a journal.

from *A Mouse's Diary*

by Michelle Cartlidge

Monday
At ballet class today we pretended to be candles on a big birthday cake. The teacher said we looked more like scarecrows than pretty candles. In the middle of the dancing I had to stop and change over my ballet shoes because they were on the wrong feet.

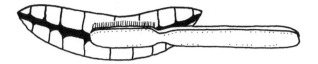

from *Goodbye, My Island*

by Jean Rogers

March 6

Teachers showed slides on toothbrushing. A toothbrush danced up and down over teeth all by itself. It made us laugh. Everyone got a new toothbrush. Everyone wanted a red one. Bits of the red handle make the best lures for bullhead fishing. It stormed for three days this week.

from *Hilary's Journal*

Buenos Aires
Dec. 31

New Year's seems to be a big celebration here. Already they have started celebrating. Today all the people in offices of the taller buildings threw their old desk calendar pages out the window onto the streets. Millions of little squares of paper saying "25 May," "20 Oct.," "5 July," etc. were fluttering down like snow. One of the streets had so much paper that it was getting caught under the black and gold taxis. We were walking over the pieces of paper that had appointments on them from the past year—very symbolic!

I'm dead tired.

from *Snapshots of Paradise*

by Adele Geras

10:00 *P.M. The Dining Room.*
Anniversary Dinner.

Everyone is smiling. What does it mean? Grandpas' smile says: I made it. I'm eighty-four and still here and so's Sarah, and these are my children, and my grandchild and great grandchildren and even a branch of the family here from England, flown over specially for the occasion, like a florist's delivery. Grandma Sarah's smile is wistful. I'm a good-looking old lady, it says, sure, but for how much longer? She seems to be glancing at Ronnie as if at her own past. Susan's smile is brave—her corset is pinching like hell. Rose's is a little forced. She is smiling at Bill, who smiles obediently back at her. Jean is enigmatic as usual, a Mona Lisa smile. Eleanor grins proudly, and so she should, looking at her sons. Harry smiles at Ronnie. Possessively. She looks happy, happy with herself and with Harry, and with good reason. Gene is smiling straight at the camera. Or, and this is more likely, at the person holding the camera. He is smiling at Fran and his eyes look as if they're pleased with what they're seeing.

from *Hey World, Here I Am!*

by Jean Little

My Journals

Real writers keep journals. I've had four.

When Mother told my sister Marilyn that I loved to write, she sent me a journal for my birthday. It was squarish and fat, with small organized pages. It had a shiny pink cover with MY DIARY written on it in scrolled, gold letters. A flimsy padlock, which would break if you looked at it, was supposed to keep it secret. Every page had two skimpy sections, with a date at the top of each. There was space enough for maybe three sentences if your handwriting was small. My handwriting scrawls. Besides, my life is too big to fit into those squinched-up pages. I gave it to my friend Lindsay Ross. She adores it. She has a smaller life. And tidy writing.

Then our teacher handed out "journals" which we had to write in every day for one month. She said she wouldn't mark them but she would read them over. I did it and, as assignments go, it wasn't bad. But, of course, you could only put down stuff that you wouldn't mind her knowing. My private life is not her affair. When I got it back, though, and saw she had written *Excellent!* on it, I felt like a fraud.

Then Dad gave me a journal. It was elegant. The pages are creamy and feel like the best art paper when you stroke them. The outside is covered with a deep blue fabric which has tiny nosegays scattered over it. I love it. Maybe, someday, my life will be elegant enough to match it. I hope so. I'm saving it carefully just in case.

My fourth journal I bought for myself. It is a hardcover book meant for writing lecture notes in. It has lots of room on every page. Some days, I write six or seven full pages about what I am feeling and thinking. Or about Emily or school. Other days I don't even pick it up or, if I do, I just write something like "Another day lived through!" I draw pictures in it now and then or paste in a copy of a poem I like.

Getting a journal is like buying shoes. You have to find the one that fits. And you are the only person who can tell if it pinches.

Writing Suggestion: Write a description of the journal that best expresses you—what it looks like, what it would have in it, etc.

Poetry

Read aloud the following selections and see what poetic thoughts arise. "If I Were My Mother" from Aileen Fisher's *In One Door and Out the Other* spurred such responses as these from the children in the American School in Amman, Jordan:

> If I were my mother we'd always fly first class.
> If I were my Mom I'd allow videos on school nights.
> If I were my Mom, I'd tell my Dad to take the job in Paris.
> If I were my mother I'd let my daughter visit her friends in Indiana during Christmas vacation.
> If I were my parents we would have a horse.

If I Were My Mother
by Aileen Fisher

If I were my mother
I rarely would make
omelet, or parsnips,
or spinach, or steak,
or carrots, or onions—
I'd much rather bake
doughnuts and pudding
and dumplings and cake.

I'd not take the trouble
to cut up a lot
of turnips—instead I'd
make jam in a pot,
and fritters, and cookies,
and pies piping hot . . .
if I were my mother.
Too bad that I'm not!

Writing Suggestion: Write down some of the things you'd do—and some you would not do—if you were your mother or father.

Most children are wary of new foods. In this poem, some foods are described as friendly, others are downright scary.

Yellow, Warm and Friendly
by Julie Fredericksen

Artichokes, peppers
pomegranates.
I am afraid
of these foods
my mother buys
and my sister eats.
Green artichoke leaves
swirled in mayonnaise,
peppers stuffed with
spicy rice.
Pomegranates bursting
with bright red seeds.
I won't touch
these colors yet.

I like friendly food
macaroni and cheese
buttered noodles
potato soup.
Yellow, warm and friendly.

Writing Suggestion: Write or tell about the secret life of your favorite foods.

In this poem from *Honey, I Love*, Eloise Greenfield provides—in just a few lines—a clear picture of Aunt Roberta and an understanding of the speaker's thoughts about her.

Aunt Roberta
by Eloise Greenfield

What do people think about
When they sit and dream
All wrapped up in quiet
   and old sweaters
And don't even hear me 'til I
Slam the door

Writing or Telling Suggestion: What is Aunt Roberta (or one of your relatives you've observed) thinking about?

Johanna Hurwitz has written many popular books. The author of *Aldo Applesauce, Hot and Cold Summer*, and *Class President*, her books have an enthusiastic following among children and, in fact, have won children's book awards in many states. In fourth grade, Johanna decided that she wanted to be a librarian and author when she grew up. She has been a school and children's librarian for thirty years and has authored as many books. Just like the fairy tales that she read as a girl growing up in the Bronx, Johanna Hurwitz' wishes have all come true.

At ten, Johanna Hurwitz wrote a poem-prediction that was published in the *New London Day* newspaper.

Books
by Johanna Hurwitz

For me to read a book is still
And always will be quite a thrill.
For me to read a book is like
A boy when he rides his new two-wheel bike.
And when a bird comes north in spring.
It's natural for him to sing.
I like to read books of science, fiction and mystery;
Books of poems, nature and history.
And what is more, I'll read until I'm grown,
And then I'll write books of my own.

Children in Westlake, Ohio contributed these original couplets on reading:

For me to read a book is cool,
A lot like diving in a pool.
by Gwen, Angela, and Carol

For me to read a book is great,
It always seems to be first rate.
by Julie and Valerie

For me to read a book is swell,
It makes me so happy I could yell.
by Jillian and Sara

For me to read a book is slick,
The one I like best is hard to pick.
by Jeff and Kevin

Writing Suggestion: Write a tribute to books or make a prediction about your career path.

Reading-to-Write Ideas in the World Around You

We often take for granted the various pieces of printed material that we read everyday. Who writes the menu in the restaurant? Who composed the ad in *Sports Illustrated*? Who drafted the notice to remind you of your dentist appointment?

Here is a list of printed items that you can collect easily in your town. Show these samples of functional writing to your young writers.

Menus from restaurants—with descriptions of the dishes
Real Estate brochures
Travel brochures
Directions to the party
Agenda for a meeting
Letter to an editor
Meeting announcement
Yearbook—quotes about class members
Brochure for a summer camp
Citation for an award
Movie review
Book review
Lost pet notice
Flap copy for a book
Complaint letter

Writing Suggestion: Write your own versions of some of these practical items.

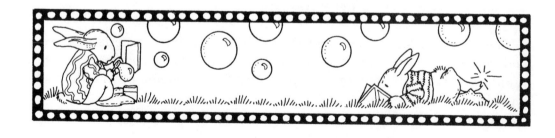

Picture Books as Story Starters

Picture books can present literature to children at the same time they kindle writing ideas. Share these books with your children and then use the suggestions for open-ended questions that accompany the annotations or let the children come up with their own ideas for writing projects or oral responses. Almost any book can be a springboard to writing.

Adoff, Arnold. *Chocolate Dreams.* Art by Turie McCombie. Lothrop, 1989.
> Poems featuring chocolate.
> > *Write or tell:* My Favorite Food

Arnold, Caroline. *Music Lessons for Alex.* Photos by Richard Hewitt. Clarion, 1985.
> Photo essay describing violin lessons.
> > *Write or tell:* My First Lesson

Bauer, Caroline Feller. *My Mom Travels a lot.* Art by Nancy Winslow Parker. Warne, 1981.
> The good things and bad things about a traveling mom.
> > *Write or tell:* The Good Things and the Bad Things about School Lunches

Butler, Dorothy. *Mr. Brown Bear Barney.* Art by Elizabeth Fuller. Greenwillow, 1989.
> A little girl describes her life with her favorite bear.
> > *Write or tell:* My Favorite Toy

Cecil, Laura. "Brown Paper" in *Stuff and Nonsense.* Art by Emma Chichester Clark. Greenwillow, 1989.
> The adventures of a piece of brown paper.
> > *Write or tell:* The adventures of a Paper Bag

Ciardi, John. *The Hopeful Trout.* Art by Susan Meddaugh. Houghton, 1989.
> A collection of humorous limericks.
> > *Write or tell:* A Limerick

Cole, Joanna. *Anna Banana.* Art by Alan Tiegreen. Morrow, 1989.
> 101 jump-rope rhymes.
> > *Write or tell:* Collect the popular jump-rope rhymes or games at your school.

Calmenson, Stephanie. *The Principal's New Clothes.* Art by Scholastic, 1989.
> This rewrite of "The Emperor's New Clothes" features a vain school principal.
> > *Write or tell:* Rewrite a well-known fairy tale using contemporary characters and situations.

dePaola, Tomie. *Strega Nona*. Art by author. Prentice, 1975.
> Big Anthony makes the magic pasta pot work, but doesn't know how to stop it.
>> *Write or tell:* The Day We Made Too Much Popcorn

Fisher, Leonard Everett. *The Great Wall of China*. Art by author. Macmillan, 1986.
> The history of the building of the Great Wall.
>> *Write or tell:* My Building Project

Fitzgerald, Rick. *Helen and the Great Quiet*. Morrow, 1989.
> A little girl listens to quiet noises in the world.
>> *Write or tell:* The Great Noise

Fleischman, Paul. *Rondo in C*. Art by Janet Wentworth. Harper, 1988.
> Each person in the audience is thinking something different as each listens to a piano piece.
>> *Write or tell:* What I Thought About When I Listened to the Radio

Florian, Douglas. *Nature Walk*. Greenwillow, 1989.
> Take a walk in the woods.
>> *Write or tell:* A City Walk

Gackenback, Dick. *Supposes*. Art by author. Harcourt, 1989.
> Play with words, e.g., "Suppose a horse had wings. He'd be a horsefly."
>> *Write or tell:* Suppose . . .

Gerstein, Mordecai. *The New Creatures*. Art by author. Harper, 1981.
> When dogs ruled the world.
>> *Write or tell:* When Giraffes Were the World's Rulers

Goldstein, Bobbye S., ed. *Bear in Mind*. Art by William Pene duBois. Viking, 1989.
> A collection of bear poems.
>> *Write or tell:* A poem about a favorite animal or collect poems about a single subject.

Greenburg, Dan. *Jumbo the Boy and Arnold the Elephant*. Art by Susan Perl. Harper, 1989.
> A boy and an elephant are switched at birth.
>> *Write or tell:* If I Were Brought Up by a Dog

Griffith, Helen V. *Plunk's Dreams*. Art by Susan Condie Lamb. Greenwillow, 1990.
> A family wonders what their dog dreams.
>> *Write or tell:* A happy dream or a frightening one.

Heller, Ruth. *Many Luscious Lollipops*. Art by author. Grosset, 1989.
> Explores adjectives in color and text.
>> *Write or tell:* Use as many adjectives as you can in five sentences.

Heller, Nicholas. *Mathilda, the Dream Bear*. Greenwillow, 1989.
> Mathilda brings pleasant dreams to sleeping animals.
>> *Write or tell:* My Dog's Dream

Hendershot, Judith. *In Coal Country*. Art by Thomas B. Allen. Knopf, 1987.
> Memories of childhood in a coal-mining town.
>> *Write or tell:* What will I remember most about my childhood.

Hort, Lenny. *How Many Stars in the Sky?* Art by James E. Ransome. Tamourine, 1991.
> A little boy and his father explore the night sky.
>> *Write or tell:* A Night Out with Dad

Isenberg, Barbara and Susan Wolf. *The Adventures of Albert the Running Bear.* Art by Dick Gackenbach. Clarion, 1982.

Here's a bear with athletic ability.
Write or tell: The Day My Dog Ran the Marathon.

Jabor, Cynthia. *Alice Ann Gets Ready for School.* Little, 1989.
Will Alice Ann be ready for her first day of school?
Write or tell: My First Day of School

Johnson, Neil. *All in a Day's Work: Twelve Americans Talk About Their Jobs.* Photos. Little, 1989.
Photo essay of twelve clerical workers.
Write or tell: I'd Like to Work as . . .

Johnston, Tony. *Yonder.* Art by Lloyd Bloom. Dial, 1988.
A tree becomes a symbol of three generations of a family.
Write or tell: What the Tree Saw

Joly-Berbesson, Fanny. *Marceau Bonappetit.* Art by Agnes Mathieu. Carolrhoda, 1989.
Marceau eats at the homes of friends while his parents are out of town.
Write or tell: Dinner at My Best Friend's House

Kamal, Aleph. *The Bird Who Was an Elephant.* Art by Frane Lessac. Lippincott, 1989.
A bird takes us on a tour of Village India.
Write or tell: A dog's view of your town.

Khalsa, Dayal Kaur. *My Family Vacation.* Potter, 1989.
A family visits Florida.
Write or tell: Our Trip

Leedy, Loreen. *The Furry News: How to Make a Newspaper.* Art by author. Holiday, 1990.
A group of animals describe how to publish a newspaper.
Write or tell: A Family Newspaper

Limburg, Peter R. *Weird! The Complete Book of Halloween Words.* Art by Betsy Lewin. Bradbury, 1989.
A dictionary of Halloween words.
Write or tell: Compile a dictionary of words associated with a holiday or hobby.

Lockwood, Primrose. *Cissy Lavender.* Art by Emma Chichester Clark. Little, 1989.
Cissy writes letters when she takes care of a gentleman's house.
Write or tell: A letter to the owner of the animal for which you "pet-sat."

Lydon, Kerry Raines. *A Birthday for Blue.* Art by Michael Hays. Whitman, 1989.
Celebrating a birthday on the road with a covered wagon.
Write or tell: The Best Birthday.

Lyon, George Ella. *Come a Tide.* Art by Stephen Gammell. Orchard, 1990.
The neighbors all dig out after a flood.
Write or tell: The Snowstorm, The Tornado, The Hurricane, The Earthquake, or . . .

Mahy, Margaret. *Making Friends.* Art by Wendy Smith. McElderry, 1990.
Two lonely people and their dogs meet and become friends.
Write or tell: How did you meet your best friend?

Mayer, Mercer. *There's a Nightmare in My Closet.* Art by author. Dial, 1968.
    A little boy frightens his nightmare.
        Write or tell: How I Got Rid of a Nightmare

McLerran, Alice. *Roxaboxen.* Art by Barbara Cooney. Lothrop, 1991.
    Children create an imaginary town from rocks and wooden boxes.
        Write or tell: What is your secret place to play?

McMillan, Bruce. *Super, Super Superwords.* Photos by author.
    Explores adjectives in their positive, comparative, and superlative degrees with color
    photographs.
        Write or tell: Make a list of your favorite words and explain why you like them.

McPhail, David. *Lost!* Art by author. Little, 1990.
    A little boy helps a lost bear find his way home.
        Write or tell: The Lost Boy

Noble, Trinka Hakes. *The Day Jimmy's Boa Ate the Wash.* Art by Stephen Kellogg.
    Dial, 1980.
    A very funny field trip.
        Write or tell: Our Field Trip

Nordquist, Sven. *Porker Finds a Chair.* Art by author. Carolrhoda, 1989.
    If you've never seen a chair, what would you do with one?
        Write or tell: How you'd use a pencil if you'd never seen one.

Parker, Nancy Winslow and Joan Richards Wright. *Bugs.* Greenwillow, 1987.
    An upbeat description of a variety of insects.
        Write or tell: The Day I Met a Black Bug

Planner, Louise. *Louise Builds a House.* Art by author. Orchard, 1989.
    Louise builds her dream house.
        Write or tell: Your Dream House

Pillar, Marjorie. *Pizza Man.* Photos by author. Crowell, 1990.
    A photo essay depicts a pizza maker.
        Write or tell: My Mom's Job

Pochocki, Ethel. *Rosebud and Red Flannel.* Art by Mary Beth Owens. Holt, 1991.
    A nightgown grows to appreciate the virtues of a pair of red flannels.
        Write or tell: The Romance Between Two Household Objects.

Precek, Katherine Wilson. *Penny in the Road.* Art by Patricia Cullen-Clark. Mac-
    millan, 1989.
    A boy finds a penny dated 1793.
        Write or tell: You found a penny dated 1944—what could it tell you about what life
        was like then.

Rice, Eve. *Peter's Pockets.* Art by Nancy Winslow Parker. Greenwillow, 1989.
    A little boy picks up found objects on a walk with his uncle.
        Write or tell: What I Found as I Walked to School

Ryder, Joanne. *White Bear, Ice Bear.* Morrow, 1989.
    If you were a polar bear.
        Write or tell: If I were a . . .

Rylant, Cynthia. *The Relatives Came*. Art by Stephen Gammell. Bradbury, 1985.
    The happy time when the relatives visited.
        Write or tell: A Visit from Aunt Gertrude

Stevenson, James. *The Worst Person in the World*. Art by author. Greenwillow, 1978.
    The worst person in the world is reformed by Ugly.
        Write or tell: My Friend, the Nicest Person in the World

Stevenson, James Walker. *If I Owned a Candy Factory*. Art by author. Greenwillow, 1989.
    The joys of owning a candy factory.
        Write or tell: If I owned . . .

Thayer, Ernest Lawrence. *Casey at the Bat*. Art by Patricia Polacco. Putnam, 1988.
    The day the baseball game is lost in Mudville.
        Write or tell: What do you see on the way to school?

Van Laan, Nancy. *Rainbow Crow*. Art by Beatriz Vidal. Knopf, 1989.
    Why the crow is black.
        Write or tell: Why Dogs Bark

Viorst, Judith. *Alexander and the Terrible, Horrible, No Good, Very Bad Day*. Art by Roy Cruz. Atheneum, 1972.
    A day when everything goes wrong.
        Write or tell: The Worst Day

Williams, Vera B. *A Chair for My Mother*. Art by author. Greenwillow, 1982.
    A family saves coins for a comfortable chair.
        Write or tell: I'm Saving for . . .

Yolen, Jane. *Owl Moon*. Art by John Schoenherr. Philomel, 1987.
    A little girl and a father take a nighttime walk in the woods.
        Write or tell: A Walk with My Father.

PART III
Promoting Poetry

Chapter 8

Teaching Children to Present Poetry

Pick a subject, any subject. Pick a language, any one of the six she spoke, and my grandmother would recite a poem . . . with gestures. In her later years in the nursing home, surrounded by a group of elderly men and women, nurses and doctors, my grandmother would recite poetry from her wheelchair. Even though the horns of busses, cars, and trucks filtered up from a busy New York City avenue, no one who listened to her heard them. Instead you felt yourself sway to waves as you stood on the deck of a ship listening to "The Rime of the Ancient Mariner."

My mother also recited poetry. My grandmother, a very friendly woman, apparently was always meeting people—in the park, in the grocery store, even on the subway. Many of these new acquaintances had odd talents and wanted to earn money by teaching. My grandmother considered taking lessons a genteel way of giving charity, and so my mother acquired all sorts of unusual accomplishments due to my grandmother's friendships. She could embroider, sing ballads, and because of a deposed duke (his claim; we never checked his lineage), she recited poetry. The tutoring that the Duke gave my mother was called elocution. I think it was supposed to improve one's speech habits. What a pity that emphasis on good speech skills has disappeared from our society.

My mother always complained that she had disliked all the extracurricular activities and she was always amazed when I begged to take lessons after school. One class I took was a theater class where we learned a whole repertoire of poems. Would you like to hear me recite "The Tomboy"? I could prove to you that if you learn something when you're ten you never forget it. Not interested? You don't know what a treat you're missing.

It's not very fashionable to require children to recite poetry from memory these days, but in your storytelling class you have the perfect opportunity to introduce children to material that can be used as a single selection in a program or can comprise an entire program. One of the great advantages to storytelling is that there is no need to coordinate with other people as you need to do in a scripted play. For the most part, each person can work on his or her presentation separately. Poetry is particularly adaptable to each person's individual style. Today, poetry books offer a wealth of material for every reading level and every taste. And the anthologies. . . . When I first started in this business thirty years ago, we had to search through many books to find a poem that matched a particular subject or that suited our personality. I had trouble with this approach because I insisted that any poem that I learned had to be funny. Of course, this was pre-Silverstein or -Prelutsky. But we did have James Thurber and Ogden Nash.

Once, in elementary school, we were given the assignment of presenting a poem of our choice. I searched through the available books in our library and not finding anything that I really loved (How many times can you get away with doing "Casey at the Bat"?), I reluctantly chose a love poem. The poem compared "My Love" to the moon and stars. On my way to school, I practiced what I thought was a tender and warm rendition with wide sweeping gestures. I should have known that the adults who were walking next to me were not smiling because I was giving such an enchanting romantic performance. When my turn came to recite I shouted to the moon and the stars and the entire class broke into guffaws of laughter. From then on, I decided that I would play just about everything I did for the Big Laugh. After all, if I was funny when I didn't even mean to be, what would I be like if I tried to make people laugh. The lesson here is that it is possible, but difficult, to change your own performance profile.

Performing Poetry

Poetry is not easy. I think of it as an advanced form of storytelling, as it requires some skill and timing. But that doesn't mean that you should wait until you are an accomplished storyteller to attempt poetry. You just start out

Students reciting "The Pig" by Ogden Nash on National Pig Day at Blessed Sacrament School in Johnson City, NY. Pig snouts are made of paper and attached with masking tape. (*Photo: Chuck Haupt*)

with short poems and build up to the lengthier and more complicated selections. Watch any seventeen-year-old learning to drive and compare her to a thirty-year-old attempting to get his driver's license and you'll understand why it's wise to encourage children to learn some poetry now. Most skills seem to come more naturally to us when we're young.

One reason that learning and reciting poetry is more difficult than, say, a folktale, is that you really must learn a poem word for word. You can't fake it by making up your own words. And this makes poetry a challenge. It also usually means that you may have to take more time to work on a poem than a story with the result that you will really know and probably always feel comfortable telling that poem. It will stick with you a lot longer than something that you learn in a hurry.

Rather than labeling poetry as more "advanced," I should have clarified and said that it is more difficult for me. In fact, I find it really hard to memorize a poem. That's probably because I tend to approach it differently than I do stories, which I may feel I "know" even before my final version has evolved. But, if I can remember pages and pages of a story with a complicated plot and lots of characterization, I certainly should be able to memorize a poem. And I have. I can still recite the two poems I learned in a drama class I took in fourth grade. So, don't even think that you can't do it, and I know your children will be able to memorize anything they choose—quickly, effortlessly, and probably permanently.

An efficient way to memorize a poem is to carry it with you wherever you go. Read it over carefully whenever you have a spare minute, and then just start saying it to yourself. When you get stuck, take a peek at the printed poem. You will want to think carefully about what the words mean to you. Your interpretation will make the poem come alive.

The poems in this and the two following chapters are divided into somewhat arbitrary, frequently overlapping sections: easy-to-learn poems for children to recite; visual poems to be used with pictures on a felt board, Velcro apron, or magnetic board; and "souvenir" poems that you can recite and match to an inexpensive token to give the children as a tangible remembrance. In the group here, I've included samples of poems that I think are particularly good to use with beginners, especially children. You will find that this short collection of poems contains several selections in which the words of the poems direct the actions to use. I chose these because I noticed that, particularly when first learning to recite poetry, no one seemed to know what to do with his or her hands.

I like to stand when I present a poem, but if you and your group experiment with sitting and standing, you'll each determine what suits you best. The only rule not to be broken—ever—is this: Give the title of the poem and the author's name both before and after you recite. It's a thoughtful gesture to your audience to also include the name of a collection in which the poem can easily be found, but it's impolite, even inexcusable, to breezily share a poem without acknowledging its creator. The only other must-do, really, is that one must always say every word as it is written in the poem. If the children (or you) miss a word in a poem, urge them not to get flustered. Stress that it's perfectly acceptable to take out a copy of the poem to see what you missed. If you're at the beginning of the verse, start again. The audience will be understanding and grateful to hear a good poem just as it was written.

A Few Coaching Hints

Your goal is to eliminate the glassy stares, rigid postures, and monotonous voices that beset those beginners who think their task is done when they simply memorize a poem. Keep encouraging your students with positively-phrased reminders like, "Marty, are you hearing and thinking about the words you're saying?" An audio and/or video tape recorder can be helpful at this stage, as such flaws as sing-songing, mumbling, or racing through lines become immediately apparent—and unacceptable—to the young reciters when they hear and view themselves.

Many children do present a poem too quickly. In fact, the listener sometimes gets the impression that the children assume that the faster they recite, the less the chance that they'll forget the words. While correcting such flaws, though, remember to find some aspect of each child's presentation that you can praise sincerely. Poetry is new to most children, and support and encouragement are essential to their efforts. Whether you're an audience of one for their first run-throughs or an anxious member of a larger audience for a recital, smile during each selection. Your young performers will be searching your face for clues to your interest and pleasure in their work.

When to Use Poetry

Absolutely anytime. Good uses for poetry are as an opening for a program, to vary the pace during a group of longer pieces, and as a catchy ending. It is also a useful way to give every member of your group a chance to perform when time is short or some tellers aren't as skilled as others at presenting complicated tales.

Choosing a Poem

Lucky you. The book world is filled with excellent poetry written just for children. There is traditional rhymed, metered poetry and free-verse; serious and nonsensical poetry—a myriad of poets and poems from which to choose. When you are searching for a poem to present next week I secretly hope that you won't find the perfect one until you have read a number of poems by a

Lonna McKeon, School Librarian at Blessed Sacrament School in Johnston City, NY, leads kindergartners in a choral poem, "The Monster's Birthday," by Lilian Moore. Gestures and movements help them to memorize words. (*Photo: Chuck Haupt*)

variety of poets. That way you'll have an opportunity to meet some of the excellent poets who are writing today as well as the wonderful poets who published years ago and who should not be forgotten.

You'll want to explore the poems of Rachel Field, Walter de la Mare, and Eleanor Farjean while you also enjoy Myra Cohn Livingston, Eve Merriam, and Arnold Adoff. My booklist of useful favorites will start you off, and then whenever you are near a library or bookstore, browse through the poetry section. You may be able to find a rare treasure in the local library when you are visiting your aunt in Purdue or Pittsburgh. Here are some of my favorites to get you and your group started on your poetry prospecting.

Hello

Hello's a handy word to say
At least a hundred times a day.
Without Hello what would I do
Whenever I bumped into you?
Without Hello where would you be
Whenever you bumped into me?
Hello's a handy word to know.
Hello   Hello   Hello   Hello.

by Mary Ann Hoberman

Imaginary Room

To fashion a room—
a room of your own—
fasten your hands
one to the other,
hollow to hollow,
as though
you were holding
a bird—
a swallow, let's say,
or a finch:
something small,
pinched,
and pressed
in the well
of your palms
like an almond
at rest
in its shell.

by Sylvia Cassedy

Note: You may want to cup your hands while reciting this poem.

Order

You mean, if I'd keep my room clean
And never stuff things under the bed
And hang up my jacket
And get straight A's
And be polite
And work hard
I could someday grow up to be President?
    Forget it!

by Myra Cohn Livingston

Note: Pause before the last line, then turn around and walk away with great dignity at the end of the poem.

What Teacher Said

"The Unicorn?!"
  said Mrs. Whist.
"The Unicorn
  does not exist.
The horse was never
  born," she said,
"Who wore a horn
  upon his head.
Oh biffle-bat,
  you silly child,
Such animals
  do *not* run wild.
I've never seen
  one *anywhere.* . . !
". . . except for *that*
  one! OVER THERE!"

by J. Patrick Lewis

Note: You may want to have a friend wearing a unicorn horn on her head appear behind you or off to your side at the end of this poem.

Bad Decision

A bull saw something red.
He gored it.
It was a fire engine.
He should have
  ignored it.

by Tony Johnston

I'm Bold, I'm Brave

I'm bold, I'm brave, I know no fear.
I'm gallant as a buccaneer.
Is that a hornet by my ear?
Gangway! I'm getting out of here!
by Jack Prelutsky

Hot Food

We sit down to eat
and the potato's a bit hot
so I only put a little bit on my fork
and I blow
whooph whooph
until it's cool
just cool
then into the mouth
nice.
And there's my brother
he's doing the same
whooph whooph
into the mouth
nice.
There's my mum
she's doing the same
whooph whooph
into the mouth
nice.

But my dad.
My Dad.
What does he do?
He stuffs a great big chunk of potato
into his mouth.
then
that really does it.
His eyes pop out
he flaps his hands
he blows, he puffs, he yells
he bobs his head up and down
he spits bits of potato

all over his plate
and then he turns to us and he says,
"Watch out everybody—
the potato's very hot."
by Michael Rosen

> *Note:* This is a perfect poem to act out while reciting; choose just one part, or mimick the speaker, brother, mum and dad, in turn.

Sing a Song of Pockets

Sing a song of pockets
A pocket full of stones
A pocket full of feathers
Or maybe chicken bones
A pocket full of bottle tops
A pocket full of money
Or if it's something sweet you want
A pocket full of honey . . .
ugh!
by Beatrice Schenk de Regniers

Chairs

Chairs
Seem
To
Sit
Down
On
Themselves, almost as if
They were people,
Some fat, some thin;
Settled comfortably
On their own seats,
Some even stretch out their arms
To
Rest.
by Valerie Worth

Puzzle

What can you do with a lap?
You can sit and wiggle your toes.
But you can't stand up with a lap,
Because when you do—
     i
      t

        g
          o
            e
              s.

by Eve Merriam

How to Make a Yawn

Open as wide
as your mouth
will go

and let out
a giant
silent
O   O   H!
by Eve Merriam

Poetry Booklist

There seems to be a new renaissance of poetry publishing. Excellent general anthologies are available as well as theme collections. Many of the books published for children are lavishly illustrated. Although some poetic purists might object to having an artist or photographer provide the images for the reader, I usually find that the art makes the poetry more accessible. In addition to the anthologies there is also an abundance of books featuring the work of a single poet. In the past ten years I've used poetry extensively both for my own theme anthologies and for an activity that I call the poetry break. The poetry break is fully explained in *This Way to Books* (Wilson, 1983), but it is simply a tactic to encourage teachers and librarians to offer poetry every day. The books listed here are those that I've used the most frequently in searching for poems for my various poetry projects. Check the shelves and card catalog in your school or public library against the list, as it may help you in filling any holes or prompt you to discover new (or old) favorites.

Adult Sources

Background material for your reading pleasure.

Anderson, Douglas. *My Sister Looks Like a Pear: Awakening the Poetry in Young People.* Hart, 1974.
Relates experiences as a poet in the school's program.

Arnstein, Flora J. *Poetry and the Child.* Dover, 1962.
Children as poets. An exploration of the relationship of the teacher and child.

Hopkins, Lee Bennett. *Pass the Poetry, Please!* Rev. ed. Harper, 1987.
Practical, lively look at children's poetry includes ideas for introducing poetry to children.

Hughes, Ted. *Poetry Is.* Doubleday, 1970.
A British poet shows how poets such as D. H. Lawrence, T. S. Eliot, and Theodore Roethke present nature and people through poetry.

Koch, Kenneth. *Wishes, Lies and Dreams: Teaching Children to Write Poetry.* Vintage, 1970
Discusses a method of teaching the writing of poetry. A companion volume is *Rose, Where Did You Get That Red?* (Vintage, 1973)—teaching great poetry to children.

———, and Kate Farrell. *Sleeping on the Wing: An Anthology of Modern Poetry with Essays on Reading and Writing* Random, 1981.
This is an anthology with essays. Emily Dickinson, Ezra Pound, William Carlos Williams are among those examined.

Larrick, Nancy. *Somebody Turned on a Tap in These Kids: Poetry and Young People Today.* Delacorte, 1971.
> A collection of essays on the joys of poetry by Jane Jordan, Karla Kuskin, Myra Cohn Livingston.

Livingston, Myra Cohn. *Climb into the Bell Tower: Essays on Poetry.* Harper, 1990.
> An articulate exploration of poets and poetry for children. Livingston is both a poet and anthologist.

Anthologies

In the "olden days" when I was a school librarian, and later, a public librarian, I wished for a children's poetry anthology to take to a desert island. My wish has now been granted, but alas, there are so many good anthologies today that now I can't choose which one to take.

Cole, William. *Poem Stew.* Art by Karen Ann Weinhaus. Lippincott, 1981.
> Humorous poetry for children. Take a look at *Oh, Such Foolishness* (Harper, 1978), as well.

dePaola, Tomie. *Tomie dePaola's Book of Poems.* Art by compiler. Putnam, 1988.
> Holidays, seasons, animals, and people, all enhanced by dePaola's distinctive art.

Dunning, Stephen, Edward Lueders, and Hugh Smith. *Reflections on a Gift of Watermelon Pickle . . . and Other Modern Verse.* Photos. Lothrop, 1967.
> An exciting collection of contemporary poetry for young adults.

Foster, John. *A First Poetry Book.* Art by Chris Orr, Martin White, and Joseph Wright. Oxford, 1979.
> The first in a series of several anthologies from Britain, this book is somewhat uneven in quality, but there are treasures here to find. The second book in this series is *Another First Poetry Book* (Oxford, 1988).

Harrison, Michael and Christopher Stuart-Clark. *The Oxford Treasury of Children's Poems.* Illustrated. Oxford, 1988.
> Humorous and serious poetry for children of all ages.

Heylen, Jill and Celia Jellett. *Someone Is Flying Balloons Australian Poems for Children.* Art by Kerry Argent. Mad Hatter (c/o Slawson Communications, San Diego, CA 92103-4316), 1983.
> Traditional and contemporary poets are represented.

Hopkins, Lee Bennett. *Surprises.* Art by Megan Lloyd. Harper, 1984.
> A selection of poems especially chosen for beginning readers.

Kennedy, X. J. and Dorothy Kennedy. *Knock at a Star: A Children's Introduction to Poetry.* Art by Karen Ann Weinhaus. Little, 1982.
> An introductory anthology with notes on form and feelings.

Larrick, Nancy. *On City Streets.* Photos by David Sagain. Evans, 1986.
> Just one of Larrick's fine collections. This one features city poems.

Lobel, Arnold. *The Random House Book of Mother Goose: A Treasury of 306 Time-less Nursery Rhymes.*
You get both the 306 rhymes *and* Lobel's color art.

Prelutsky, Jack, ed. *The Random House Book of Poetry for Children.* Art by Arnold Lobel. Random, 1983.
The favorite. 572 poems, a subject index, and you get Arnold Lobel's art, too.

_____. *Read-Aloud Rhymes for the Very Young.* Art by Marc Brown. Knopf, 1986.
Especially chosen for younger children, this outstanding anthology will be enjoyed by adults, too. Brown's art is a perfect complement to the selections.

Rosen, Michael. *The Kingfisher Book of Children's Poetry.* Illustrated. Kingfisher, 1985.
Eve Merriam, Dorothy Aldis, and Mary Ann Hoberman are among the American poets represented in this British collection. There is also a subject index in this volume.

Sullivan, Charles, ed. *Imaginary Gardens: American Poetry and Art for Young People.* Abrams, 1989.
Poetry illustrated with American art.

Pictures to Share

Art and poetry just seem to complement each other. We have an abundence of beautifully illustrated poetry books to share with children. Although some may cringe at the idea of imposing someone else's pictorial interpretation of a poem, such books can enhance the poetry while making poems more accessible to a wider range of children.

Andersen, Hans Christian. *The Swineherd.* Translated by Naomi Lewis. Art by Dorothee Duntze. North-South, 1987.
Gloriously sophisticated art for this classic Andersen tale.

Baylor, Byrd. *The Best Town in the World.* Art by Ronald Himler. Scribners, 1983.
". . . that town where everything was perfect."

Carroll, Lewis. *Jabberwocky.* Art by Graeme Base. Abrams, 1989.
A lush interpretation of the poem from *Through the Looking Glass* with double-spread paintings.

Degen, Bruce. *Jamberry.* Art by author. Harper, 1983.
With each line rhyming with the word berry, this is an exuberant nonsense poem and happy pictures.

Farber, Norma. *How Does It Feel to Be Old?* Art by Trina Schart Hyman. Dutton, 1979.
The advantages and disadvantages of old age are described in words and pictures.

Frost, Robert. *Birches.* Art by Ed Young. Holt, 1988.
Muted art gives room for your own imagination. Compare this with Susan Jeffers' artistic interpretation of the same poem. (Dutton, 1978).

Grimes, Nikki. *Something on My Mind*. Art by Tom Feelings. Dial, 1978.
  Each full page portrait is accompanied by a short poem featuring families and feel-ings.

Greenfield, Eloise. *Daydreamers*. Art by Tom Feelings. Dial, 1981.
  Tom Feelings' portraits of black children are accompanied by a poetic text.

_____. *Under the Sunday Tree*. Art by Amos Ferguson. Harper, 1988.
  Life in the Bahamas. The vibrant art works perfectly with Greenfield's poems.

Highwater, Jamake. *Moonsong Lullaby*. Photos by Marcia Keegan. Lothrop, 1981.
  An original native American lullaby with full color photographs of people and sce-nery.

Lenski, Lois. *Sing a Song of People*. Art by Giles Laroche. Little, 1987.
  A celebration of city people.

Lewis, Richard. *In a Spring Garden*. Art by Ezra Jack Keats. Dial, 1965.
  Japanese haiku from morning to night.

The Little Dog Laughed and Other Nursery Rhymes. Art by Lucy Cousins. Dutton, 1990.
  Mother Goose offerings with big, bold, brightly colored art.

Livingston, Myra Cohn. *Space Songs*. Art by Leonard Everett Fisher. Holiday, 1988.
  Outer space is explored by a distinguished artist and poet. This winning combination has also teamed to give us *Sky Songs* (Holiday, 1984), *Earth Songs* (Holiday, 1986), *Sea Songs* (Holiday, 1986).

Longfellow, Henry Wadsworth. *Paul Revere's Ride*. Art by Nancy Winslow Parker. Greenwillow, 1985.
  Parker's clearly defined art illuminates this famous story poem.

Pomerantz, Charlotte. *If I Had a Paka: Poems in Eleven Languages*. Art by Nancy Tafuri. Greenwillow, 1982.
  Each of these poems uses a few foreign words.

Prelutsky, Jack. *Beneath a Blue Umbrella*. Art by Garth Williams. Greenwillow, 1990.
  Short poems and full page art, this is a companion volume to *Ride a Purple Pelican* (Greenwillow, 1986), which features nonsense verse about place names.

Shaw, Nancy. *Sheep in a Jeep*. Art by Margot Apple. Houghton, 1986.
  Hilarious art matched to a funny read-aloud book.

Sing a Song of Sixpence. Art by Tracy Campbell Pearson. Dial, 1985.
  Delightfully illustrated, a pleasure to view.

Singer, Marilyn. *Turtle in July*. Art by Jerry Pinkney. Macmillan, 1989.
  Domestic and wild animal poems and full page art for each poem.

Thompson, Pat, comp. *Rhymes around the Day*. Art by Jan Ormerod. Lothrop, 1983.
  Ormerod uses three pre-schoolers as background figures depicting this collection of nursery rhymes.

Westcott, Nadine Bernard. *Skip to My Lou*. Art by adapter. Little, 1989.
  The traditional folksong gaily illustrated.

Whipple, Laura, ed. *Eric Carle's Animals Animals*. Art by Eric Carle. Philomel, 1989.
  Each of the animal poems is illustrated with Carle's double-spread art.

Willard, Nancy. *A Visit to William Blake's Inn: Poems for Innocent and Experienced Travelers.* Art by Alice and Martin Provensen. Harcourt, 1981.
Visitors to the Inn range from the Cat of Cats to a wise cow.

Some Poets

The work of the following poets is consistently well-written. Just one offering for each is listed here, but most of these writers have several books for children, and as you identify your group's favorite poems, you can check your library for their other collections.

Ahlberg, Allan, *Please Mrs. Butler.* Puffin, 1983
Best known as a picture book author, Ahlberg writes about school and playtime.

Cassedy, Sylvia. *Roomrimes.* Art by Michele Chessare. Crowell, 1987.
Places, each beginning with a letter of the alphabet.

Ciardi, John. *The Hopeful Trout and Other Limericks.* Art by Susan Meddaugh. Houghton, 1989.
Humorous limericks by a popular children's poet.

Cummings, E. E. *Hist Whist and Other Poems for Children.* Art by David Calsada. Liveright, 1983.
This American poet is better known for his adult poetry. These selections have been especially chosen for their child appeal.

de la Mare, Walter. *Peacock Pie.* Art by Louise Brierley. Holt, 1969, 1989.
Enduring poems from a master poet.

de Regniers, Beatrice Schenk. *The Way I Feel . . . Sometimes.* Art by Susan Meddaugh. Clarion, 1988.
Children's ups and downs are offered in short, upbeat poems.

Giovanni, Nikki. *Vacation Time.* Art by Marisabina Russo. Morrow, 1980.
From "Tommy's Mommy" to "Rainbows," these are poems with lilting rhythms.

Glenn, Mel. *Back to Class.* Photos by Michael J. Bernstein. Clarion, 1988.
Outstanding poems illuminate the inner thoughts of high school students and teachers.

Greenfield, Eloise. *Honey, I Love and Other Poems.* Art by Diane and Leo Dillon. Crowell, 1978.
Poems to make you feel and remember.

Janeczko, Paul B. *The Place My Words Are Looking for: What Poets Say About and Through Their Work.* Bradbury, 1990.
Contemporary poets discuss their poetry and give examples of their work.

Kuskin, Karla. *Near the Window Tree.* Harper, 1975.
Notes precede each of these poems, the subjects of which range from bugs to friends

Lee, Dennis. *Alligator Pie.* Art by Frank Newfeld. Houghton, 1975.
Lee is known for his nonsense rhymes.

Lewis, J. Patrick. *A Hyppopotamusn't and Other Animal Verses*. Art by Victoria Chess. Dial, 1990.
Unexpected animal poetry.

Livingston, Myra Cohn. *There Was a Place and Other Poems*. McElderry, 1988.
The thoughts and feelings of children with family problems, such as living with divorced parents, meeting fathers' girl friends, and dealing with lonely moms.

Merriam, Eve. *Chortles*. Art by Sheila Hamanaka. Morrow, 1989.
Just one of Merriam's superb collections. Her trademark: a remarkable use of language.

McCord, David. *One at a Time: His Collected Poems for the Very Young*. Art by Henry B. Kane. Little, 1980.
McCord's work is the quintessence of children's poetry. A subject index is included.

Milne, A. A. *When We Were Very Young*. Art by Ernest H. Shepard. Dutton, 1924, 1961, 1988.
It is still a pleasure to introduce a child to Milne. Also delightful is *Now We Are Six* (Dutton, 1927, 1961, 1988).

Moore, Lillian. *Think of Shadows*. Art by Deborah Robinson. Atheneum, 1980.
Shadows on the playground, in a tunnel, Ground Hog Day.

Moss, Jeff. *The Butterfly Jar*. Art by Chris Demarest. Bantam, 1989.
Funny and poignant. Gives Silverstein some competition.

Nash, Ogden. *Custard and Company*. Art by Quentin Blake. Little, 1980.
From Nash, the supreme humorist, here are selections for children—and everyone else.

Pomerantz, Charlotte. *The Tamarind Puppy and Other Poems*. Art by Byron Barton. Greenwillow, 1980.
Poems in English with a few Spanish words.

Prelutsky, Jack. *The New Kid on the Block*. Art by James Stevenson. Greenwillow, 1984.
Prelutsky's poems are humorous, bouncy, and happy; they have great appeal to children.

Rylant, Cynthia. *Waiting to Waltz: A Childhood*. Art by Stephen Gammell. Bradbury, 1984.
Portraits in poetry of a spelling bee, swearing, and people from the poet's childhood. More of this author's haunting poems from a youthful perspective are found in *Soda Jerk*, for which Peter Calanotto did the artwork (Orchard, 1990).

Silverstein, Shel. *Where the Sidewalk Ends*. Art by author. Harper, 1974.
The A-1 humorous collection.

Simmie, Lois. *Auntie's Knitting a Baby*. Art by Anne Simmie. Orchard, 1984.
Lots of fun and some serious thoughts, too.

Stevenson, Robert Louis. *A Child's Garden of Verses*. Art by Michael Foreman. Delacorte, 1985.
Numerous artists have illustrated this classic collection. This is a sophisticated interpretation of the well-known poems.

Viorst, Judith. *If I Were in Charge of the World and Other Worries.* Art by Lynne Cherry. Atheneum, 1981.

The joys and worries of childhood. Some spoofs of fairy stories are also included.

Worth, Valerie. *All the Small Poems.* Art by Natalie Babbitt. Farrar, 1987.

Every poem is a gem of simplicity. Featured are animals and objects such as magnet, kitten, fence, and pie.

Themes

These are some individual poets and anthologists who have pinpointed various subjects and themes.

Adoff, Arnold. *All the Colors of the Race.* Art by John Steptoe. Lothrop, 1982.

Thoughts and feelings of a child with a black mom and a white dad.

_____. *Chocolate Dreams.* Art by Turi MacCombie. Lothrop, 1989.

For chocolate lovers everywhere.

_____. *Sports Pages.* Art by Steven Kuzma. Lippincott, 1986.

Training, injuries, playing, winning and losing, individual and team sports are all covered.

Bauer, Caroline Feller. *Windy Day: Stories and Poems.* Art by Dirk Zimmer. Lippincott, 1988.

Poems and stories on weather themes. Similar themed anthologies include *Rainy Day* (Lippincott, 1986), and *Snowy Day* (Lippincott, 1986), *Halloween* (Lippincott, 1989).

Bennett, Jill. *Spooky Poems.* Art by Mary Rees. Little, 1989.

These are humorous poems featuring a Halloween theme.

Brewton, Sara, John E. Brewton, and John Brewton Blackburn. *Of Quarks, Quasars and Other Quirks: Quizzical Poems for the Supersonic Age.* Art by Quentin Blake. Crowell, 1977.

The Brewtons have edited many collections. This one features poems about television, think tanks, and IBM.

Cole, Joanna, and Stephanie Calmenson. *Miss Mary Mack and Other Children's Street Rhymes.* Art by Alan Tiegreen. Morrow, 1990.
Rhymes for hand-clapping, ball-bouncing, counting-out.

Dahl, Roald. *Rhyme Stew.* Art by Quentin Blake. Viking, 1990.
An irreverent look at some old folktales in rhyme.

Esbensen, Barbara Juster. *Words with Wrinkled Knees: Animal Poems.* Art by John Stadler. Crowell, 1986.
When the name or word for the animal becomes as important as the animal.

Fleischman, Paul. *Joyful Noise: Poems for Two Voices.* Art by Eric Beddows. Harper, 1988.
Poems about insects, to be presented with two voices.

Goldstein, Bobbye S. *Bear in Mind: A Book of Bear Poems.* Art by William Pène duBois. Viking, 1989.
The theme is bears, the art is by the bear expert.

Gordon, Ruth. *Under All Silences: Shades of Love.* Harper, 1987.
Kenneth Patchen, Paul Verlaine, Rainer Maria Rilke. Love poems for young adults.

Greenberg, David. *Slugs.* Art by Victoria Chess. Little, 1983.
Not all adults will like this slightly gross, funny look at slugs, but children love it.

Hoberman, May Ann. *Bugs.* Art by Victoria Chess. Viking, 1976.
A celebration of insects.

Hopkins, Lee Bennett. *Click, Rumble, Roar: Poems about Machines.* Photos by Anna Held Audette. Crowell, 1987.
Hopkins is a master collector of themed poetry. Animals, holidays, bedtime poems and city poems can all be found in his other individual collections.

Janeczko, Paul B., ed. *The Music of What Happens: Poems that Tell Stories.* Orchard, 1988.
Story poems for young adults.

Kennedy, X. J. *Brats.* Art by James Watts. Atheneum, 1986.
One verse poems describing a variety of brats.

Knudson, R. R., and Mary Swenson. *American Sports Poems.* Orchard, 1988.
Baseball, football, soccer, volleyball and more represented by poems.

Larrick, Nancy. *Cats Are Cats.* Art by Ed Young. Philomel, 1988.
A lovely package of art and poetry—all about cats.

Marzollo, Jean. *Pretend You're A Cat.* Art by Jerry Pinkney. Dial, 1990.
Poems about pretending, accompanied by pictures showing various animals and children imitating them.

Merriam, Eve. *Halloween ABC.* Art by Lane Smith. Macmillan, 1987.
Sophisticated Halloween poetry for older children and young adults.

O'Neill, Mary. *Hailstones and Halibut Bones.* Art by John Wallner. Doubleday, 1989.
The classic poems about colors reissued with new color art.

Prelutsky, Jack. *It's Halloween.* Art by Marilyn Hafner. Greenwillow, 1977.
Prelutsky has written several holiday books, all published by Greenwillow, featuring easy-to-read poems, including *It's Christmas* (1981), *It's Thanksgiving* (1982), *It's Valentine's Day* (1983).

Sneve, Virginia Driving Hawk. *Dancing Teepees: Poems of American Youth*. Art by Stephen Gammell. Holiday, 1989.
Short poems collected from the oral tradition of native Americans.

Steig, Jeanne. *Consider the Lemming*. Art by William Steig. Farrar, 1988.
Excellent use of language and wit to describe animals from the beaver to the penguin.

Streich, Corrine, ed. *Grandparent's Houses*. Art by Lillian Hoban. Greenwillow, 1984.
Grandmothers and grandfathers from around the world.

Turner, Ann. *Street Talk*. Art by Catherine Stock. Houghton, 1986.
City poems: people and places (the museum), street painting.

Yolen, Jane. *Best Witches: Poems for Halloween*. Art by Elise Primavera. Putnam, 1989.
A prolific author gives us her views on Halloween.

Chapter 9

Visual Poetry

If you're not familiar with using visual props in poetry presentations, the following poems paired with art will give you a good sampling with which to experiment. After duplicating the pictures accompanying each poem, mount them on posterboard and use watercolors or whatever media you prefer to paint them. You can type up the poem and attach it to the back of your picture to serve as a prompter when you recite the poem. The pictures can also be displayed on felt, magnetic, or Velcro boards, or you may choose to make a set for each of the children in your group to take home and use when reciting the poems for their families and friends.

It's usually wise to use just one visual poem in a presentation with other verse, and all of these selections can be presented in traditional poetry recitations, as well as in visual format.

Hippopotamus

You see

> wheels on a car
> and on a train
> wheels on a truck,
> and a jumbo plane.

You see

> wheels on a van,
> a bike, a bus,
> but you don't see wheels
> on a Hippopotamus—

UNLESS SHE'S ROLLER SKATING.

by Robert Heidbreder

Another Snake Story

I saw a snake go by today
Riding in a Chevrolet;

He was long and he was thin
And he didn't have a chin;

He had no chin, but what the heck,
He had lots and lots of neck.

by Lois Simmie

Note: Make the snake's neck by folding the carboard or paper in accordion-style, using Velcro to attach it to the back of the car. As you recite the last couplet, release the tape to extend the neck.

The Pear Tree

I love our old pear tree,
Our old gnarled pear tree.
It doesn't bear apples
And it doesn't bear pears,
So it has lots of room
For the bears.

So up in the pear tree
Where the pears are not—
The nice juicy pears
That the tree hasn't got—
Lives a family of bears
As fierce as can be.

They're wild old bears
But they're scared of me.
'Cause whenever I shout
To the top of the tree,
"Bears, Bears,
You better watch out,
I'm coming up stairs—"

You can hear them growl,
The way bears do,
"Come on up stairs
We're not afraid of you."

But they're scared all right
'Cause they never stop
To play or fight.
When I reach the top.
They're out of sight.

I wouldn't hurt the silly old bears.
I like them better than apples or pears
In our old pear tree
That doesn't grow apples
Or doesn't grow pears,
But leaves lot of room
For me and the bears.

by E. Elizabeth Longwell

Note: Put small pieces of Velcro (the hook part) on branches of the tree. Put loop pieces of Velcro on the backs of the bears. When reciting the poem, place the bears in the tree.

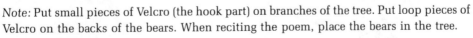

Sometimes I Wish I Was a Bear

Sometimes I wish I was a bear
real big and white and furry
I'd roar and growl and
show my claws
I'd scare folks in a hurry
I'd sit up on my haunches
and wave my paws around
and then when I got tired
I'd snooze—
stretched out on the ground.

But
maybe I could have more fun
pretending I'm a collie,
a little tiny poodle
or a French pug fat and jolly
but heck!
Who wants to chew on bones
and maybe even get fleas
I think I'll stay just like I am
Because, well,
I Like Me.

by Nonie Borba

Note: Make these masks with cutout areas in the pupils of the animals' eyes and put on first the bear mask, then the dog, as you recite the poem. You can attach a handle to the side of the mask for easier manipulation, or just hold the mask itself as you recite.

Dogs and Cats and Bears and Bats

Mammals are a varied lot;
some are furry, some are not;
many come equipped with tails;
some have quills, a few have scales.

Some are large, and others small;
some are quick, while others crawl;
they prance on land, they swing from trees;
they're underground and in the seas.

Some have hooves, and some have paws;
some have fangs in snapping jaws;
some will snarl if you come near;
others quickly disappear.

Dogs and cats and bears and bats,
all are mammals, so are rats;
whales are mammals, camels too;
I'm a mammal . . . so are YOU!

by Jack Prelutsky

Note: Use the pictures to illustrate the last verse and point to your listeners or hold up a mirror for them to see themselves as you say the last line.

Ready for Winter

I have a fur cap
  And mittens, just new.
My coat is so heavy
  No cold can get through.

With stout leather boots
  And stockings, wool—red,
I shall keep nice and warm
  From my toes to my head.

My nose? Never fear!
  I've a scarf round about
That leaves only space
  For my eyes to peep out.
by Clarice Foster Booth

Note: Use a flannel board or a Velcro board or apron to present this poem. Start out with the figure of the little boy, then add each item of clothing as it's mentioned in the poem. Be sure to color the stockings bright red!

Greedy Dog

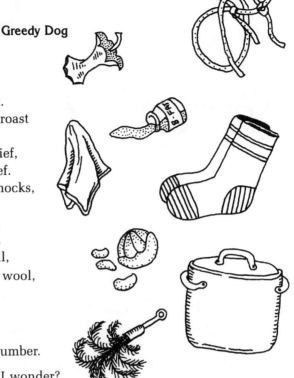

This dog will eat anything.

Apple cores and bacon fat,
Milk you poured out for the cat.
He likes the string that ties the roast
And relishes the buttered toast.
Hide your chocolates! He's a thief,
He'll even eat your handkerchief.
And if you don't like sudden shocks,
Carefully conceal your socks.
Leave some soup without a lid,
And you'll wish you never did.
When you think he must be full,
You'll find him gobbling bits of wool,
Orange peel or paper bags,
Dusters and old cleaning rags.

This dog will eat anything,
Except for mushrooms and cucumber.

Now what's wrong with those, I wonder?
by James Hurley

Note: Make the dog's stomach a circle of clear acrylic. On the back of the figure, attach a paper bag or envelope with the front cut out to fit around the clear opening for the stomach. As you mention each item that the dog eats, drop it into the bag, so that it shows through the clear "stomach."

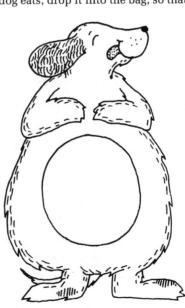

Chapter 10

Souvenir Poetry

Everyone welcomes a present, but when you give a gift to an adult you sometimes wish it could fulfill some secret longing: a sports car, a trip to Zanzibar, or a mansion by the sea.

Children are thrilled to receive even the simplest and least expensive (translate that to cheap or free) gifts.

It's fun to find a poem to suit a clever souvenir, or a souvenir to go with a poem you would like to share. It's extra nice for the waiting-at-home parents to see some visible sign of what went on at Book Time at the library.

Here are some suggestions that I've found helpful in using this approach to poetry:

1. Distribute the souvenirs at the last possible minute, so that the tokens don't get lost or damaged even before the child leaves your facility.

2. Letting the children reach into a cloth bag or a box held above their sight line heightens the excitement of the gift. If you don't have gifts that are all the same size and shape, remind the children that, while they may trade with someone else, the magic for them is in the item they pulled out of the bag or box.

3. After reading the poem, show the souvenir that the group will receive. Then, read the poem once again, holding the remembrance for them to see. This simple technique allows you to use a souvenir poem as a theme for an entire program, even if the remainder of the books or poems you are presenting have nothing at all to do with marbles or feathers (or whatever you've

222

chosen to give out). If you recite the short poem keyed to the gift at intervals between other selections, it will in itself give structure to your program.

4. When you see the perfect souvenir (on sale, on the beach, or in the garden) run to the poetry collection in your library for a poem to compliment your theme. There are wonderful poems dealing with almost any subject you can imagine.

Following are some poems and souvenir suggestions that you can use yourself or that might prompt other creative pairings of poems and small keepsakes.

Beach Stones

When these small
stones
were
in clear pools and
nets of weed

tide-tumbled
teased by spray

they glowed
moonsilver,
glinted sunsparks on
their speckled
skins.

Spilled on the
shelf
they were
wet-sand jewels
wave-green
still flecked with
foam.

Now
gray stones
lie
dry and dim.

  Why did we bring them home?
by Lillian Moore

The Playground

I went to the playground
I played on the swings.
I played on the ground
And did lots of things.

I slid down the slide
And whizzed down like a rocket
Then picked up some stones
to take home in my pocket.

by Carmen Coupe

Souvenir: Small stones

Stamps

You can lick 'em
   and stick 'em,
And send them away
Or keep 'em on hinges
   In an album's OK.

You can trade 'em,
   parade 'em,
Or save 'em forever;
Compare 'em and share 'em,
   most any endeavor.

You can buy 'em,
   or sale 'em,
From most anywhere;
Collect any color
   and size to compare.

You can display 'em,
   or lay 'em
Under a lamp.
What are they?
I'll they you:
   The Postage Stamp!

by Linda G. Paulsen

Stamps

I collected stamps
Papa gave me a big bagful
I didn't collect stamps anymore.
by Siv Widenberg

Souvenir: Postage stamps

Paperclips

A jumbled sight,
The sheets I write—
  High time for paperclips
To take a bite
And clasp them tight
  Between bright bulldog lips!
by X. J. Kennedy

Souvenir: paperclips

Paperclip Relay

After reciting the poem, and before you distribute the paperclips that will be the souvenirs for the group, you and the children might enjoy trying this race.

You need: two boxes of paperclips
a group of eager children

How to: Divide the children into teams of five. Give each person a paperclip and have each team form a line. The first person passes the paperclip to the person behind, who fastens the two together. The third in line fastens his or her paperclip to the two already linked, and passes all three on to the next person. The first team that finishes their chain wins. You can reverse the process, too, having the children race to detach the clips, one at a time. The first team to undo their chain wins that round, and at the end, each child will be holding a souvenir paperclip.

Flying a Ribbon

What is your favorite mystery?
>   It's the wind.
Where does the wind go?
>   It goes where it wants to go.
Can you hear it?
>   Only if it's in a hurry.
>   When the wind is quiet,
>   it runs through the street
>   in sneakers.
How do you know the wind's secret?
>   I tie a long white ribbon
>   to the end of a stick
>   and when the wind comes by
>   it makes the ribbon fly
>   in its direction.

by Kathleen Fraser   *Souvenir:* ribbons

If You Find a Little Feather

If you find a little feather,
a little white feather,
a soft and tickly feather,
   it's for you.

A feather is a letter
from a bird,
and it says,
"Think of me.
Do not forget me.
Remember me always.
Remember me forever.
Or remember me
at least
until
the little feather
is lost."

So . . .
. . . if you find a little feather,
a little white feather,
a soft and tickly feather,
   it's for you.
   Pick it up
     and . . .
       put it in your pocket!
by Beatrice Schenk de Regnier

   Souvenir: feathers (purchase them at a crafts shop)

BALLOONS!

A balloon
is a wild
space animal,

restless pet
who bumps and butts
its head
on the cage walls
of a room—

bursts
with a bellow,
or escapes slowly
with sighs
leaving a limp skin.

Balloons on the street
fidget
in fresh air,
strain
at their string
leashes.

If you loose
a balloon,
it bolts home
for the moon.
by Judith Thurman

   Souvenir: balloons

Marbles

Marbles picked up
Heavy by the handful
And held, weighed,
Hard, glossy,
Glassy, cold,
Then poured clicking,
Water-smooth, back
To their bag, seem
Treasure: round jewels,
Slithering gold.
by Valerie Worth

Marbles

Immies.
Purees.
Agates.
Shooters.
In a circle.
In a row.
Immies.
Purees.
Agates.
Shooters.
Knock one out
or down a hole.
Immies.
Purees.
Agates.
Shooters.
If I win,
I keep them all.
by Kathleen Fraser

Souvenir: marbles

from Houses from the Sea

When we took our pails and shovels
and went down to the sea
the waves ran up to meet us
as if glad that we had come.
They made a fizzing bubbling sound
as the lacy edges of white foam
swirled around our feet
And then
the sea rolled back down the beach.

My sister called to it:
She called to it and said,
"Come back!
Oh, please come back and play with us!"

As if it heard our call
the sea came running back.
But
again it slipped away
as if pulled back down the beach
by some hand we could not see.

Even though our friend, the sea,
did not stay and play
it brought us treasures
and left them lying on the sand for us.

We found two moon shells
so smooth and round
they fittend in our hands
the little animals that once lived inside
and used them for their home,
were gone;
the shells were ours to keep—
these little houses that came in from the sea.

by Alice E. Goudey

Shells

The bones of the sea
are on the shore,
shells
curled into the sand,
shells
caught in the green weed hair.
All day I gathered them
and there are always
more.

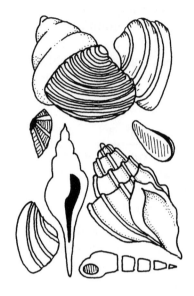

  I take them home
  magic bones of the sea,
  and when
  I touch one,
  then I hear
  I taste
  I smell the sea
  again.
by Lilian Moore

She Sells Sea-shells

She sells sea-shells on the sea shore;
The shells that she sells are sea-shells I'm sure.
So if she sells sea-shells on the sea shore,
I'm sure that the shells are sea-shore shells.
Anon.

Souvenir

I bring back a shell so I can always hear
the music of the ocean when I hold it to my ear.

then I feel again the grains of sand
trickle sun-warm through my hand

the sea gulls dip and swoop and cry
as they dive for fish then climb the sky

the sailboats race with wings spread wide
as the wind spins them round and they glide ride glide

my lips taste a crust of salty foam
and sandpipers skitter and crabs scuttle home.

where I build a castle of Yesterday
the high tide washes away away

while I keep the shell so I can always hear
the music of the ocean when I hold it to my ear.
by Eve Merriam

Souvenir: sea shells

PART IV

Active Programming with Books for Fun

Chapter 11

Grand Openings or Great Closings

Although I use the following ideas most often to create an impact at the beginning or a lasting impression at the end of my presentation, this chapter could simply be titled Attention Getters, since these ideas can be used anytime your program—or your day—is dragging a bit. Perhaps you are in the middle of a complicated explanation of a math process and you think you have lost the attention of your students. Or maybe you'd like to end your own working day with a memorable hype for books. You can just whip on your black-fabric-puppet stage and recite a poem. Whip it off and go back to your math lesson.

These ideas can work well in unexpected situations. My friend Penny is the wife of a navy captain. She often speaks at naval functions where all the women are dressed in their best. In her Chanel suit, dainty hat, and white gloves she looks like the perfect naval wife. After she is introduced as the speaker, she demurely takes off her gloves. One of them has the clown sleeve attached (p. 242) and the red, white, and blue fabric sets off at first nervous giggles and then honest, delighted laughter, as all tension is broken.

I admit to using these ideas advantageously, even when the occasion is not book-related. The Library Cheer'' in *Presenting Reader's Theater* (Wilson, 1987) and the ''Read Cheer'' on page xix have been so successful in my programs that I thought I would try the same approach in another situation. We are doing some remodeling on our house. It's been torn up for weeks. Every day the work folks promise to come and don't or come as the day is ending. Yesterday, when the truck pulled up at noon, just in time for them to break for lunch, I ran out with my pom poms and flags and did a welcoming cheer. Did it work? Not exactly. They still haven't come today. Do you think we'll always have a hole in the wall?

Just because you have used these ideas once don't hesitate to repeat them. They can be used many times, featuring different books and poems. In fact, the telephone, decorated book jacket, or a host puppet are often used every day in libraries and classrooms, where the props become cues to the children that something fun is coming that has to do with books.

Collect ideas that will help you add variety and liveliness to your book promotions. Next time you attend a really good lecture take note of how the speaker gets and keeps your attention. Here are a few quick and easy lead-ins—or sign-offs—to try:

In the Spotlight

Turn off the lights, and place the book you are featuring on a table. Now, put the book in a spotlight by directing the light of a flashlight on it. Announce the title and author, and you're ready to share the book.

Aquarium

No fish in your aquarium? Put a book into the empty container and you have a crystal house for your featured book.

Bring on the Books with Music

Before you announce the title and author of the featured book, ring a bell, strike a cymbal, triangle, or a small gong to bring on the book with fanfare.

A Present

Gift wrap the book you are featuring and then make a ceremony of opening the present: the book of the day.

On a Pedestal

Use a sculpture pedestal or a music stand to display the book of the day, which you've covered with a cloth. As you begin, ceremoniously remove the cloth to reveal the book.

Food

Offer cookies or other food that is appropriate to the theme of the selection before or after a book talk or story. You will be sure to be remembered with love.

Serve Judith's Peanut Butter Cookies (the recipe is on p. xviii) to accompany a reading of *World Famous Muriel and the Scary Dragon* by Sue Alexander with art by Chris L. Demarest (Little, Brown, 1985).

Fan

Do you own a fan that you purchased at the county fair, one that your great-grandmother used, or one you bought yesterday at the import store? Use it to introduce a book.

Open the fan and, at the same time, slip the book you will introduce behind the fan. Close the fan and Ta! Ta! there is the book.

Frame Poetry

Use a posterboard frame to introduce a book, story or poem. Once you make the frame in any shape you like, it is reusable as a prop, whenever you want to open or close a program or to add a visual element to a poetry presentation.

Here are several sample frames that you may want to duplicate and a poem to use with each frame. Remember that the frame does not have to be used with poetry. You can stick your own head in the frame and introduce your story.

Window Frame

Outside

I
am inside
looking outside
at the pelting
rain—
where
the outside world
is melting
upon my window
pane.
by Lilian Moore

Heart Frame

I Like You

Although I saw you
The day before yesterday,
And yesterday and today,
This much is true—
I want to see you tomorrow, too!
by Masuhito (8th Century)

Picture Frame

Mom

Hilary drew a picture of her Mom
Short unkempt hair
Colored glasses
faded lips and
a fake smile.
Do I really look like that?
by Caroline Bauer

TV Screen

Last Laugh

They all laughed when I told them
I wanted to be

A woman in space
Floating so free.

But they won't laugh at me
When they finally see
My feet up on Mars
And my face on TV.
by Lee Bennett Hopkins

Hat Tricks

Use your favorite hat as a signal that book-sharing time or book break is about to begin. A special hat, whether outrageous, book-themed, or just extravagantly decorated, can be created for this purpose. Some storytellers have derived their use of a hat as a story prompt from the African story-hat tradition. Small objects on the hat represent stories to tell. You might want to translate this into a hat that represents one or more particular stories in your repertoire or one that speaks of books or fairy tales in general. Time for a story? Put on your hat and read aloud.

Pom Poms

These are available from a toy store or athletic-supply house. I use pom poms along with Garrison Keillor's Library Cheer (*Presenting Reader's Theater*, Wilson 1987) or the "Read Cheer" on page xix.

Fabric Puppet Stage

This is the ultimate attention getter. You are bogged down in an explanation of the new guidelines for purchasing and your committee is falling asleep. Or, the children have become hyper-crazy in your semi-quiet library. Quick: throw on your puppet stage and recite a poem or give a short book talk. A few seconds later, when you take off the stage you will have the full and rapt (if startled) attention of the committee or class.

This is not literally a stage, but since I use it with puppets, I think of it as a puppet stage. It is simply a black piece of fabric long enough to cover you from head to toe, with two eye holes cut in it so that you can observe the audience while they stare at you. I have used this successfully as an opener when I walk into a room, or onto a stage with the fabric draped over me and begin my presentation with two puppets discussing the virtues of reading. You can give a book talk or tell any kind of story while wearing the fabric puppet stage, but it should be short, because unless you are wearing a microphone or your voice will sound faint and muffled and you will not be heard that well. Finger plays and hand puppets both work well with this approach. I also use this with the following hand story as a finale to my talks:

It Takes Two

There was once a hand.	(Show your hand to audience.)
He was very proud because he could do so many things.	
He could point;	(Point.)
he could count one, two, three, four, five;	(Show each finger.)
he could stay "stop";	(Hold up hand palm outward.)
he could scratch himself;	(Use little finger to scratch next finger.)
he could say "come here";	(Beckon with index finger.)
he could wave goodbye;	(Wave.)
he could shake himself;	(Relax fingers, shake hand.)
he could chastise;	(Point and shake a finger.)
he could be tough;	(Make a fist.)
but he was very sad	(Let fingers droop down.)
because he couldn't make any noise.	
Then the ring finger told the thumb about a noise the first three fingers could make. The hand tried it;	(Snap your fingers.)

but the hand was dissatisfied.
Then one day the hand met another
 hand.   (Bring other hand in view.)
They discovered they could make a
 noise together.   (Clap hands.)
The moral of this story is: (Take off puppet stage and look right at
                                           audience.)

It takes two hands to clap.

Puppets

This is just to remind you that the introduction of a puppet at the beginning or end of a presentation will always be a hit. See the puppetry chapter, pp. 250–287 for ideas.

The Clown Sleeve

To get the most impact from this attention-grabber, you stand up in front of your group with poise and dignity, greet them, and proceed to remove your gloves. The first one slides off easily, but the second glove keeps coming and coming with more and more colorful material as you continue to pull.

You need: two white gloves, made of jersey knit fabric, 60 inches by 16
             inches.

How to: Sew a tube of fabric and attach it to one of the gloves. This can be

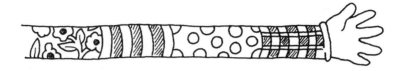

divided into four lengths, each one of a different color. Put the glove on and hide the extra fabric with a blazer or shirt.

Everyone thinks this is fun—children and adults. It helps add to the surprise if you are dressed rather formally, perhaps in a suit, although this is a classic clown caper and they are usually in costume.

Paper-Tear Star

For this opening gambit, a newspaper is folded and cut while you discuss how reading makes everyone a star (or give any other introduction you like that connects reading and books with stars). When the newspaper is unfolded the audience sees the cutout of a star.

You need: Doublefold sheet of newspaper.
              Scissors

How to: 1. Before your presentation, fold the newspaper as shown in the diagram. As you start your performance, open the paper and refold it in front of the audience.
              2. Cut on dotted line and open to show star.
              3. To show off the star—and you—to advantage, put your head through the opening in the newspaper star.

Hint: To fold the newspaper efficiently each time you use this idea, a template is handy. Since it took me a considerable amount of time to figure out how to do this the first time, I've provided an outline drawing to use as a pattern for the template. This pattern can be made from a piece of posterboard cut with thirty-six-degree angles for the points. Fold the newspaper around the template, creasing well at each fold. Remove the template and re-fold the paper until ready to use.

Patter: Make up your own patter to suit your particular circumstances. For instance the star could be given any time one of your students does good work in reading. I use a doublefold from the sports section of the newspaper and I usually say something like this while I fold the paper, cut, and then reveal the star:

"When you browse through the sports section of the local newspaper you always see smiling faces of athletes being awarded prizes for their feats in sports. I congratulate them, but at the same time I wish that there were more prizes available for people who read. People that read science books, fantasy, historical fiction, biographies, adventure stories. I think people should be given prizes just about anytime for reading. How about a *star* for the reading that you did today. Congratulations."

Juggling Scarves

This is for all of you who have always wanted to know how to juggle. If you've even taken a course at your local community center as an adult and failed to learn how to juggle three balls at once, you'll find this is a much easier juggling project and one that looks colorful and graceful.

You need: Three chiffon scarves in contrasting colors—any size is okay.

Time: 5 to 10 minutes of practice, depending on your dexterity.

How to: When I asked my husband and my daughter for help in explaining how to juggle, they both agreed that it was more difficult to describe how to do it then to actually do it. Their suggestion: "Tell them to put one scarf in one hand and two scarves in the other hand, and just try it." This is good advice—trying it is important—but here are a few preliminary tips.

Start with one scarf, holding it in the center, palm down. Throw it into the air, aiming up and across the body and catch it with the other hand, also palm down. Now, try the same action, beginning with the other hand. You need to be able to throw and catch the scarves easily with both hands.

Next, hold one scarf in each hand, palm down. Throw the scarf in your right hand, and after you have released it, throw the scarf in your left hand, catching each scarf in the opposite hand from that with which you threw it. Practice this maneuver for a few minutes until it feels comfortable. Now, you can add the third scarf and really look like an expert. Here's what you do: Place

two scarves in your right hand, one in your left. Scarf #1 should be placed between the thumb and forefinger of the right hand, scarf #2 is in the left hand, and scarf #3 should be held with the last two fingers of the right hand.

Throw scarf #1, and as soon as it is in the air toss scarf #2 (the scarf that is in the left hand). Catch scarf #1 in your left hand and throw scarf #3 with your right. As soon as you release #3, you will catch #2 with you right hand, your left hand will be throwing #1 again.

It sounds complicated, but it really takes only a few minutes (trust me) to master the rhythm of releasing a scarf to throw with one hand while the other hand is catching the last one thrown. The chiffon scarves float in the air before they fall, giving you plenty of time to catch and throw. The best advice is still my husband's: just try it.

Bags and Bags

I've used this idea to introduce books all over the world, and in every school—whether in Nepal, Syria, Taiwan or Indiana—the children are intrigued. It's such a simple idea, and one that can be used over and over.

You need: Five bags—laundry bags or pillow slips work well.

How to: In the bag that will be the last opened (the innermost bag), put the book you will be introducing, or a slip of paper with the title and author of the book or an object that you will use to introduce the book. Or, you may want to put a puppet or other object that you're going to use to tell the story in that last-opened bag. Put the bag within a bag within a bag within a bag. Then, simply stand in front of your group and without saying anything start opening the bags. Open, peel off, and toss the outermost bag first, then each successive bag, working from the outside and tossing the bags willy-nilly on the floor until you reach the last bag. Open it and show the book or object to the group. By the time you get to it, their interest is rivetted.

The Jogging Suit and Music Stand

I use this as a finale to my lectures or book sharing.

You need: A warm-up jacket or sweatshirt imprinted at the tee shirt shop with the words READING IS NO SWEAT

A portable band-music stand. Borrow one from the school band or get one at the local music store.

A paperback book

How to: At the end of the program, while you are speaking, put on the warm-up jacket, music stand, and book and jog off the stage.

Patter: "Remember, You must think books at all times. You can always read no matter what you are doing. When you go home this evening and put on your track suit for your evening run. Think Books!"

Riddle, Riddle

If you work with children in the second or third grades you have been subjected to "Want to hear a riddle?" numerous times. You've probably heard them all, many times. The children, however, haven't heard them and, if they have, they will take pleasure in the fact that they "know that one." Here's an idea for presenting riddles more formally that involves the audience and gives them a chance to read aloud.

You need: A selection of your favorite riddles printed in large letters on cards. The answers should be printed on the reverse side of the card.

How to: Children are chosen to stand in front of the group and hold the riddle so all can see it. The audience reads the riddle and the child flips the card over to reveal the answer.

After you have gone to the trouble of making the riddle cards, you will want to use them more than once. You can. Even though you have heard these riddles over and over again, keep in mind that children are always ready to hear them again . . . and again. The cards can also be used on a bulletin board.

Some samples for you to use today:

WHAT IS TAN, HAS FOUR FEET, AND IS FOUND IN ALASKA?
A LOST CAMEL.

HOW DO YOU SPELL MOUSETRAP IN THREE LETTERS?
C-A-T

WHY ARE YOU TIPTOEING PAST THE MEDICINE CHEST?
I DON'T WANT TO WAKE THE SLEEPING PILLS.

WHAT HAS GONE FOREVER?
YESTERDAY.

WHEN IS IT BAD LUCK TO HAVE A BLACK CAT FOLLOW YOU?
WHEN YOU ARE A MOUSE.

WHY ARE YOU JUMPING ON THE POTATO PATCH?
I'M TRYING TO GROW MASHED POTATOES.

Puppet Playing the Xylophone

Use this idea anytime as an attention getter.

You need: A hand puppet
           A toy xylophone (available in any toy shop)

How to: A puppet looks alive while playing an instrument. A xylophone is the perfect choice because anyone can play. Use your musical puppet to introduce a story or to accompany the group while singing simple songs. If you are not an accomplished musician (or even a beginner), don't worry, toy xylophones are usually packaged with color-coded tunes such as "Row, Row, Row Your Boat" and "Happy Birthday." You and your children can make up words to some of these simple tunes.

Decorated Book Jacket

Whether you are telling a story, presenting a poem, or giving a book talk, it is good policy to have the book you're promoting available. In this way, children can see that the story is from a printed source and they can also check the book out to read for themselves.

Sometimes you do not have a copy of the book on hand, or even if you do you may want to use this idea to provide added visual appeal.

You need: Craft beads
              Glittery fabric
              A ring binder

How to: Sew the craft beads onto fabric and glue the fabric to a ring binder to create a fantasy book cover.

If you don't sew you can use any luxurious fabric from the fabric shop. You can also purchase a handmade decorated book jacket from Sharon Caldwell P.O. Box 816, Newberg, Oregon 97132

Everyday, after you have read aloud or told a story, pick up the fantasy book jacket and say simply, "The story I just told you is (give the title) by (give the author)." If you make it a habit to credit the author, your students will realize that books are written by Real People.

The Telephone

You pretend that you have received a telephone call. The audience hears your side of the conversation. This enables you to answer imaginary questions, such as, "What books do you suggest I bring on my trip?" or "What are you going to tell the sixth grade in your talk today?"

The ring of the telephone gives a sense of urgency to what you have to say.

All you need: A toy telephone borrowed from a preschool child or purchased in a toy shop will work fine for this one-sided conversation. My telephone has its own ring, giving a bit more urgency to my "call."

WE LOVE BOOKS Color Card

Three separate color cards are shown to the audience. A paper bag is shown to be empty. The cards are put into the bag and are removed one by one. One of the cards has disappeared and a fourth colored card appears with the words WE LOVE BOOKS printed on it.

You need: Four pieces of colored poster board, one red, one white, one blue, and one yellow. (For a large audience, use 8″ × 10″ pieces, for a small group, 3″ × 5″ cards are adequate.)

Glue

Paper bag

Materials for lettering

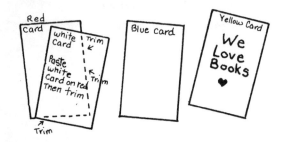

How to: First, you will need to prepare a "fake" card. Take two different-colored cards, in this case the red and the white, and paste them together at an angle, trimming the overhang, as shown in the diagram, so that one side shows red and white, the other solid red. The yellow card should be lettered with the words WE LOVE BOOKS. Conceal the card with the letters printed on it behind the fake card (made of the two sheets). The remaining colored card, blue in this example, is placed on top of all the others. Fan the cards out so that the audience sees three colors: two on the fake with the third on top; the lettered card should be completely hidden behind the fake.

Patter: "Please help me with this trick. The magic words are 'We Love Books'. Let's practice the magic words." Children shout, "We Love Books". "That's good, but I think we could use a bit more enthusiasm. Let's try again." Children shout "WE LOVE BOOKS". "I have here three cards: red, white, and blue." Fan the cards out revealing the fake—red/white—and the blue card. "This is my book bag". Show the empty bag with the other hand. Put it down on the table. "I'm going to place the cards in my book bag." Put the cards in the bag. "Here they are again: The red (take out the fake showing the one-color side and place it face down on the table); the blue (show the blue card); and now what is left in my book bag?" Children shout WHITE.

"No this is a yellow card." Bring it out, showing the empty bag. Show the solid color side. When the children ask you—usually in a shout to turn the card around say "We need the magic words. What are they?" Children shout WE LOVE BOOKS as you turn the card around revealing the words WE LOVE BOOKS.

Chapter 12

Puppets Show the Way to Books

Phanna, from Cambodia, found a "friend" in the library with whom he could play even before he knew much English.

I was bored. Waiting for a plane in Aberdeen, Scotland, I sauntered into the gift shop. Quietly, I removed a puppet from the rack and tried it on my hand. I thought that I was communicating alone with the hedgehog when I looked up to see a man watching me. I had the hedgehog clap her hands and bow in his direction. Nice man—we had a lovely chat until the plane arrived. I bought the puppet just in case I got lonely at the next stop on my itinerary. It's so easy to make friends with a puppet.

In the Moscow airport, the X-ray machine picked up a medal in my carry-on bag as I was exiting through customs. "Open your case," said the uniformed officer. Instead of simply showing him the medal, I put my hand into my Crictor snake puppet and had him pick up the medal, "He was awarded the medal for bravery," I said. A second inspector came over to admire Crictor before I passed through the gate to the bemusement of the Czech tourist group behind me.

I wonder why travel guides never suggest that travelers carry a puppet with them to make friends. It always works for me.

Puppets are extremely versatile and can be used for a variety of purposes in your book program. They can introduce a story, a poem, or a theme. They can tell jokes, ask riddles and recite poetry. They can be characters in a play, or narrate a story.

First, you will need a puppet. Almost anything that can be articulated works. While you are reading this, examine the palm of your left hand. Do you see the face there? It's smiling isn't it? Now, look at the palm of your right hand—that poor Joe is frowning. Try to make Joe, in your right palm, smile using your left palm-puppet. Now, let both of your hands droop downwards. Let the legs (index and third finger) march along the surface of a table. Your thumb, curved toward the hand can look like an arm.

You can use your index fingers to talk to each other. Are you practicing in a public place? That's fine. Maybe your "face puppet" will want to talk to the people that are staring at you.

Now take out your water-soluble markers or water colors and paint outlines of your puppet on one of your hands. A friend can paint the other hand.

You're ready to graduate into household articles: a wooden spoon, a paper cup, or a paper bag can be puppets too. You get the idea. Almost anything works as a puppet. But it's no use having a puppet without giving the puppet an action or a voice. Think of the possibilities for creative writing. You already have a character. Start infusing your character with a personality.

Mistakenly, we often think that puppets are used effectively only with younger children, but I have not found this to be the case. I also use puppets with young adults and with adults. When I lived in Portland, Oregon, I purchased a Trailblazer basketball-star-puppet at a craft fair, and it was admired by all ages—the perfect book-lure.

Using Puppets to Promote Literature

Introduce a Book or Program

Do you have a favorite puppet? You can use it as your book-program mascot. He can introduce a theme or particular story. You'll find a puppet useful to introduce yourself to your audience or to introduce the audience to the puppet, and therefore to each other. It's fun to infuse your puppet with a particular personality. He might be shy, agressive, or pompous.

Some puppeteers prefer not to have their puppets talk out loud. All dialogue is directed to the puppeteer, who imparts the puppet's message to the audience. This obviates the need for changing voices, and also focuses attention on you, the puppeteer, and on the story or book the puppet is telling you about.

If you are using your puppet to introduce and/or close a program, you might want to have a place to put the puppet when you are finished with him. This can be a box that becomes his bed, or he can sit in his own chair and listen to the stories. I tend to use the tactic of putting my puppet away— to sleep or off to work—rather than leaving him in view of the audience. He can be distracting to the children and I think the contrast of his active role to the limp, inert doll takes away from the realistic effect that you create when he is interacting with you.

As you and your puppet introduce your program, you and your audience might find that your puppet is quite knowledgeable. He may refer to other books on the same subject that he has enjoyed, or may already have read the book you are presenting and can tell the audience about a memorable character or incident. Thus, the puppet is acting as a host to the program and he can also be used to close the program by reacting to the book or story and repeating the title and author.

Give a Booktalk

I have several puppets that represent particular titles. I own a Babar puppet ("borrowed" from my daughter), a Pippi Longstocking puppet, and a Paddington Bear puppet. (These are all handpuppets. After getting the strings for marionettes hopelessly snarled, I use any marrionettes I'm tempted to acquire for display only.) These character puppets are perfect to introduce their own books, but any puppet can talk about any book. She can always say, "I read an intriguing book last night . . . ," or, picking up a book, "I wonder what this is about. It has a picture of a bear on the jacket."

Recite a Poem

I really like the idea of a puppet reciting poetry. All eyes are on the puppet so that you have your students' attention. Now, recite the poem of your choice. There is the danger that the puppet may be so disarming that she distracts from the words of the poem, but if you use the same puppet often to recite, she becomes your Poetry Puppet. The audience will soon be listening attentively to the words and feeling the meaning of the poem.

Tell a Joke, Ask a Riddle

Most of the riddles that children like seem quite silly to adults. In addition, many popular riddles and children's jokes are often durable retreads from your own childhood—or even from your grandparents' youth. They could even be considered the private property of children, who instinctively discover that their classmates and the library's collection of humor books are sources of material. On the other hand, it's satisfying to offer a joke or two yourself, and your puppet allows you to do so without intruding a too-adult voice. And, if a puppet does the telling, you can blame him for the self-satisfied groans from your all-knowing audience.

Tell a Story

While it can be cumbersome for a puppet to narrate a lengthy or sophisticated story, it can tell a short anecdote or narrate a folktale very effectively. You may find that you have a puppet that represents a character in a story and you can narrate the story while manipulating the puppet to match the action.

When I tell "The Tiger's Minister of State" by Harold Courlander (page 261–263), I use a rabbit puppet (these are usually easily available in toy stores in the spring). At the end of the story, I slip the rabbit on my hand and finish the story.

Be in a Play

When you think of puppets, you generally think of them interacting with other puppets in a scripted play. It is exciting to put on a full-fledged production, complete with puppet actors, stage, scenery, and lighting. However, this does take considerably more time and usually additional people who can coordinate the puppet-making, and act in the play.

Although children enjoy creating puppets and manipulating them, it is sometimes difficult to find enough jobs to involve everyone in your group. I solve this problem by preparing several short plays using transitional material in between. In this way, a much larger group can take part in the presentation than the number of specified roles suggests. For instance, one puppet can introduce a play. Another can introduce the characters. Still others can recite a poem, tell a joke, or attempt several tongue twisters between the short plays or skits. A great advantage of giving several short plays rather than one long one is that rehearsing for the big performance can be done with the cast of each small group separately instead of a cast of thirty-five children all on the stage at the same time.

Just as some horse lovers enjoy grooming the horse more than riding or a camera enthusiast may be more interested in acquiring the equipment than taking pictures, so it can happen that there are children who take more joy in the creation of the puppet and the stage than in actually performing in a play. There are children who would prefer to work on the publicity, invitations or lighting rather than on learning lines and rehearsing for a performance. There are some parents who always try to treat their two children equally. They feel that they must buy the same T-shirt for each child. I don't think it is necessary to feel that every child in the program must be in the spotlight; those with supporting roles can have their chance to shine another day and take pride in their contribution today.

The idea of working with puppets is to give children a chance to become familiar with this form of theater. The size and age of your group, the time and space limitations, and other logistical factors will determine whether you will be the puppeteer or the children will manipulate the puppets. In any case, puppets should be treated with respect because, manipulated with skill, they become REAL.

Selections

Using your hand as a puppet, tell the following story. At the end of the story, show the audience the back of your hand and point the index finger and little finger up while keeping the other fingers down.

Why Rabbits Have Long Ears

Princess Rabbit loved to listen to stories. She loved to tell them, too. She was always nagging her Nanny to tell her a story. Rabbit was known to hop under the dining room table when there was a banquet in session in hopes of hearing a well-told tale. She listened with great concentration whenever the rabbit youngsters were told bedtime stories. However the best storytellers were the professional taletellers who gathered nightly at the town square.

Princess Rabbit wanted desperately to attend these sessions, but her father, the King of Rabbits, was very protective. Rabbit was not allowed outside without an escort. Young rabbits were forbidden to leave the warren at night. It so happened that Rabbit's bed chamber was located directly under the storyteller's gathering place. Every night she strained and strained to hear the storytellers. If she stretched her ears as far as they would reach, she could just barely make out the words of the stories.

After several months of stretching her ears skyward the Rabbit's ears had grown tall and upright. The King admired his daughter's long ears and suggested that all rabbits work on their hearing. If you see a rabbit today, you will notice that the King's advice was followed.

Rabbits have long ears, like this, (hold up two fingers forming a V) and they love to listen to a good story.

Some Types of Puppets

As you already have discovered, even your hand can be used as a puppet. Puppeteers use simple kitchen utensils, such as wooden spoons and paper plates, as well as intricately-crafted hand puppets and marrionettes. You can experiment with some of the easy-to-make puppets and use them with a group of children to see if you are interested in pursuing this style of presentation.

The easiest puppets to buy and use are plush hand puppets sold at most toy shops. As discussed above, these puppets can introduce books, tell jokes, ask riddles—or even assign homework (let your children complain to a puppet about "too much work, Ms. Harris.")

Many presenters become discouraged because once they have a puppet they cannot easily find material to use with it. Here are some stories that work well with easily-operated puppets.

Mitt Puppets

This is a simple glove-type puppet that can be made of paper or cloth. If you start with this basic shape, make it out of felt, and add eyes only, it becomes what I call an "anything puppet" because it can represent virtually any character. If you tell your audience that the puppet is a pig, or a monster, an old man or a witch, they will believe you—because you said so.

A simple shape can take on individual characteristics by creating puppets with facial features. The story below, "The Clever Man," can be told as a traditional tale without visual enhancement, it can be adapted to a reader's theater format, or it can be told with mitt puppets by reproducing the portraits of the King and Sri Than and mounting them onto cloth or paper mitts and using the mitt puppets to illustrate the action of the story. Notice that this is not scripted as a play, but uses the puppets almost as one might show illustrations in a book. Although the puppets are not essential in telling the tale, this is simply an alternate way of presenting the story and will be useful to those programmers who would like to vary their presentations.

The Clever Man, a Story from Thailand

Storyteller: This story comes to us from Thailand, known for centuries as Siam. The story is called The Clever Man.

In a small village by the river there lives a man call Sri Than. The people in the village think he is the cleverest man in the region. They brag about him to travelers. Eventually the King heard about Sri Than. The King did not believe that there could possibly be someone as smart, or even smarter than he, the King.

The King rode an elephant to the small village by the river, but he dressed in peasants' clothes so that he wouldn't be recognized. Sri Than was hauling fish from the river in a reed basket. He looked up and saw a strange man riding an elephant into town.

{Put the puppets on your hands and continue to tell the story. Hold up the puppets representing the character who is speaking.}

Sri Than admired the elephant. "Greetings," he said,

"That's a fine elephant you're riding."

"He belongs to the King. I am a groom in the stables there. I've been sent here to find the man they call, Sri Than."

"I am Sri Than. What business have you with me?"

"The King has heard that you are a very clever man. I have been sent to see if this is true."

Sri Than was a very modest man and so he replied, "There is no one in the kingdom as smart as the King."

"That is for me to decide." said the King. "Tell me, do you think you could somehow get me to jump in the river?"

"I doubt that I could do that" said Sri Thanochai, "But I might be able to make you come out of the river if you were already in the river."

"Let's see if that is possible."

The King jumped into the river.

"Here I am. I am in the river. See if you can get me to come out."

"There is no need for a further test. I got you into the river after all. Now you come out whenever you want."

The King was amused. He walked out of the river wringing wet.

"You are every bit as clever as they told me you are. It is good to know that there are men like you in Siam. I would like to reward you with the elephant that I rode here."

"Thank you", said Sri Than, "But what will the King say when you return without the elephant?"

"He will tell everyone that he has met Sri Thanochai who made the King of Siam jump into the river. Enjoy your new elephant."

Rod Puppets

The patterns given here were designed by Lynne Jenning to be used with the story, "The Scholar," a tale from Bangladesh that I collected. It can be told, as shown here, with rod puppets, adapted for use with mitt puppets, or told in traditional style. These patterns can be transferred to paper or poster-board, and put together with glue or staples. Or they can be painted onto fabric with fabric paint. To make these patterns into rod puppets:

1. Photocopy the designs onto card stock or thicker board.

2. Color them.

3. Cut out all designs; fold and glue the boat together, cutting on the dotted lines in the boat, folding on the dashed lines. Tabs should be bent in, then glued or taped, so that the boat will look like the drawing below.

4. Use wooden barbecue skewers as rods with which to manipulate the puppets. Glue or tape them in place:

a. behind the oar to just beneath the hand-hold

b. under the forward boat seat

c. to the middle of the back of the swimming-man puppet

d. to the arms of the scholar (if you wish to have him gesture)

5. For arm connections, it is best to use heavy thread, knotted at one end. Draw thread through the arm, through a small (no more than one-quarter inch diameter) fabric circle used as a washer (felt is a good choice here), and then through the shoulder. Knot the thread tightly on the back of the puppet. The left arm in the pattern belongs to the turbaned scholar; make two right arms to use for the boatman and the swimmer. After the boatman's arm is attached, glue the oar to his hand so that he is gripping the oar.

Performance Ideas: You can make a stage from a shoebox or longer box in which you have made a one-inch-wide slit, extending almost the length of one long side of the box. Tape waves in place, with calm sea in front, storm waves behind, attached to rods which players can move up into the slit in the stage as the storm rises in the story. At first, the boatman slowly skulls the boat on the calm sea, then as the storm mounts, hidden performers can make the boat rock and eventually sink. After it has sunk, the swimming boatman rises until he can just be seen behind the waves, his arms spinning on their rod as he swims for shore. The scholar has disappeared from sight at this point.

If you wish to use the puppets for a classroom performance, lay a grid over the pattern to enlarge it and use a table turned on its side to use as a stage and to screen your performers. Or, if you wish, perform the puppet play in the open without a stage, *bunraku* style. You can adapt these tips to your own needs, facilities, and unique performance style.

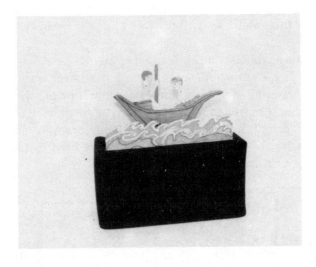

The Scholar: A Story from Bangladesh

A learned scholar was visiting a small village in the Bangladesh countryside.

Continuing on his journey he stopped at a boat landing and hailed a ferry. The boat was propelled by a single oar wielded by a lanky peasant dressed in an illfitting shirt and patched trousers.

The trip was slow and the scholar could not keep silent for very long. "Have you read anything of value lately?" asked the scholar.

"No. Can't say as I've read anything. I've never learned to read", answered the ferryman.

"Ah," replied the scholar. "What a pity. All the great thoughts of our learned philosophers are in books. All of knowledge can be found in books."

The two lapsed into silence. Once again the scholar could not remain silent. He asked the boatman "And what mathematical solutions have you studied this week?"

"Sorry, sir," drawled the boatman. I've never bothered with math. I don't even know how to add or subtract."

"Ah," replied the scholar. "What a pity. Many of the greatest thinkers have spent their lives studying the theories of mathematical equations. Perhaps you know something of science?'

"No, your honor," said the boatman to the scholar. "I'm not sure what the word means."

"Ah, what a pity," returned the scholar. "Without a knowledge of science we would not know about the chemical balances of the world, the intricacies of the human body or the phenomena of nature.

"Ah," said the boatman seizing on the one word he understood. "Speaking of nature, do you see those big black clouds forming overhead?"

"Yes. I have been observing them," replied the scholar.

"Well, those clouds mean a storm is coming. A storm means we will have rain. Rain means this small boat will tip over. I hope you can swim, sir," said the boatman.

"No," said the scholar. "I never learned to swim."

"Ah, what a pity. I've never learned to read. I've never learned to add or subtract. I know nothing of science. But I do know how to swim."

At that moment it started to rain very hard. The small boat, rocked by the wind and heavy torrent, tipped over. The boatman swam to safety.

As for the scholar—well, sometimes it doesn't help to know how to figure out a mathematical equation.

Hand Puppets

Hand puppets are available in most toy or gift shops. In fact, you may have purchased one of these because it seemed to "call to you" from a puppet tree in such a store. Now that you own it, consider using it as your book mascot. The puppet can also narrate a story or poem. The story below, "The Tiger's Minister of State," uses a hand puppet only at the end to focus attention on the hero of the story. The rabbit hand puppet can be found in most toy shops or can be ordered from the resource list at the end of this chapter.

This story is particularly well-received by adults and young adults, and is especially enjoyable at election time.

This version is printed exactly as it was collected by Harold Courlander. Tell it as a traditional literary story, slipping the puppet on your hand when the rabbit appears in the story. Until it is needed, the puppet can be stored in a colorfully printed gift bag on the table, maintaining the element of surprise.

The Tiger's Minister of State
*A Shan Tale from Burma**

Word went through the forest one day that Kyar the tiger, king of animals, needed a chief minister of state. So, from the places where they lived, Wet-wun the boar, Myauk the monkey, and Yon the rabbit set out for the tiger's house. Coming from different directions, they arrived on the same day. They gathered before Kyar's gate and waited until the king saw fit to let them in.

The tiger king at last came out of his house, looking lean and hungry.

"Who are these people standing before my gate?" he asked his servants.

"They are Wet-wun the boar, Myauk the monkey, and Yon the rabbit," his servants replied. "They are applying for the job of minister of state."

"Let them in," Kyar the tiger said.

The servants opened the gate, and the three animals entered and sat on the ground before the king.

"It is true, as you have heard, that I need a new minister," the tiger said. "However, the one I select for this position must have the gift of being able to say the right thing at the right time. My last minister didn't have the ability."

*From *The Tiger's Whisker and Other Tales of Asia and the Pacific* by Harold Courlander (Harcourt Brace and World, 1959). Copyright © 1959, 1987 by Harold Courlander.

"I have the ability," Wet-wun the boar said.

"No, I have the ability," Myauk the monkey said.

"On the contrary, it is I who have the ability," Yon the rabbit said.

"Well, since you can't agree, I'll have to ask you to pass an examination," Kyar the tiger said. "He who speaks most wisely will be my minister. Boar, come forward."

The boar came forward.

The tiger opened his mouth and asked him: "Is my breath sweet or not?"

The boar smelled the king's breath. It was foul. But he was eager to please Kyar, so he said: "Oh Great King, never have I smelled such a sweet breath! It is like fruit blossoms in full bloom!"

"Ah, just as I thought," the tiger said. "You are a flatterer. A flatterer has no regard for the truth, but only for his own welfare. Such a man would be a danger to me and my kingdom." And he pounced on the boar and ate him.

Then Kyar called on the monkey to come forward.

"Is my breath sweet or not?" he asked, opening his mouth wide.

The monkey was more cautious. He smelled the tiger's breath. "Hm!" he said.

"Well?" Kyar asked.

"Just a moment," the monkey said, and he sniffed again.

"Answer the question," the tiger ordered.

"Oh Great One," the monkey said at last, "you will see that I am no flatterer. You can always rely on me for the truth. For your breath indeed smells very bad."

"Smells bad, did you say?" the tiger asked, his eyes opening very wide.

"Yes, quite offensive. Please don't ask me to sniff again."

"So! It is just as I suspected," the tiger king said. "You are the kind of person who speaks directly, without any regard for anyone's feelings. It is this kind of minister that creates arguments and bad feelings everywhere. Such a man is a menace to the community."

And Kyar the tiger pounced on Myauk the monkey and ate him. As he finished eating, he wiped his mouth and turned to Yon the rabbit.

"Now it is your turn," he said. "Is my breath foul, as the monkey said, or sweet, as the boar said?"

He opened his mouth, and the rabbit came forward and sniffed. As he sniffed, his nose twitched. He sniffed and twitched in front of the tiger's mouth, but gave no answer.

"Well, what is it? Foul or sweet?" the tiger demanded.

The rabbit came a little closer, his nose twitching violently. At last he said: "Oh King, how unfortunate I am!"

"What is the trouble?" Kyar asked.

"I have a terrible cold," the rabbit replied. "I can't smell a thing one way or the other."

The tiger smiled.

"You are the man to be my minister!" he said. "For an ordinary person a sense of smell is important. But one who deals in affairs of state is better off without one."

And he appointed Yon, the rabbit, to be his minister of state. The rabbit is still the tiger's minister of state. And day in, day out, he twitches his nose to show the king that he still has a cold and can't smell a thing one way or the other.

Stick Puppets

These are simply pictures, usually mounted on posterboard and attached to a handle. They are the easiest puppets to manipulate, since all the puppeteer does is hold the handle and move the puppet slightly while the character is speaking. I use this type of puppet extensively when presenting to young children, who seem to be drawn into the story instantly when the figure is held up. Patterns for this type of puppet follow in the programs designed around dinosaur puppets.

Using Dinosaur Stick Puppets for a Dinosaur Day Program

Dinosaurs, and anything at all connected with dinosaurs, continue to be popular with youngsters. We don't know all of the reasons for which dinosaurs died out, and neither are we sure just why children are so captivated by them. I do remember, though, that none of the fascinating exhibits I saw as a child at the Smithsonian Institute in Washington, D.C. was as awesome as the huge skeleton of a dinosaur that filled the entire room. The poet Lillian

Moore must have been intrigued by a similar exhibit when she wrote "To the Skeleton of a Dinosaur in a Museum." You can mount the drawings of the dinosaurs as they once looked and of the dinosaur skeletons, shown on pages 268 and 269 to make illustrations or turn them into stick puppets that can be used to present this poem and the other dinosaur-themed selection here. Use a duplicating machine to enlarge the drawings, then color them in a gray-green color and glue the pictures onto poster board. If you attach a painted stick or dowel to the backs of the pictures, the children can move them appropriately as they recite.

You can use two different casts for the two book talks, and a third cast can recite the dinosaur poems, so that your whole group can be involved in this program.

Select other dinosaur poems to present from these collections:

Hopkins, Lee Bennett. *Dinosaurs*. Art by Murray Tinkelman. Harcourt, 1987.

Most, Bernard. *Four and Twenty Dinosaurs*. Art by author. Harper, 1990.

Prelutsky, Jack. *Tyrannosaurus Was a Beast*. Art by Arnold Lobel. Greenwillow, 1988.

DINOSAUR FACTS

Players: 4

Triceratops   Tyrannosaurus   Compsognathus   Stegosasaurus

ALL: We are dinosaurs.
TRICERATOPS: Some of us lived over 225 million years ago.
TYRANNOSAURUS: 65 million years ago we no longer existed.
COMPSOGNATHUS: What happened?
STEGOSAURUS: No one really knows

TRICERATOPS: My name is Triceratops (try-SAIR-uh-tops). I have horns on my head that are three feet long. There is a big shield of bone covering my shoulders. My jaw looks almost like a parrot's beak. Don't worry, I only eat plants.

TYRANNOSAURUS: My name is Tyrannosaurus (tye-RAN-uh-saur-us). I do eat meat. I'm frightening because I'm so big. I can get up to fifty feet long, the length of three cars, and twenty feet high. My teeth are each seven inches long, bigger than your hand.

STEGOSAURUS: My name is Stegosaurus (steg-oh-SAW-rus). I am long too. I have flat plates along my spine, and a very small head. My back legs are much longer than my front legs. I use my long tail as a weapon. I lived 150 million years ago.

COMPSOGNATHUS: I am Compsognathus (KOMP-sow-nay-thus). I am small, about the size of a hen. I run fast so that I can catch lizards, which I swallow whole. I'm not big, but I'm still a dinosaur. We can't all be giants.

TRICERATOPS: If you would like to find out more about us, go to your library and check out some books about dinosaurs.

TYRANNOSAURUS: Read about us in *On the Tracks of Dinosaurs* by James O. Farlow with art by Doris Tischler (Watts, 1989).

COMPSOGNATHUS: And read about us in *The News about the Dinosaurs* by Patricia Lauber with art by a variety of artists (Bradbury, 1989).

STEGOSAURUS: We are also in *Album of Dinosaurs* by Tom McGowan with art by Rod Ruth (Checkerboard, 1987).

ALL: See you in a book.

Production note: Each player holds the stick puppet of the dinosaur he or she represents while speaking. Substitute titles of the dinosaur books that your library owns at the end of the book talk.

WE LOVE DINOSAURS

Players: 4

Dinosaur 1   Dinosaur 2   Dinosaur 3   Dinosaur 4

ALL: We love dinosaur books.

DINOSAUR 1: What a vacation. The Laskeys went to Montana to search for dinosaur fossils. They dug up bones that had been buried for 67 million years. You can read all about it in *Dinosaur Dig* by Kathryn Laskey with photos by Christopher G. Knight (Morrow, 1990).

ALL: We love dinosaur books.

DINOSAUR 2: How many different dinosaurs have been found? Scientists think that there were about 350 different kinds of dinosaurs. If you read *New Questions and Answers about Dinosaurs* by Seymour Simon with art by Jennifer Dewey (Morrow, 1990), you'll find out the latest discoveries about us.

ALL: We love dinosaur books.

DINOSAUR 3: Alfred Watkins found three dinosaur eggs on the beach. They hatched and then the Watkins had three small dinosaur children, but they grew and grew and GREW. For fun read: *Dinosaur Eggs* by Francis Mosley with art by the author (Barrons, 1988.)

ALL: We love dinosaur books.

DINOSAUR FOUR: Daniel and Julia Creath were part of the great hunt. They looked for dinosaur bones when palentologists were in competition to find the biggest bones. Now, years later Julia is in the museum and she sees "Daniel's dinosaur." You'll enjoy *My Daniel* by Pam Conrad. (Harper, 1989.)

ALL: We love dinosaur books. You will too.

More Dinosaurs Books to Enjoy

Carmine, Mary. *Daniel's Dinosaurs.* Art by Martin Baynton. Scholastic, 1990.
     Daniel imagines dinosaurs everywhere he goes.

Hennessy, B. G. *The Dinosaur Who Lived in My Backyard.* Art by Susan Davis. Viking, 1988.
What if . . . dinosaurs lived in your backyard?

Lauber, Patricia. *Living with Dinosaurs.* Art by Douglas Henderson. Bradbury, 1991.
The author of *The News about Dinosaurs* describes other creatures who lived seventy-five million years ago.

Mansell, Dom. *If Dinosaurs Came to Town.* Art by author. Little, 1991.
An oversize book showing what might happen if dinosaurs visited a city.

Nolan, Dennis. *Dinosaur Dream.* Art by author. Macmillan, 1990.
A little boy and a baby dinosaur journey back to the Jurassic period in history.

Oram, Hiawyn. *A Boy Wants a Dinosaur.* Art by Satoshi Kitamura. Farrar, 1990.
Alex insists that he wants a unique pet: a Massospondylus from the dino-store.

Schlein, Miriam. *Discovering Dinosaur Babies.* Art by Margaret Colbert. Macmillan, 1991.
Schlein tells how scientists discovered the life of baby dinosaurs and how they may have lived.

Watson, Clare. *Big Creatures from the Past.* Art by Robert Cremins. Design and paper engineering by Keith Moseley. Putnam, 1990.
Information about dinosaurs are accompanied with pop-up pictures. The creatures really look big!

Brachiosaurus by Jack Prelutsky

Players: 4

DINOSAUR 1: Brachiosaurus by Jack Prelutsky

DINOSAUR 2: Brachiosaurus had little to do
but stand with its head in the treetops and chew,
it nibbled the leaves that were tender and green,
it was a perpetual eating machine.

DINOSAUR 3: Brachiosaurus was truly immense,
its vacuous mind was uncluttered by sense,
it hadn't the need to be clever and wise,
no beast dared to bother a being its size.

DINOSAUR 4: Brachiosaurus was clumsy and slow,
but then, there was nowhere it needed to go,
if Brachiosaurus were living today,
no doubt it would frequently be in the way.

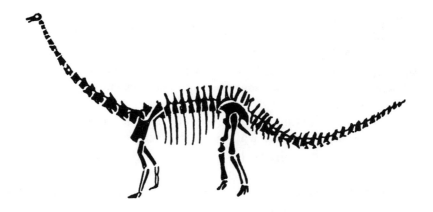

**To the Skeleton of a Dinosaur
in the Museum by Lilian Moore**

Players: 4

Dinosaur 1   Dinosaur 2   Dinosaur 3   Dinosaur 4

DINOSAUR 1: "To the Skeleton of a Dinosaur in the Museum"
DINOSAUR 2: by Lilian Moore
DINOSAUR 1: Hey there, Brontosaurus!
    You were here so long before us
    Your deeds can never bore us.
    How were the good old days?
DINOSAUR 2: Did you really like to graze?
    Did you often munch
    With a prehistoric crunch
    On a giant tree—or two—or three
    For lunch?
DINOSAUR 3: As you went yon and hither
    Were you ever in a dither
    When your head and distant tail
    Went different ways?
DINOSAUR 4: Did you shake the earth like thunder
    With your roars and groans
    I wonder. . . . Say, it's hard
    To have a conversation
    With your bones.

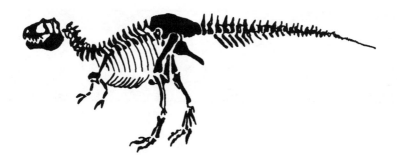

Production note: Use this poem with the dinosaur-skeleton stick puppet, making the puppet in sections. Have each player memorize his or her verse. The first player holds up the head, the second player the neck, the third holds the body, and the fourth player adds the tail to complete the dinosaur skeleton. Another method of presentation would be to have one child read the poem while four others hold up the sections of the dinosaur skeleton.

Questions for a Dinosaur by Patricia Hubbell

Players: 2

DINOSAUR 1: Questions for a Dinosaur

DINOSAUR 2: by Patricia Hubbell

DINOSAUR 1: O Stegosaurus
    if you saw us,
    would you be
    against or for us?

DINOSAUR 2: Would you shout,

BOTH: "Hooray, we're linked!"

DINOSAUR 2: Or would you wish
    We were extinct?

A DAY FOR DOGS—A Themed Puppet Program

There are children in this country who have never seen a real live cow or a goat, but everyone has seen a dog. Americans love their dogs. In the city or in the country children can observe the real thing. In fact I think it is easier to see dogs in the city than in the suburbs where they tend to live in backyards surrounded by fences. In our cities the dogs are walked several times a day and even if you don't own a dog you can vicariously enjoy them.

My family spent the last year living in France with our dog. In France and in Germany dogs are really treated well. They can go into hotels and restaurants and receive the same service as do human guests with their own tariffs and special meals. In a cafe in France you can request "un bol a TouTou" and a bowl of drinking water will be brought for your dog to enjoy.

Juvenile authors have written many books featuring the exploits of dogs. These book range from the realistic fact-filled books to the pure fantasy. Authors have written stories about our 'K9' friends for the very youngest readers as well as more sophisticated novels for young adults.

For this sample program I've chosen stories, poems and riddles dealing with dogs that are fun to tell using puppets, and I've also included an idea for an easy-to-make, walk-around puppet stage. These selections work well with all age groups so that you can offer this program as a family or community event. I've tried to be selective in the bibliography, listing only some of my favorite dog books that you might want to choose for a book exhibit or to recommend to those children who are eager to read more about dogs. The bookmark can be duplicated as a souvenir of the program.

Dog Puppet in Box

This is an easy idea that appeals to all ages and is effective for introducing stories, reciting poems, and is especially fun for presenting riddles. You can ask the riddle, then let your dog puppet (I've named mine Bisquit) answer the riddles.

You need: An empty dog biscuit box

A dog hand puppet (available at any toy store)

A selection of riddles like those below printed on small cards

How to: Open the dog biscuit box on both ends and, wearing your dog hand puppet, put your arm through the box, so that the dog peeks out of the top of the carton. Then, ask him some of these dog riddles:

What did one flea say to the other when they left the theater?

Do you want to walk home or take a dog?

How does a dog get down from a tree in the summer?

She climbs onto a leaf and waits for fall.

Who wears a coat all winter and pants in the summer?

A dog.

When is a black dog with white spots most likely to come into a house?

When the door is open.

If you call a tail a leg, how many legs does a dog have?

Five.

No, only four. Calling a tail a leg doesn't make it a leg.

(This has Been Attributed to Abraham Lincoln)

How do you keep a dog from barking in the back seat?

Move him to the front seat.

What is the outer part of a tree called?
Don't know.
Bark.
Woof. Woof.
Write a sentence with at least 25 words:
Here Spot, Spot, Spot, Spot, Spot, Spot, Spot, Spot, Spot Spot, Spot, Spot, Spot, Spot, Spot, Spot, Spot, Spot, Spot, Spot, Spot, Spot, Spot.
After the riddles, you can use your dog puppet with your favorite hat to present this short poem.

Riddle Hat

Dr. Seuss has a cat
   in his hat
Now what do you think
   of that
If you think that sounds like
   a riddle
Well, my hat has a dog
   in the middle.
            by Nonie Borba

Stories to Tell or Read Aloud

One of my students, Mary Norman, told *The Tail That Wagged the Dog* by Robert Kraus in my storytelling class with a stuffed dog, but it also works well with a hand puppet, which can be easier to manipulate to fit the action of the story. Any floppy dog with a nice tail will do, but both Mary and I went on an extensive search for the perfect dog. I have a whole collection of "perfect" dogs to tell this story, and my current favorite dog is actually a puppet (available from Alyce Ruth, RR1, PO Box 55, Woodbine, Iowa 51579). To tell this story using a stuffed animal or puppet simply tell the story letting the actions in the story dictate your dog's movements. For instance, take hold of the dog's tail, using it to swing Leo when he is happy (quickly) and sad (slowly).

The Tail Who Wagged a Dog

by Robert Kraus

Once upon a time there was a tail who wagged a dog.
The dog's name was Leo.
His tail didn't have a name,
but usually he was called Leo's tail.
Whenever Leo's tail was sad, he wagged Leo.
Whenever Leo's tail was happy, he wagged Leo.
Whenever Leo's tail just felt like it, he wagged Leo.
Sometimes Leo's tail even wagged him when he was asleep.

Leo's tail always wagged him without warning.

It was really getting Leo down. He was the laughing stock of all the dogs in
   the neighborhood.

"I would say this is a clear case of the tail wagging the dog," said a beagle.

Leo also became the laughing stock of all the cats in the neighborhood, as
   well as all the mice, not to mention all the birds and the bees.

Leo was so depressed that he slunk away with his tail between his legs.

Finally, Leo went to see a vet.

The vet gave Leo a complete examination but for some reason Leo's tail did
not wag him at the vet's.
Too smart.
Leo's tail was too smart.

But as soon as Leo left the vet's office,
his tail started wagging him like crazy.

Leo went home
and plunged
into a hot bath.

He soaked and soaked and soaked, figuring a good soaking might help.

But when he got out of the tub and started to shake himself off, his tail started
   shaking him.

Leo took to his bed.

But Leo's tail just wagged Leo, bed and all.

"There must be a reason why my tail wags me," thought Leo.
"There must be a reason—there must!
But what could it be?
AHHHHHHHH—I've got it!"

"The reason my tail wags me," said Leo,
"is because he thinks *he's* the dog and *I'm* the tail.
I've just got to show him who's the dog!"

"I've also got to show my tail show's the boss," said Leo.

And he chased his tail and chased his tail faster and faster and faster until he caught it!

Then Leo bit his tail as hard as he could.

"Ouch!" said Leo.

"Ouch!" said Leo's tail.

Biting his tail really hurt. "It's probably hurting my tail more than it's hurting me," thought Leo and he bit even harder.

"Stop biting me," said Leo's tail.

"Stop wagging me," said Leo.

"I'll stop wagging if you'll stop biting," said Leo's tail.

"I'll stop biting if you'll stop wagging," said Leo.

And so now *Leo* wags his tail, which is the way it always should have been, and Leo is very happy.

    So is Leo's tail.

      The End

Invisible Dog Puppet

Use a rope, leash, and collar—and your invisible-dog puppet—to tell "No Dogs Is Not Enough," starting out with the rope trailing along behind you, then switching to the leash and collar (borrowed from your or a friend's real dog),which you can hold up at the end of the story. The same leash and collar can then be used to recite "Invisible Dog" by Nonie Borba.

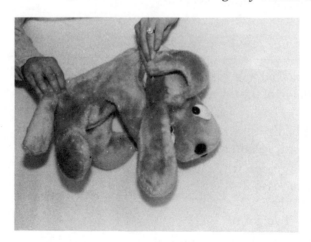

No Dogs Is Not Enough

by Linda Leopold Strauss

Tony wanted a dog.

Tony's mother said no.

Mrs. Lawlor who lived up the street promised Tony one of Snuffy's puppies—if Tony's mother said yes.

Tony's mother said no.

"I have enough to do already," she told Tony, "without taking care of a dog."

The Lawlors were going to put an ad in the paper to sell Snuffy's puppies, even the brown puppy with the white nose. Tony had to find a way to change his mother's mind.

The next morning, after he got dressed, Tony found a rope. He made a loop at one end and a smaller loop at the other end that he held in his hand. Then he ran downstairs, trailing the rope behind him.

"I'm going to walk Nosey before breakfast," Tony told his mother.

His mother stared at him.

"Nosey. My dog," said Tony. "Isn't she cute?" And he went out the back door, pulling the rope behind him.

"Now, Tony . . . ," began his mother, but Tony was gone.

When he came back in the kitchen, he looped the rope over the back of his chair. "Down, Nosey," he said. "Down, girl. Sit."

Tony's father leaned over to look at the floor next to Tony's chair. He looked at Tony. "Are you feeling all right?" he asked.

"Fine," said Tony. "Nosey's fine, too. She's a good dog, isn't she, Dad?"

"You'd never even know she's there," said Tony's father.

Tony was very busy after school. He took the money he had been saving from his allowance and walked Nosey to the corner store. He bought dog food and a red dish to put it in, a leash, and a real leather collar. When he got home, he put the dog food and a bowl of water in the kitchen.

"Mom?" said Tony. "Nosey's such a good dog. Can she sleep in my room tonight?"

"Absolutely not," said Tony's mother firmly. "No dogs in the bedroom." Then she laughed out loud. "You and your imagination!"

After a few days, the neighbors got used to seeing Tony walk around the block with a leash and a real leather dog collar. Tony walked Nosey twice a day, rain or shine, and every morning he put fresh food in her new red bowl. Tony's mother had to admit that Tony took good care of Nosey.

"If I can take care of Nosey," Tony told his mother, "I can take care of any puppy."

"Perhaps," said his mother, "but we have Nosey now. One dog is enough."

Early the next morning, Tony came down to the kitchen. "Have you seen Nosey?" he asked his mother. "I can't find her anywhere."

He walked over to the red dish. "Nosey hasn't touched her food," he said in a worried voice. "She must have got out."

"But how?" asked Tony's mother. "You had her with you at bedtime. I saw her myself." She turned to Tony's father. "Didn't you, dear?" she asked.

Tony's father looked at her and shook his head, "You and your imagination!" he laughed. "You and that dog!"

Right after breakfast, Tony went out to search for Nosey. He walked up driveways and behind garages and down the hill to the playground.

"Nosey," he called, but Nosey didn't come.

"Maybe we should put an ad in the paper," suggested Tony's mother at lunchtime.

"What would we say Nosey looked like?" Tony wanted to know.

There was no doubt about it, Nosey was doing to be hard to find.

"We won't find her," said Tony, and he was right.

"I hate to admit it," said Tony's mother at dinner, "But I think I miss Nosey."

"We could get another dog," said Tony quickly.

"What if Nosey comes back?" asked his father. "Your mother says one dog is enough."

"Nosey is not coming back," said Tony. "And no dogs is not enough."

"Not coming back?" said his mother. "That's a different story." She looked at Tony. "I see in the paper that Lawlors' puppies are still for sale."

"Brown ones," said Tony's father. "One with a white nose."

Tony held his breath.

"It's a nice night," said Tony's father. "Let's take a walk to the Lawlors'."

"And don't forget the leash and collar," said Tony's mother.

Invisible Dog

I'm going strolling with my dog
as you can plainly see
What's that?
You can't?
For heaven's sake
He's almost as big as me
He always minds me very well
He sits!
He stays!
He lies!
You still can't see him?
Glory Be!
He's here, right in front of your eyes
I hope you can at least see the leash.
by Nonie Borba

The following poem was written by a third grader in Norwalk California. It can be presented by a child using a dog puppet or a favorite stuffed animal and can be recited in English or Spanish—or both.

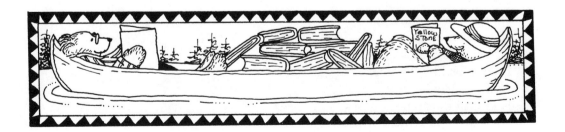

My Dog

Mi perrito
más bonito
tiene miedo
de San Diego
porque es
Mexicano y el
otro es Americano.
Pobre de mi perrito
tiene miedo de
San Diego.

My dog,
so cute.
He's scared
of San Diego
since he's
Mexican and the
others American.
My poor dog,
He's scared of
San Diego.
by Sandra Espinoza
Edmondson School, Norwalk, CA

These two poems are fun to use with a stuffed dog or a dog hand puppet, as they both have plenty of action and emotions for your dog to mime.

Mad Dog

I gave Ruff a bone,
So it's really absurd
For him to expect
What is meant for a bird.
The suet I hung
(But not high enough!)
On the tree for the birds
Was stolen by Ruff.
So I snatched back the bone
He dropped by the tree,
And that is why Ruff
Is as mad as can be.
                by Grace Cornell Tall

April Is a Dog's Dream

april is a dog's dream
the soft grass is growing
the sweet breeze is blowing
the air all full of singing feels just right
so no excuses now
we're going to the park
to chase and charge and chew
and I will make you see
what spring is all about

by Marilyn Singer

Other stories and poems in this book that can work well with hand puppets in a dog-puppet program are "Sometimes I Wish," by Nonie Borba, page 218; The Greedy Dog," by James Hurley, page 221; and "Why Dogs Have Cold Noses," page 177.

Posters and Bulletin Boards

On your bulletin board or blackboard, post the following quote, attributed to Groucho Marx:

OUTSIDE OF A DOG
A BOOK IS MAN'S BEST FRIEND;
INSIDE OF A DOG, IT'S TOO DARK TO READ.

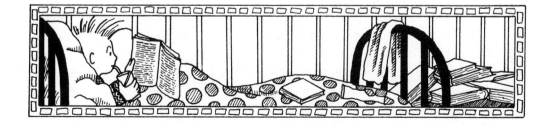

For a poster to accompany your dog-puppet program, you can use this cartoon. Or, enlarge the picture-strips of the cartoon and mount them on cardboard, cut into pieces as a jigsaw puzzle and let the children reassemble it to enjoy the joke afresh.

Dog Books

Writers of children's books must love dogs, or maybe they just fake it very well. It's difficult to select a manageable booklist from the wealth of wonderful books about canines, but here are some personal favorites to start your search. Do be sure to check your library, too, for older titles that I haven't included here. No doubt this trend of doggie books will continue, so be on the watch for new dog titles your children will love. You might want to reproduce the dog bone here, type the titles of the books and poems you're presenting in your dog-puppet program and others you think your group will enjoy, and post it on your "Dog Day."

Beginning Readers

Lexau, Joan M. T. *The Dog Food Caper*. Art by Marilyn Hafner. Dial, 1985.
Miss Hays, the witch, helps solve a mystery.

Porte, Barbara Ann. *Harry's Dog*. Art by Yossi Abolafia. Greenwillow, 1984.
Harry's father is allergic to Harry's dog.

_____. *The Take-Along Dog*. Greenwillow, 1989.
Read Alone adventures with Benton, a take-along dog.

Rylant, Cynthia. *Henry and Mudge*. Art by Suçie Stevenson. Bradbury, 1987.
First in a series featuring a HUGE dog and his friend Henry.

Picture Books

Adoff, Arnold. *Friend Dog*. Art by Troy Howell, Lippincott, 1980.
Adoff's poetry describes a dog's relationship with a young girl.

Barracca, Debra and Sal Barracca. *The Adventures of Taxi Dog*. Art by Mark Duehner. Dial, 1990.
Taxi is adopted by a New York City cabdriver.

Bogart, Jo Ellen. *Daniel's Dog*. Art by Janet Wilson. Scholastic, 1990.
Daniel uses an imaginary dog to adjust to a new baby in the house.

Brenner, Barbara. *A Dog I Know*. Art by Fred Brenner. Harper, 1983.
Poetic portrait of a boy's dog.

Catalanotto, Peter. *Dylan's Day Out*. Art by author. Orchard, 1990.
A Dalmatian plays soccer with a group of penguins and skunks.

Cuyler, Margery. *Freckles and Jane*. Dover, 1961.
Jane learns to respect Willie's dog.

Day, Alexandra. *Carl Goes Shopping*. Art by author. Farrar, 1989.
Wordless story shows a large dog as Nurse with a baby.

_____. *Paddy's Pay-Day*. Art by author. Viking, 1989.
An Irish terrier spends a day in town.

Durrell, Gerald. *Keeper*. Art by Keith West. Arcade, 1990.
Explore Durrell's private zoo with Keeper, a dog who lives there.

Ernst, Lisa Campbell. *Ginger Jumps*. Art by author. Bradbury, 1990.
Large format features a circus dog who finds a home with a little girl.

Gackenbach, Dick. *What's Claude Doing?* Art by author. Clarion, 1986.
Claude is tempted by other dogs to leave his vigil of staying with a sick boy.

Gerstein, Mordicai. *The New Creatures.* Art by author. Harper, 1991.
When dogs ruled the world, they discovered a strange breed of creatures.

Griffith, Helen V. *Plunk's Dreams.* Art by Susan Condie Lamb. Greenwillow, 1990.
Imagine what a dog dreams.

Hill, Eric. *Where's Spot?* Art by author. Putnam, 1980.
Lift the flap and look for Spot the Puppy. First in a colorful series.

Isele, Elizabeth. *Pooks.* Art by Chris Demarest. Lippincott, _____.
Pooks plays the maestro's piano in a simple spoof.

Jeram, Anita. *It Was Jake!* Art by author. Little, 1991.
Danny's dog Jake is the naughty one. Or is he?

Keller, Holly. *Goodbye, Max.* Art by author. Greenwillow, 1987.
Can a new puppy replace Max?

Kellogg, Steven. *Tallyho, Pinkerton.* Art by author. Dial, 1982.
A lovable Great Dane disrupts a hunting class. You'll find more tales of Pinkerton in *Pinkerton, Behave!* (Dial, 1979) and *A Rose for Pinkerton* (Dial, 1981).

Khalsa, Dayal Kaur. *Julian.* Art by author. Potter, 1989.
Julian loves to chase anything that moves.

Marshak, Samuel. *The Pup Grew Up.* Art by Vladimir Radunsky. Holt, 1989.
A picture book translated from the Russian is a poem in which a woman's small dog is replaced by a Great Dane in a train's baggage compartment.

Mahy, Margaret. *Making Friends.* Art by Wendy Smith. McElderry, 1990.
Mrs. deVere and Mr. Derry meet in the park with their dogs.

Matthews, Petra. *Theodor and Mr. Balbini.* Art by author. Harper, 1988.
Mr. Balbini's dog begins to talk and demands French lessons.

O'Neill, Catharine. *Mrs. Dunphy's Dog.* Art by author. Viking, 1987.
When James, the dog, discovers that he can read he becomes a "news hound".

Oxenbury, Helen. *Our Dog.* Art by author. Dial, 1984.
Hilarious art and short text make this a walk and a dog bath that's fun.

Parker, Nancy Winslow. *Poofy Loves Company.* Art by author. Dodd Mead, 1980.
A rambunctious dog misbehaves when company comes.

Rand, Gloria. *Salty Dog.* Art by Ted Rand. Holt, 1989.
A dog watches a boat being built.

Rayner, Mary. *Marathon and Steve.* Dutton, 1989.
Marathon hates to run.

Rylant, Cynthia. *Henry and Mudge and the Bedtime Thumps.* Art by Susie Stevenson. Bradbury, 1991.
Mudge is a huge dog, Henry is a small boy. This is one in a series of early readers featuring their adventures.

Seligson, Susan and Howie Schneider. *Amos: The Story of an Old Dog and His Couch.* Art by Howie Schneider. Little, 1987.
An old dog propels his couch through the city. Very funny. Another by the same author is *The Amazing Amos and the Greatest Couch on Earth* (Little, 1989).

Schwartz, Amy. *Oma and Bobo*. Art by author. Bradbury, 1987.
Grandma teaches Alice's dog manners.

Sharmat, Andrew. *Smedge*. Macmillan, 1984.
Smedge leads a double life as family dog and business man. Funny.

Shyer, Marlene Fanta. *Stepdog*. Art by Judith Shermer. Scribners, 1983.
Terry's dad remarries and he must adjust to a "stepdog" in the family.

Waber, Bernard. *Bernard*. Houghton Mifflin, 1982.
When Bernard's "parents" split up he feels unloved.

Wahl, Mats. *Grandfather's Laika*. Art by Tord Nygren. Carolrhoda, 1989.
"Everything that lives must die sometime." The death of a beloved dog.

Wahl, Robert. *Friend Dog*. Art by Joe Ewens. Little, 1989.
A little boy and a puppy enjoy their first day together.

Weller, Frances Ward. *Riptide*. Art by Robert J. Blake. Philomel, 1990.
An adventurous golden retriever rescues a girl from the sea.

Young, Ed. *The Other Bone*. Art by author. Harper, 1984.
Wordless picture book shows a dog's dream of a fine bone.

Poetry

Cole, William. *Good Dog Poems*. Art by Ruth Anderson. Scribners, 1981.
A collection of eighty-eight poems about dogs. Humorous and poignant.

dePaola, Tomie. *The Comic Adventures of Old Mother Hubbard and Her Dog*. Harcourt, 1981.
The nursery rhyme illustrated with warmth and humor.

Hopkins, Lee Bennett. *A Dog's Life*. Art by Linda Rochester Richards. Harcourt, 1983.
Dog poems in a picture book format.

Livingston, Myra Cohn. *Dog Poems*. Art by Leslie Morrill. Holiday, 1990.
Poems by X. J. Kennedy, Valerie Worth, John Ciardi.

Nonfiction

Ancona, George. *Sheep Dog*. Photos by author. Lothrop, 1985.
Discusses the use of dogs as herders.

Cohen, Susan and Daniel Cohen. *What Kind of Dog Is That? Rare and Unusual Breed of Dogs*. Photos. Dutton, 1989.
The Shar-Pei and the Xoloitzcuintli are among the breeds described.

Cole, Joanna. *A Dog's Body*. Photos by Jim and Ann Monteith. Morrow, 1986.
Examines a dog's body in a photo essay.

Fischer-Nagel, Heiderose. *A Puppy is Born*. Photos by Andreas Fischer-Nagel. Putnam, 1985.
Color photos show the arrival and puppyhood of wirehaired dachshunds.

McCloy, James. *Dogs at Work*. Art by Sheila Beatty. Crown, 1979.
Dogs and their work.

Pinkwater, Jill and D. Manus Pinkwater. *Superpuppy*. Clarion, 1972.
Choosing, buying and training a dog.

Poortvliet, Rien. *Dogs*. Abrams, 1983.
An artist treats us to an album of paintings and sketches of all breeds of dogs.

Pugnetti, Gino. *Simon and Schuster's Guide to Dogs*. Edited by Elizabeth Meriwether Schuler. Simon, 1980.
Dogs of 320 breeds illustrated in color and described.

Silverstein, Alvin and Virginia Silverstein. *Dogs: All About Them*. Photos. Lothrop, 1986.
Discusses breeds and dogs in science and sports.

Longer Books

Ahlberg, Allan. *Woof!* Art by Fritz Wegner. Viking, 1986.
The adventures of a boy named Eric who turns into a Norfolk terrier.

Armstrong, William H. *Sounder*. Art by James Barkley. Harper, 1969.
A boy and his coon dog search for his father in the deep South.

Benjamin, Carol Lea. *The Wicked Stepdog*. Crowell, 1982.
A Golden Retriever makes life miserable for Louise when her father remarries.

Bethancourt, Ernesto. *The Dog Days of Arthur Cane*. Holiday, 1976.
Arthur turns into a dog and discovers it's a dog's life.

Cirker, Blanche. *Five Great Dog Novels*. Dover, 1961.
Take this along on a trip and you'll have a heartwarming cry through *Bob, Son of Battle*, *The Call of the Wild*, and more.

Cleary, Beverly. *Ribsy*. Art by Louis Darling. Morrow, 1964.
Ribsy escapes a bath and gets lost in this classic.

————. *Strider*. Art by Paul O. Zelinsky. Morrow, 1991.
In this sequel to *Dear Mr. Henshaw*, Leigh Botts shares a dog with a friend.

Cresswell, Helen. *Absolute Zero: Being the Second Part of the Bagthorpe Saga*. Macmillan, 1978.
Zero becomes a TV star. *Ordinary Jack* (Macmillan, 1977) introduces this charmingly stupid canine.

Dejong, Meindert. *Along Came a Dog*. Art by Maurice Sendak. Harper, 1958.
The friendship between a dog and a red hen.

Dillon, Barbara. *What's Happened to Harry?* Art by Chris Conover. Morrow, 1982.
Harry is transformed by a witch and becomes a poodle.

Gardiner, John Reynolds. *The Stone Fox*. Art by Marcia Sewall. Harper, 1980.
Willy enters a sled dog race that he must win. This is geared to children aged 9–12.

Gipson, Fred. *Old Yeller*. Harper, 1956.
Travis, a 14-year-old, shows courage and determination on the frontier.

Haas, Jessie. "The Greyhound." In *The Sixth Sense and Other Stories*. Greenwillow, 1988.
Can a racing greyhound be saved from death?

Jones, Diana Wynne. *Dogsbody.* Greenwillow, 1975.
    The dog star, Sirius, comes to earth as a dog. This intriguing fantasy features an Irish girl and the dog star, Sirius.

Kaplan, Marjorie. *Henry and the Boy Who Thought Numbers Were Fleas.* Art by Heidi Chang. Macmillan, 1991.
    A dog helps a boy unlock the mysteries of math.

Kjelgaard, Jim. *Big Red.* Art by Farrell Collett. Scholastic, 1957.
    A memorable Irish Setter hunts a killer bear with Danny. A favorite.

London, Jack. *The Call of the Wild.* Macmillan, 1963 (first published by Macmillan, 1903)
    Meet Buck, the famous dog of the Far North.

Morey, Walt. *Kavik the Wolf Dog.* Art by Peter Parnall. Dutton, 1968.
    Kavik searches for Andy across 2,000 miles.

Parker, Nancy Winslow. *The Spotted Dog.* Dodd, 1980.
    A witch turns a baby sister into a dog and she wins at the dog show.

Rawls, Wilson. *Where the Red Fern Grows.* Bantam, 1961.
    It's a tear jerker, but you'll want to read about a boy and his dogs.

Rylant, Cynthia. "Retired." In *Every Living Thing.* Art by S. D. Schindler. Bradbury, 1985.
    A retired school teacher and a dog named Velma make friends with children on a playground. In the same collection of stories, "Stray" will also be of interest.

Singer, Marilyn. *The Fido Frame-up.* Art by Andrew Glass. Warne, 1983.
    Samantha Spayed tells how she is the dog behind the detective Philip Barlowe.

Steig, William. *Dominic.* Art by author. Farrar, 1972.
    Dominic seeks adventure in a sophisticated novel.

Taylor, Theodore. *The Trouble with Tuck.* Doubleday, 1981.
    A blind Golden Labrador is led by a seeing eye dog.

West, Colin. *Monty, the Dog Who Wears Glasses.* Art by author. Dutton, 1990.
    Monty wears glasses to keep him from bumping into things.

Puppets: A Booklist for Adults

Adachi, Barbara C. *Backstage at Bunraku: A Behind-the-Scenes Look at Japan's Traditional Puppet Theatre.* Photos by Joel Sachett. Weatherhill, 1985.
    An overview of the body-size Japanese puppets.

Baird, Bill. *The Art of the Puppet.* Photos. Macmillan, 1965.
    Puppets and puppetry around the world with a wealth of full color photographs.

Beaton, Mabel and Les Beaton. *Marionettes: A Hobby for Everyone.* Dallas Puppet Theater Press, 1948, 1989.
    Full treatment for the marionette.

Champlin, Connie. *Puppetry and Creative Dramatics.* Art by Nancy Renfro. Renfro Studios, 1980.
    A good introduction to using puppets in unscripted drama.

Currell, David. *The Complete Book of Poetry*. Plays, 1974.
History, puppet types, the show.

Engler, Larry and Carol Fijan. *Making Puppets Come Alive: A Method of Learning and Teaching Hand Puppetry*. Photos by David Attie. Demonstration puppets by Paul Vincent Davis. Taplinger, 1973.
Excellent directions for articulating your puppet.

Feller, Ron and Marsha. *Paper Masks and Puppets: For Stories, Songs and Plays*. The Arts Factory, Seattle, WA, 1985.
Drawings and photographs make this book useful.

Fling, Carol and Frank Ballard. *Directing Puppet Theater*. Resource Publications, San Jose, CA, 1989.
Step-by-step guide to production.

Grater, Michael. *Paper Mask-Making*. Art by author. Photos by Geoffrey Goode. Dover, 1967.
Animal masks: tiger, cat, rat, bird, donkey.

Hanford, Robert Ten Eyck. *The Complete Book of Puppets and Puppeteering*. Art by Ted Erik. Sterling, 1976.
General overview of puppetry in America, with history and description of puppets.

Hawkesworth, Eric. *Puppet Show to Make: How to Entertain with All Kinds of Puppets*. Supreme Magic, 64 High St., Bideford, Devon, England. _____.
Detailed instructions on how to make puppets and theaters with sample shows for each kind of puppet.

Hunt, Tamara and Nancy Renfro. *Pocketful of Puppets: Mother Goose Rhymes*. Renfro Studies, 1982.
Mother Goose puppets made from cups, boxes and paper bags.

Kominz, Laurence R. and Mark Levenson, eds. *The Language of the Puppet*. Pacific Puppetry Center, Tears of Joy Theater, Vancouver, WA.
Advanced presentations at the UNIMA conference on the nature of puppetry.

Magon, Jero. *Staging the Puppet Show*. Art by author. Charlemagne Press, 1384 Hope Road, No. Vancouver, V7P 1W7, Canada. 2nd ed., 1976, 1989.
Professional descriptions of lighting and staging.

Mahlmann, Lewis and David Cadwalader Jones. *Folk Tale Plays for Puppets*. Plays, 1980.
Folktales scripted for puppets.

Malkin, Michael R. *Traditional and Folk Puppets of the World*. Photos by David L. Young. Barnes, 1977.
Description and photos of puppets from around the world.

Marks, Burton & Rita. *Puppets and Puppet Making: The Plays, the Puppets, the Production*. Plays, 1982.
Short original scripts and simple puppet directions.

Masson, Anne. *The Magic of Marionettes*. Art by author. Annick, 1989.
Marionettes are considered more difficult than hand or finger puppets. This is a beginner's book of marionettes.

Painter, William M. *Story Hours with Puppets and Other Props.* Shoe String, 1990.
Ideas for presenting children's literature with easy to find and make puppets. Another good resource by the same author is *Musical Story Hours: Using Music with Storytelling and Puppetry.* (Shoe String 1989).

Pittman, Jeanne W. *Fanciful Finger Friends from Sea and Shore.* Art by Lynne W. Jennings. Pittman, 3821 Voltaire St., San Diego, CA 92107, 1989.
Felt puppet patterns for creatures from the sea. Another by this author is *Fanciful Felt Finger Friends* (Pittman, 1989).

Ross, Laura. *Holiday Puppets.* Art by Frank and Laura Ross. Lothrop, 1979.
Directions for making holiday characters using rod puppets, hand puppets and marionettes.

Ross, Laura. *Puppet Shows: Using Poems and Stories.* Art by Frank Ross, Jr. Lothrop, 1970.
Text and production notes for Mother Goose rhymes, and books.

Sierra, Judy. *Fantastic Theater: Puppets and Plays for Young Performers and Young Audiences.* Wilson, 1991.
Directions for making and manipulating shadow and rod puppets and scripts for puppet plays adapted from rhymes, folksongs, myths and folktales.

Sims, Judy. *Puppets for Dreaming and Scheming: A Puppet Source Book.* Art by Beverly Armstrong. Early Stages, Walnut Creek, CA, 1978.
Using egg cartons, hand and finger puppets in classrooms.

Sullivan, Debbie. *Pocketful of Puppets: Activities for the Special Child with Mental, Physical and Multiple Handicaps.* Art by Nancy Renfro. Renfro, 1982.
Emphasis on puppets for the special child.

Sylwester, Roland. *The Puppet and the Word.* Art by author. Concordia, 3558 S. Jefferson Avenue, St. Louis, MO 63118, 1982.
Using simple puppets with Bible stories. A similar work by this author is *Teaching Bible Stories More Effectively with Puppets* (Concordia, 1976).

Tichenor, Tom. *Tom Tichenor's Puppets.* Art by author. Abington, 1971.
Hand puppet plays and marionettes plus the author's personal philosophy.

Wilt, Joy, Gwen Hurn and John Hurn. *More Puppets with Pizzaz: Fifty Novelty and String Puppets Children Can Make and Use.* Creative Resources, Waco, Texas, 1977.
Each puppet is illustrated with step by step photos.

Wright, Denise Anton. *One-Person Puppet Plays.* Art by John Wright. Libraries Unlimited, 1990.
Short scripts and simple patterns to produce one-person puppet shows.

Wright, John. *Rod, Shadow, and Glove: Puppets from the Little Angel Theater.* Photos. Robert Hale, 1986.
Puppet construction, costumes, scenery, production. An advanced book.

Chapter 13

There's Magic in Reading

So there I was in India, being driven from New Delhi to a school in the mountains five hours away. We were inching our way through cars, bicycles, bullocks, rickshaws, and pedestrians when I looked up and saw the glass from the window on the driver's side crumbling into the car. A bus had slowly plowed into our car.

In India, it doesn't take much to gather a crowd, but an accident involving a car with diplomatic plates and a female foreigner is a real magnet. We had at least three hundred curious people gaping at the car and bus. We also had at least fifty policemen holding back the crowd.

I probably should have been feeling a little bit apprehensive, but mostly I was as curious as the onlookers, and I just happened to have with me a pocket version of the color-changing-silks trick. I simply couldn't resist the audience. I casually ran a red silk through my hand and it changed to a yellow silk. Was I a hit in Meerut!

As a magician, even an amateur, I know that you should never repeat a trick a second time to the same audience, but the folks in Meerut wanted to see this trick again and again, so I showed it to them. We gave one of the policemen a ride to the next town where I parted with the trick in exchange for a brass pot he offered me.

Yes, that was a day of adventure. I only feel badly that I broke my own rule. Everything you do should be directed to promoting books. If only I had had some books to share with the curious crowd. Oh well, maybe next time.

Actually, if you become interested in using magic to promote leisure reading, I assure you that you don't need to stage an accident to attract an attentive audience. Children, young adults, and adults are always intrigued by a magic trick. Even if you don't want to perform yourself, you may want to engage a magician to come to your classroom or library to perform. Don't expect him or her to introduce literature to your group, however. You can introduce the magician with books, or use a few minutes at the end of the show to booktalk magic books or books that might relate to the magicians patter.

Ask your dad or cousin if they ever owned a magic set and chances are the answer will be "yes," and that answer may even be accompanied by a story telling how he once was the Greatest Magician in the World. For many years, a magic set has been a very popular present to give to young boys. Even today, the three magic clubs I belong to are heavily membered with men, many of them elderly, who have had a passion for magic since they were nine-year olds. As for women, I'm not sure why this has traditionally been largely a male interest, but of course, now this is changing. The barriers have fallen and a Japanese woman, Princess Tenko, recently won the Magician of the Year award.

What is the universal appeal of conjuring? It must be that despite the technical advances in the world today, most people, regardless of age, enjoy believing in magic. After a magician performs a trick, you will see people in the audience whispering among themselves: "How did he do that?" or "I know how that was done."

Children really love it when you do a magic trick. They are astonished and intrigued. They love to badger the magician and often brag to their

friends that they know how the trick was accomplished. Offering a trick, or better yet offering the chance to learn how a trick is done will have children, right through high school, lining up for a chance at a glimpse into the world of magic. Remember, though, that preschoolers can be the toughest audiences for magicians. Since they still think that all of life is magical, they may seem less impressed by a mere magic trick.

Naturally, you will want to use the magic tricks to lead children into reading. I like to key my magic to a particular book or poem or to reading in general. If you find a trick that you want to perform and you can't come up with a book connection you can always booktalk magic books. Or, you can introduce any book and then say, "I think reading is as magical as any magic trick. Here's a trick I've enjoyed." Hopefully your audience will appreciate the trick and be even more eager to read, as you will become associated with the "magic of books."

You should be forewarned: The problem with conjuring is that it *is* magical. You may find yourself completely involved with the world of magic. I'm sure you have been to lectures where the front row fills up last. At magic conventions, the people who send their reservations in first get the seats in the front rows. At a Las Vegas magic convention, I tried to squeeze my husband into a better seat and we practically caused a riot, started by a member of my own club who had obtained his seat a year in advance. He certainly didn't want anyone usurping it.

Don't get the impression the magicians are any crazier than any other group of people in love with a hobby. I think they are, as a whole, really quite warm and welcoming. If you'd like to learn more about magic and magicians, write to the International Brotherhood of Magicians and The Society of American Magicians (you'll find these addresses on page 322) to inquire if there is a member club in your area. If there is a magic shop near you, the owner should also be able to help you find a club.

If you attend a club meeting, you will find that the amateur and professional magicians are constantly trying to hone their skills. Almost every meeting involves a lecture or workshop. At the conventions, you will see clusters of magicians watching a fellow conjuror manipulate coins or cards.

Now that you're anxious to learn some tricks, perhaps you are wondering what educational benefits of magic you might list for your library director or school superintendent in order to sell the idea of using magic to promote reading. For starters, magic really leads children to reading, as almost every trick has been revealed in a book or pamphlet; students of magic must learn to read instructions carefully, interpret them, and perform with poise for their family and friends—all lessons that are applicable to many other fields as well. And, once a fledgling magician has mastered a trick, he or she really must find an audience and perform the trick. Children, even the most timid, will develop a sense of worth and a new confidence through this process.

Writing skills can also be developed through an interest in magic. It is, after all, not the trick which creates the dramatic effect, but the way it is presented. Most children will want to write down the patter (what is said while performing) to accompany each trick and, with practise, will be able to adapt the patter to their individual performance styles.

In addition, magic helps children develop manual dexterity, as most tricks require some manipulation. The most advanced form, sleight of hand, requires constant and faithful practice.

Magic is guaranteed to garner the undivided attention of any audience as it involves mystery, invention, manipulation, performance, articulation, entertainment—skills which will whet an appetite for reading.

How to Begin

In the following section there is a selection of tricks for you to try. They are all easy to prepare and perform, and use household objects. It is interesting to note that despite incredible technological advances—from the micro chip to my very favorite modern invention, the fax machine—the magic fraternity and their magic tricks have remained fairly stable. Tricks that were performed in the Middle Ages, such as the Cups and Balls, are still being presented. You can start with some of the tricks given here, and then check out a pile of magic books from the library. Browse through them looking for an appealing trick. Reading a magic book is like reading a cookbook, as once you know some basic terms you will be able to understand the directions.

Another way of introducing yourself to the basics of magic is to find someone to help you who already performs tricks. Put a notice up in your school or library asking for a magic guide and no doubt several children and adults will come to your aid. You can visit a local magic shop, or make a point of looking for one when you are on a trip. Ask the clerk for simple tricks that are easy to perform. Written directions will be enclosed with the trick, but the salesperson will usually be happy to demonstrate the trick for you, as well.

Teaching Children and Adults to Perform Magic

You may want to incorporate a magic trick or two in your storytelling class to expose the group to the dramatic potential of the art of conjuring. You don't really need to know more than one trick to introduce the idea of magic, as a single trick done well and with style will be enough to spark the interest of those who wish to pursue the study of magic.

Particularly when working with children, it's necessary to be certain that your group understands the importance of keeping the secrets of the tricks to themselves. Explain to them that handling the responsibility of a trick is part of being a magician. The trick loses it's impact once the secret is revealed. Equally important is the presentation of the trick.

For theatrical effect, some magicians develop a character to use when presenting magic. Many older magicians adopted Chinese names and costumes capitalizing on the image of the mysterious east. You will find sorcerors, comic drunks, bumbling professors, and of course, the elegantly attired, black-tie magicians appearing and reappearing in magic shows. Still other magicians perform with a musical background only.

After presenting a magic trick, you might provide each student with his or her own apparatus (rope, or paper and scissors, for instance) and let them experiment on their own, encouraging each to come up with an individually-tailored presentation idea. Or, you could demonstrate the trick and send everyone home with written directions for at-home study and refinement.

In the following pages you will find directions for tricks, stories to read aloud or tell, poems, and a resource list to help you begin an adventure in magic.

A Magical Story to Share

This is the perfect story to share before you perform a trick or teach a trick. Kirby typifies the anxious, got-to-show-it-to-someone amateur magician who tries to perform before he or she has learned and practised. You will also find that it is a very effective tale to relate when you want your children to pay attention to directions.

Watch Out!

by Bruce Coville

"I'm home!" yelled Kirby Markle, bursting through the front door of his house. Without waiting for an answer, he pounded up the stairs and dashed into his bedroom. Flopping down onto his bed, he tore open the box he had bought at that strange store he found when he took the new shortcut home.

Inside he found a second box. "THE CAVE OF THE GNOME," proclaimed bold, black letters written across the top.

Underneath, in smaller print, it said, "Fool Your Family! Amaze Your Friends! A Fascinating Device for Both Amateur and Professional Magicians."

Kirby examined the box with wide eyes. Maybe this would finally be the trick he got to work. The old man who had sold it to him said it was especially good for someone like him, who was in a hurry to learn magic.

Fumbling with the tape that held the box shut, Kirby tore open the flaps and held the box upside down over his bed.

Out tumbled a cave made of papier-mâché.

A look of uncertainty crossed Kirby's face. He couldn't see any way that this was going to make things disappear.

"Kirby! Supper!"

Kirby sighed. He really didn't want to go to supper now. He wanted to figure out how to make this trick work.

"Just a minute, Mom!"

He began reading the directions.

"Kirby!"

"All right, all right. I'm coming!" Kirby shoved the directions into his pocket and bolted down the stairs.

As soon as supper was over, Kirby asked his mother and father to come into the living room. "I have something I want to show you," he said.

He herded them through the door and onto the couch, then raced back upstairs to grab the cave.

"I got a new trick today," he announced, as he hurtled back down the steps, two and three at a time.

Kirby's parents exchanged smiles. Kirby wanted so badly to be a magician. But he had never yet gotten a trick to work properly. He was always so eager to show them off that he never took the time to learn how to do them right.

"Did you read the directions yet?" asked his mother.

"Sort of," said Kirby. "It's gonna be great. Now, I need something to put in the cave. Can I have your watch, Dad?"

Kirby's father looked properly doubtful. "Will I get it back?" he asked.

"Oh, Dad."

"Well, okay," said his father, smiling. "But be careful with it. It's quite expensive."

He took out his pocket watch and gave it to Kirby.

"Now, watch this," said Kirby. He put the watch in the cave. Then he rolled the little papier-mâché boulder across the front of it. Putting his right hand on the cave he read the magic words off the instruction sheet, at the same time giving the top a little twist to the right. He smiled to himself. The twist must be what activated the mechanism that would hide the watch.

BOOM!

The noise was so loud it actually shook the windows. A puff of smoke rose from the cave, and the red flames licked out around the little boulder.

Kirby snatched his hand away. "Ow!" he cried.

Mr. and Mrs. Markle looked at each other nervously.

Trying to act casual, Kirby removed the boulder from the front of the cave.

The watch was gone.

"Presto kazam!" he said with a big smile. "A genuine magic trick!"

Kirby's parents applauded dutifully. But his father had a worried look on his face. "Why don't you bring it back now?" he said gently.

"You bet!" said Kirby. He put the boulder back in front of the cave and twisted the top to the left.

Nothing happened.

He tried it again.

Nothing happened.

He twisted it to the right.

Nothing happened.

Kirby snatched up the directions and began reading frantically through them. Suddenly he turned very pale.

"What is it, Kirby?" asked his mother

*   *   *

Gregory Gnome was puttering about in his cave when he heard the bell ring. A greedy smile crossed his face, and he ran to the loading platform.

The smile faded a little. Another gold watch. Well, it was better than a kick in the pants, he thought with a shrug. Taking the watch to the storage area, he tossed it into a box already close to overflowing with watches. He really would have to have a cave sale soon to turn some of this junk into usable cash.

"Gregory!" said a voice behind him. "Aren't you ashamed of yourself, taking advantage of all those children?"

Gregory winced. His face took on an injured expression. As he turned to his wife, he pulled a sheet of paper from his pocket. As he turned to his wife, he pulled a sheet of paper from his pocket. "Look at these directions," he said. "Read the paragraph to me."

It was his wife's turn to sigh. "I don't have to read it," she said. "I know it by heart: 'Once an object is placed in the Cave of the Gnome, it can never be returned. So please be sure to use only objects that have no real value.'"

"Well, there it is," said Gregory, looking soulful. "It could hardly be any plainer, could it? All I wanted to do was give kids a toy they could have some fun with. Can I help it if not one out of twenty is smart enough to read the directions before he tries to use the thing? Can I?"

No matter how hard he tried to look serious, Gregory could not hide the greedy smile that twitched at the corners of his mouth.

* * *

The little papier-mâché cave was in tiny pieces all over Kirby's living-room floor.

Of papier-mâché there was a lot. Of the gold watch, not a trace.

"Kirby," said Mr. Markle, "come with me. I want to have a little talk with you."

Slowly, very slowly, Kirby followed his father out of the room.

Share the Magic of Books

The following tricks take little preparation, but you will have to *practise* a good deal before you perform them.

Before you even look at the first trick, please raise your right hand and declare out loud (no fingers crossed, please):

"I promise never to reveal the secret of these tricks!"

Of course, teaching a new group of magicians with new styles of presentation is a different matter: You're spreading the magic not revealing it. And, even if some of your students know the trick you've chosen, remember that it's *how* you present the trick that makes it entertaining.

One exercise that's valuable when teaching magic to a group of children is to have the students practise the trick until all are proficient with it, then have each member of the class create an individual line of patter that makes the presentation meaningful for them. I try to key all of my magic to books, so every magic trick is accompanied by a poem, story or comments that are related to books.

THE APPEARING RABBIT TRICK

THE TRICK: You show a newspaper. Roll it up and a rabbit comes out of the newspaper. Then you show the newspaper again.

YOU NEED: two sheets of newspaper
glue
paper or felt rabbit (directions for fold-and-cut rabbit follow trick)

PRE-PERFORMANCE PREPARATION:

Glue two double sheets of newspaper together leaving a pocket as shown in figure 1.

Trace the rabbit on the next page onto paper or felt and cut it out.

Put the rabbit into the pocket (figure 2).

HOW TO: 1. Show the audience both sides of the newspaper. Put your hand over the pocket as you show it.

2. Roll the paper to form a cone (figure 3, 4, 5).

3. Reach into the paper cone and pull out the rabbit.

4. Unroll the paper and show it empty again.

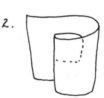

PATTER: As you all know, every magician needs a rabbit. My rabbit is a "Reading Rabbit." He lives in the newspaper (show the newspaper). He likes to read as much as I do (start rolling cone as you talk). He reads books about other rabbits and some of his favorites are: (mention or show your favorite books on rabbits). Just before supper he comes to visit, so I can read him a story. (Remove rabbit from pocket and show the newspaper again by holding it up and showing both sides.)

Fold-and-Cut Reading Rabbit

This is an easy, anyone-can-do-it, fold-and-cut project. In addition to using the Reading Rabbit with the newspaper trick above, you can make this rabbit or the rabbit sock-puppet below your magician's assistant for any magic program and a mascot for any rabbit stories or programs you present.

Follow the diagram below, cutting along the dotted lines after making all folds as shown. Snip the dark triangles before unfolding for the rabbit's eyes, nose, and mouth. You can use scraps of paper or felt for the front paws and book and glue them to your rabbit.

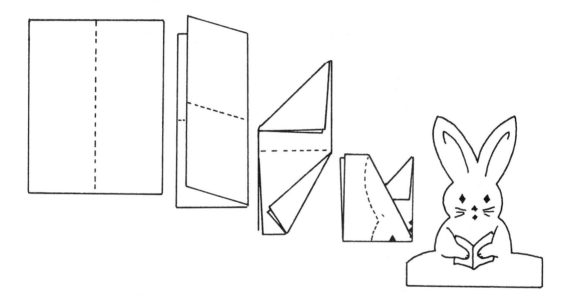

Magician's Rabbit Sock Puppet

Since most magicians' puppets appear from within their top hats, you might want to make this rabbit puppet and magician's hat, designed by Lynne Jenning, to use when you tell stories about magic or to set the mood for any other trick you will perform for your group.

Cut sock at edge of ribbing as shown at left. Stuff toe of sock with cotton or other soft stuffing material to make head. Insert a wooden dowel into head and secure at "neck" (A in drawing at left) with rubber band.

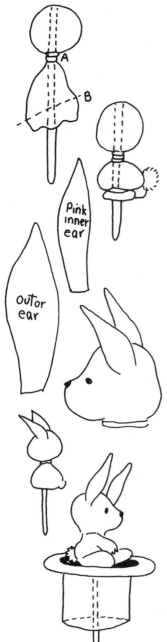

Stuff body to dotted line B, securing with rubber band. Then wrap each half of material below B around a small wad of stuffing, using the rubber band at B to make a loop around each half and secure the two "feet"; glue to body and dowel to hold in place, if necessary.

Glue a fabric pompom for a tail.

Cut a set of two inner ears from pink felt, cloth, or paper and two outer ears from slightly larger white felt, cloth, or paper. Glue each pink inner ear to a white outer ear, then glue one completed pink-and-white rabbit ear to each side of head.

Sew a few stitches to make indentations for the rabbit's eyes, then add pieces of pink felt or two pink beads for the eyes. Use pink felt or a small pompom for the nose. Elaborate on the features or add others, such as a felt mouth, black stitches sewn next to mouth or short, thin pieces of wire inserted through fabric on either side of mouth for whiskers, as desired.

For Magician's Hat, cover salt or oatmeal box with black paper. Make a brim for the top hat of stiff black paper or black cardboard. Cut a hole the diameter of the dowel in the bottom of the box (the crown of the top hat) for the rabbit's dowel handle to go through.

Put the rabbit into the hat, holding the dowel beneath the hat and push the rabbit puppet up to make him 'appear' and pull down on the dowel to make him 'disappear'.

Now that you have several tricks featuring rabbits and you have your Reading Rabbit and your sock-puppet rabbit, you'll have lots of opportunities to display and share the following books:

Fiction

Adams, Richard. *Watership Down*. Macmillan, 1972
A long (400+ pages) saga about a group of rabbits in search of a new home and a better life.

Howe, Doborah and James Howe. *Bunnicula: A Rabbit-Tale of Mystery*. Art by Alan Daniel. Atheneum, 1979.
The story of a vampire rabbit told by Harold, the dog.

Lawson, Robert. *Rabbit Hill*. Art by the author. Viking, 1944.
Will the new folks be planting folks? This is a read-aloud classic.

Michels, Tilde. *Rabbit Spring*. Art by Kathi Bhend. Translated by J. Alison James. Hourcourt, 1986.
Enjoy Silla and Rahm's first litter of rabbits.

Williams, Margery. *The Velveteen Rabbit*. Art by William Nicholson. Doubleday, 1975.
This story of a stuffed toy that is loved so much that it comes alive has many illustrated versions. Nicholson's art is the original offering.

Folklore

Aardema, Verna. *Rabbit Makes a Monkey of Lion*. Art by Jerry Pinkney. Dial, 1989.
Rabbit and her friends fool the king of the jungle. This is a picture book to look at and share.

Castle, Caroline. *The Hare and the Tortoise*. Art by Peter Weevers. Dial, 1985.
Aesop's fable retold with watercolor paintings.

Harris, Joel Chandler. *Jump! The Adventures of Brer Rabbit*. Art by Barry Moser. Adapted by Van Dyke Parks and Malcolm Jones. Harcourt, 1986.
These Brer Rabbit stories are presented with sophisticated art and text to share with middle- and upper-grade children. Just as wonderful is the sequel, *Jump Again! More Adventures of Brer Rabbit*, by the same author and artist (Harcourt, 1987).

Jaquith, Priscilla. *Bo Rabbit Smart for True: Folktales from the Gullah*. Art by Ed Young. Philomel, 1981.
Folktales featuring a clever rabbit from the Gullah people of America.

Lester, Julius. *The Tales of Uncle Remus: The Adventures of Brer Rabbit*. Art by Jerry Pinkney. Dial, 1987.
Excellent short retellings of the Brer Rabbit tales. Others in this series to look for are *More Tales of Uncle Remus* (Dial, 1988) and *Further Tales of Uncle Remus* (Dial, 1990).

Martin, Rafe. *Foolish Rabbit's Big Mistake*. Art by Ed Young. Putnam, 1985.
Rabbit panics when he hears a loud noise. Adapted from a Jakarta tale.

VanWoerkman, Dorothy O. *Harry and Shellburt*. Art by Erick Ingraham. Macmillan, 1977.
>   This version of the classic race is for beginning readers.

Picture Books

Anderson, Lena. *Bunny Party*. Art by the author. R&S/Farrar, 1987.
>   In this small-size wordless picture book, a rabbit prepares a special meal for a small child. The same format is followed in *Bunny Surprise* (1986) and *Bunny Story* (1987).

Brewster, Patience. *Rabbit Inn*. Art by author. Little, 1991.
>   Pandora and her husband Bob and assorted animal guests prepare the inn for a very special visitor.

Caldwell, Mary. *Morning, Rabbit, Morning*. Art by Ann Schweniger. Harper, 1982.
>   A short text and lively art show rabbits as they stretch, scratch, jump and thump. For the preschool story time.

Lionni, Leo. *Let's Make Rabbits*. Art by the author. Pantheon, 1982.
>   A pencil and a collage rabbit make friends.

Newberry, Clare Turlay. *Marshmallow*. Art by the author. Harper, 1942.
>   A cat learns to accept the new bunny in his house. The charcoal drawings won a Caldecott honor award.

Potter, Beatrix. *Peter Rabbit*. Art by the author. Warne, 1987.
>   This story of a naughty rabbit is still the old-time favorite of children and their parents.

Wahl, Jan. *Rabbits on Roller Skates*. Art by David Allender. Crown, 1986.
>   This contains a lively chant for beginning readers, "dipping, slipping, dashing, splashing. Rabbits on roller skates!"

Zolotow, Charlotte. *Mr. Rabbit and the Lovely Present*. Art by Maurice Sendak. Harper, 1962.
>   A rabbit helps a young girl find the perfect present for her mother.

The Classic Cut-and-Restore Rope Trick

There are so many different rope tricks that some magicians confine their repertoire of tricks to the manipulation of rope, or others may limit themselves strictly to working with cards or coins. This is one of the most frequently performed rope tricks.

THE TRICK: The magician shows a length of rope. She cuts it in half and restores it to its original state.

YOU NEED: A length of rope
                        Scissors

PRE-PERFORMANCE PREPARATION:

The more supple your rope, the easier the trick. If you choose to use clothesline, select a line that has a removable inner core, as the hollow line will palm more easily. If you can't find a workable rope, you can order some "magicians' rope" from one of the suppliers listed at the end of this chapter. Be generous in the amount of rope you order, as the trick is more difficult if the rope is very short, and it becomes shorter with each demonstration of the trick. Start with a three-foot length of rope.

HOW TO:

(Go very slowly while learning the trick, following the directions step by step)

1. Grasp one end of the rope in your left hand between the thumb and the index finger. Now take the other end of the rope and hold it with the same two fingers.

2. You will now have a long loop hanging below your left hand. With your right hand, take this loop and place it against the palm of your left hand.

3. This is the critical move for the success of the trick. You will place the loop on top of the right end of the rope in your left hand, marked X in figure 1. Now, with your right hand, bring the section marked X up to form a loop above your left hand. Since the back of your hand faces the audience, they believe they see the main loop that they watched you make at the beginning of the trick, but what they are actually viewing is the small loop you made at the end of the rope (figure 2).

4. At this point, either you can cut the loop that is visible above your left hand, or you can invite a member of the audience to do so. You will have four ends sticking up for the audience to see (figure 3).

5. Drop the two long ends of the rope. You are now still holding two ends, and to the audience (who watched you cut the loop), it looks like you are holding two pieces of rope. Actually, you are holding

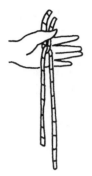

only a short piece of rope that is wrapped around the original length of rope (figure 4).

6. Now, let the audience watch you tie the two ends of the short piece of rope (the cheating rope) together above your hand. It will appear that you are rejoining the cut rope (figure 6).

7. Show the rope with the knot in the middle (don't worry if it's not exactly in the middle of the long rope).

8. Now grasp one end of the rope in your right hand (practised magicians do this maneuver with the left hand, before it seems to be the right hand to the audience, and therefore, looks more natural. I find it easier to do this smoothly with my right hand), and coil it around that hand while passing the rope through your left hand. When the knot arrives in your left hand, slip it off while you continue to coil the rope length. Palm the knot in your hand as you show the restored rope.

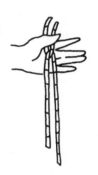

9. There are some fancy, sleight-of-hand techniques for getting rid of the knot in your left hand, but the easiest and most convincing tactic is simply to hold up the "restored" rope to capture the audience's attention as you slide the knot into a pocket and take your bow.

PATTER: Learning the Ropes of Writing a Book

(Say each paragraph while you perform the action in the direction above, mentioned in parentheses.)

Most people think that an author sits down and writes, "Once upon a time . . ." and continues to write and write and write until she comes to "and they lived happily ever after. The End." (direction #1.)

In reality, though, an author usually finds that somewhere, maybe right in the middle of the manuscript, there is a paragraph she really dislikes (directions #2, #3, #4) and decides to cut it out altogether (direction #5).

When she rereads the story, the author may see that the

paragraph she just cut was the best writing of the whole piece, so she puts it back in (directions #6 and #7).

Now, the author proudly sends the finished story to her editor, who says, "We love your story, but we hope you'll be willing to take out that one lengthy passage." The author wants the book to be published so she takes that section out again (direction #8). The book is published, and of course, it's a great success. The End (direction #9).

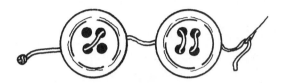

The Button Trick

"Round as an apple,
Flat as a chip,
Got four eyes
And can't see a bit."
A button riddle

I love this trick because it is *easy*, mistake-proof—and magical. You can use it with the riddle above or after you have shared one of the following stories, books, or chants:

"Hi, My Name Is Sew." In *Presenting Reader's Theater* by Caroline Feller Bauer. Wilson, 1987.
A nonsense chant about a button factory.

Lobel, Arnold. "A Lost Button." In *Frog and Toad Are Friends*. Harper, 1970.
In this story, Toad loses a button and Frog helps him find it.

Reid, Margarette S. *The Button Box*. Art by Sarah Chamberlain. Dutton, 1990.
A child explores Grandma's button box.

Spoph, Kate. *Introducing Fanny*. Art by author. Orchard, 1991.
Mararita and Fanny decorate a doll with buttons.

Taback, Simms. *Joseph Had a Little Overcoat*. Random, 1977.
Joseph's coat wears out and he uses the fabric to make a jacket, a vest, a tie, and a button. A version of this story based on a folksong can also be found in *Just Enough to Make a Story* by Nancy Schimmel (Sisters Choice, 1982).

Ueno, Noriko. *Elephant Buttons*. Harper, 1973.
An elephant "buttons out" to become other animals.

BUTTON TRICK

THE TRICK: A member of the audience chooses a button from a bag. The magician identifies which button the person chose.

YOU NEED: A cloth bag

A collection of 20 buttons of different colors and shapes.

A collection of 20 buttons all exactly the same size, shape and color

A nylon thread

A clear jar or plastic bag

PRE-PERFORMANCE PREPARATION:

String the different-colored buttons on the clear thread letting it form a circle of colorful buttons. Put the loose same-colored buttons into the jar, along with the threaded buttons.

HOW TO:

1. Show the audience the jar of buttons

2. Show that the cloth bag is empty, turning it inside out and back again

3. Dump the buttons from the jar into the bag

4. Palm string of buttons in right hand while holding bag of same-colored buttons.

5. Ask someone to put her hand into the bag and choose one button, cautioning her, "Don't let me see it."

6. You tell the audience which color button was chosen.

PATTER: I've been collecting buttons for years. I keep my favorite buttons in this jar (show the jar). I have quite a rapport with my buttons, as they are my friends. If I put them into this bag (show bag, turning inside and out), they will always call out to me, even if someone takes one of them. I'll just put my collection in the bag (dump the buttons in the bag and reach into the bag, holding onto the threaded buttons. Hold them in your right fist inside the bag, holding the bag slightly above the eye level of the person you ask to assist you).

Now, I'm going to have—what's your name? I'm going to have Hilary assist me. Please put your hand into the bag and take out one button. Don't let me see it. Do you have a button?

Ladies and gentlemen, Hilary could have chosen a red button, a blue button, a small button, a big button, a square button, but she took out a round red button with four holes. Is that correct? Yes, it is! A little applause for my faithful button collection, please.

HINTS:
—Don't give the audience too much time to ponder on the jar of buttons—just flash them a glimpse of it.

—Make sure the button-chooser doesn't have too much time either. Whip the bag away as soon as she has chosen.

—Make sure that you get the button back again so you can repeat the trick at another time and place. Or, you can let the chooser keep the "magic" button as a souvenir.

In fact, you might want to give everyone a magic button to take home. Tell the group how to use their magic buttons: "Hold the magic button in your left hand. Close your eyes. Make a wish. Of course, you may not get your wish immediately, but just keep wishing whenever you have your button handy."

ANOTHER IDEA:
Replace some of the buttons with glittery beads or rhinestone buttons and perform this trick when you tell "The Sack of Diamonds" (pp. 146–147), referring to the beads as the diamonds the old woman shoots into the sky.

Some Games the Children Can Play with a Button Collection:

Count them
Divide them by color
Divide them by size
Line them up to make a train
Make a collage, pasting them onto cardboard
Stack them into towers
Find any "twins"
Find any "triplets"

Make circle
Make square
Teach them tricks: "sit," "stay"
Give them names
Tell them a story
String them on a thread
Write a story about their "aunt" on your sweater
Sew one on a hat
Sew some on a t-shirt
Sing a song to them
Play checkers with them
Hide one behind your back and have a friend guess which one it is
Make a necklace
Sew some onto a ribbon
Balance one on your nose
Balance one on your toes
Trade them with a friend
Play "I Spy"
"Hide" them by placing them in plain view but in unexpected spots and have
   a friend list how many she can find.
Put them in a line and measure it
Subtract all of one color and measure the line again
Make them sit still while you read a book

What else can you do with buttons?

Peter's Paper Clip Trick

My husband, Peter, showed me this trick. It works for him 100% of the time. It works for me two out of three times. Try it and see how you do with it. Children love to show this one to their friends, and you can use it with the poem on page 225.

THE TRICK: Two paper clips jump from a folded dollar bill and mysteriously link together.

YOU NEED: Two paper clips
A one-dollar bill

HOW TO: 1. Fold the dollar bill into the shape of an S.

2. Use the paper clips to hold it as shown in sketch.

3. Quickly pull the ends of the bill in opposite directions.

4. Three cheers! The paper clips are joined together.

PATTER: Have you ever used a paper clip as a bookmark? Here's something else you can do with a paper clip. These two paper clips are friends. They are separated by this evil old dollar bill that keeps them apart. But look: when they get the bill out the way, they can live together forever.

THE POSTCARD NECKLACE

THE TRICK: The magician shows an ordinary picture postcard and declares that she can turn it into a necklace—and does by cutting and folding the card.

YOU NEED: A standard postcard or an index card or posterboard cut to 5″ × 7″

Scissors

HOW TO: 1. Fold the card in half lengthwise (fig. 1).

2. Cut seven slits in the folded edge, each extending half the width of the card (fig. 2).

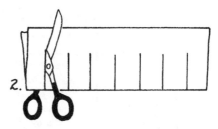

3. Turn the card over and cut seven more slits in the unfolded edge between the original slits, each going halfway into the card (fig. 3).

4. Cut along the folded edge only where the dotted line is shown in figure 4.

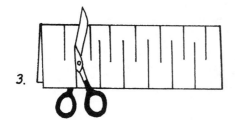

3.

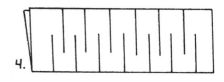

4.

5. Unfold the card (do this gently to avoid rips).

6. Put the finished necklace over your head and take a bow.

PATTER:

I like to make my patter last through the whole trick, but as it takes a bit of practise to wield a scissors while talking, you might prefer to give an introductory "set-up" for the trick, then do the cutting (to some recorded background music, if possible). I've included both versions here for you to choose. The introductory version of the patter is:

I just received this postcard from a magician. He said that, if I cut it up just right, his card would become a beautiful necklace for me to wear. Let's see if he's right. (Perform trick, then show and wear necklace.) It's true!

The longer variation that I use as I cut the card is:

You probably all learned to read years ago. You probably read all sorts of books: fantasy, historical fiction, poetry, biographies, fairy tales. If you read fairy tales, you probably know a lot about magic. So, you may not be too surprised to learn that I just received a postcard from my fairy godmother yesterday. (Hold up postcard and show that it has writing on one side, a photo on the other.) Here's what it says:

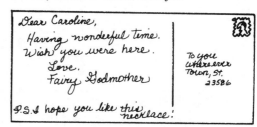

Since all I received was this postcard, I figure the necklace must be in here somewhere. (Pick up the scissors and cut while talking.)

I really do think that reading is magical. Imagine being able to take those little black symbols and turn them into words in your head. Books can take you into the future or back into history. They can teach you all about the life cycle of the squirrel or about nuclear fission. With a book you can find out how to play football or fix a clock.

Reading is also magical because you can do it when you're eight or eighty. You can do it for eight minutes or eight hours a day.

Next time your fairy godmother sends you a postcard that says, "I hope you like this necklace," you'll know that the necklace really is in the postcard. (Unfold the finished necklace and put it on.) Wear it in good health. (Take your bow.)

THE POPCORN TRICK

Use this trick when you tell "Paul Bunyan and the Popcorn Blizzard" (my retelling of this classic follows these instructions) or when you read or tell "The Huckabuck Family and How They Raised Popcorn in Nebraska and Quit and Came Back" in *Rootabaga Stories, Part II* by Carl Sandburg with art by Michael Hague (Harcourt, 1989).

THE TRICK: A bowl of popcorn turns into a popcorn necklace.

YOU NEED: A bowl

Popcorn to fill the bowl

A needle with a large hole, such as an embroidery needle

String

A paper shopping bag

(Optional: a book about popcorn to share)

PRE-PERFORMANCE PREPARATION:

Make a popcorn necklace by taking whole kernels of popped corn and stringing them together with needle and string to form a necklace, using as much popcorn for the necklace as it takes to fill the bowl you've chosen for this trick. Arrange the pre-strung necklace in the bowl so that it looks like a bowl of loose popcorn, ready to eat. Put a few loose kernels of popcorn on top of the necklace in the bowl.

HOW TO:

1. Show the audience the bowl of popcorn. Take a few loose kernels from the bowl and eat them (be sure to have a glass of water handy, as popcorn easily gets stuck in your throat). Throw a couple of loose kernels up in the air.
2. Hold a paper bag up and show that it's empty.
3. Place a string in the bag.
4. Pour the popcorn into the bag. (Practise this maneuver so that the popcorn doesn't spill over or get caught on the bag, thus revealing the trick.)
5. Pull out the popcorn necklace.

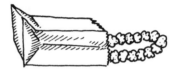

PATTER:

(Do this trick after you've finished telling "Paul Bunyan and the Popcorn Blizzard.") I love stories about popcorn. And I really love to eat popcorn. I like it with salt, with sugar, or just plain like this. (Show bowl of popcorn.) I even like to wear popcorn. Maybe you'd like to wear some popcorn jewelry, too. All you need is some popcorn. (Throw a couple of kernels in the air and eat one or two.) And some string. (Hold up the string.) And of course, your Magic Maker. (Show that the paper bag is empty.) I put the string into the bag (do it), then I pour the popcorn in on top. (Hint: If you use a square-bottomed grocery bag, you can stand it on a table and use both hands to direct the popcorn and keep the string from draping on the bag as you pour.) And—KAZAM! (Or use your favorite magical word.) Here is my necklace. (Put it on or hold it up; if you like, hold up the bag again to show it's empty, though any kernels you didn't throw or eat will remain in the bag).

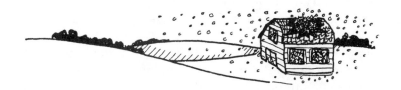

Paul Bunyan and the Popcorn Blizzard

Paul Bunyan—you know who he is, don't you? He was a big fella with a gigantic blue ox. Paul was a logger. He had a logging camp up in the North Woods. In fact, Paul had camps all across America. You could have run into him 'most anywhere, especially if there were trees around—and the bigger the better.

Well, the time I want to tell you about is when Paul, you see, he had set up camp in the desert down there in the Southwest. It was summer and blazing hot, not at all like the cool forest up in Maine (or was it Oregon?) where his men had been working last. It was hot in the desert and Paul's men were mighty sluggish. They would do just about anything to get cool.

Babe the Blue Ox would wave his tail back and forth, making a giant fan for twenty men at a time. They would line up and catch the breeze. If you visit down South, around there in Arizona, you'll see where Paul dragged his ax behind him one scorching hot day. It left a big hole in the desert. Today, we call that hole the Grand Canyon.

No one wanted to do any work; no one even wanted to move. The men just sat around panting. Paul decided to do something to get his men back into action. He hitched up Babe to his wagon. The wagon was so huge that 100 men could stand in its shadow and get a bit of shade. Paul drove Babe up into Iowa, where he discovered a whole barn filled with corn. He bought that whole barn from the farmer who owned it and put it into his wagon.

As he started back down to that desert, the sun was blazing on the roof of the barn. The barn jiggled back and forth in the wagon. The corn stored in the barn started to pop. By the time Babe pulled the wagon into camp, the corn was snapping and crackling in the barn. Since the popcorn had no place to go, the roof flew right off, and it rained popcorn. It was a regular blizzard.

The men thought, "Snow!" and put on their snow clothes, pulled on mittens and started a snowball fight with the white popped kernels. Slim Jim thought it would be fun to build a snowman and the men scooped up hand-fuls of popcorn and built a snowman that looks just like Paul. The wind whipped the popcorn around in a swirling cloud. It looked and felt just like a snowstorm, and neither Paul nor Babe told them it was popcorn. Of course, they must have figured it out for themselves, because Cream Puff Fatty started shoveling up the "snow" and piling it high on the cookhouse table. Between crosscountry skiing and snowball fights, they ate their fill of freshly popped corn. That's when Paul said, "We're going home. Time to move up North and get some work done."

They moved camp with Babe at the head of a long column of men dressed for a winter blizzard, smack in the middle of the blazing hot desert.

If you're traveling through the Southwestern desert, look down at your feet. You might just find a few handfuls of popcorn there still—ready to eat.

CHOOSE A BOOK I

THE TRICK;   The magician predicts which book will be chosen.

YOU NEED: The Reading Rabbit from the Appearing-Rabbit Trick (p. 296)

Three books of your choice

Three pieces of paper

An envelope

Rubber cement (You can use rubber cement to lightly glue the predictions to the rabbit or book. It is easy to remove when you are finished.)

PRE-PERFORMANCE PREPARATION:

Choose three books that you would enjoy sharing with your audience. For instance, *My Place in Space*, by Robin and Sally Hirst with art by Roland Harvey with Joe Levine (Orchard); *The Bridge Dancers* by Carol Saller with art by Gerald Talifero (Carolrhoda); and *Barn Dance*, by Bill Martin, Jr. and John Archambault with art by Ted Rand (Holt).

Write "You chose *My Place in Space*" on a piece of paper and use rubber cement to lightly glue it to the back of the Reading Rabbit (the rubber cement can be easily removed from the Reading Rabbit after the trick)

Then write "You chose *Barn Dance*" on another slip of paper and lightly attach it with rubber cement to the back of *Barn Dance*.

Finally, write "You chose *The Bridge Dancers*" on a third piece of paper, put it in an envelope, seal it, and put it on the table with the books.

HOW TO: Place the three books on a table. Invite someone from the audience to "Choose the book I will share with you next."

Then give the following direction to the person selected to make the choice, "Place this Reading Rabbit on the book you choose." If the person picks *My Place in Space* turn the Reading Rabbit over and show your prediction. If she chooses *Barn Dance* turn all three books over showing your prediction glued to that book. If she chooses *The Bridge Dancers*, tell her to open the envelope and read your prediction. Take your bow and share the chosen book by reading aloud or giving a booktalk.

PATTER: This morning I am going to share one of these books with you. Who would like to help me choose which one? (Choose someone). I'm going to lay these three books on the table. Marge will choose from *My Place in Space*, *Barn Dance*, or *The Bridge Dancers*. Please place this Reading Rabbit on the book of your choice. (Read the prediction.)

Incidentally, you can use this opportunity to tell something about each of the books and then read or booktalk the chosen book.

CHOOSE A BOOK II

This is another way of having a volunteer choose a book and the magician confirms the choice. This version of Choose a Book calls for an assistant who knows the secret of the trick.

THE TRICK: Six books are laid out on the floor or a table. The magician leaves the room or turns his back while a volunteer points to the book she chooses. The magician identifies the book.

YOU NEED: Six books that you would like to share with a group.

An assistant who knows the secret of the trick.

PRE-PERFORMANCE PREPARATION:

Lay six books on a table or floor (if your group will see them better) in the pattern as shown. Explain the trick

to your assistant. The pattern of the books represents the features on a face.

HOW TO: After the book is chosen your assistant signals the book choice to you by touching the part of her face that represents the book chosen. Remember that the assistant is touching her own face and the magician needs to transfer the signal to the correct side. For instance if the assistant tugs at her right ear, the magician must realize that he is seeing a mirror image of the face. The book chosen is the one to the right of the pattern. Easy and fool proof, you can repeat this trick again. Pick your confederate carefully. He or she needs to be able to keep a secret.

PATTER: I'd like to share a book with you, but I couldn't decide which one of these to read to you. I'm going to lay them here on the table. Eric, would you help me please? I'm going to turn my back and you point to the book you would like me to share with you today. Say, "Ready" when you have pointed to the book. Eric, you have chosen *Monsters* by Russell Hoban with art by Quentin Blake (Scholastic). I'll show it to all of you and read some of it. (Before you tell the audience which book Eric chose, you may want to give one sentence annotations on the other five books. This will give your confederate lots of time to make the identifying action. If you find it more magical to make your revelation quickly, you may want to do your mini-booktalk before Eric chooses. Then, after announcing the selection, take your bow and share the chosen book.)

THE GROWING TREE

An obvious story to use with this paper-tree trick is Jack and the Beanstalk, since the tree looks exactly like the stalk that Jack really did climb. It would also work with Sleeping Beauty, since a forest grows up around the castle. This trick is also perfect to use with any book about a tree, forests or gardening, such as "The Talking Tree" (on page 317).

THE TRICK: The magician shows a roll of paper. He makes a few cuts into the roll and pulls out a paper tree.

YOU NEED: A roll of paper. You can use wallpaper, shelf paper, newspaper, or any roll of paper.

Scissors or heavy duty shears.

PRE-PERFORMANCE PREPARATION:

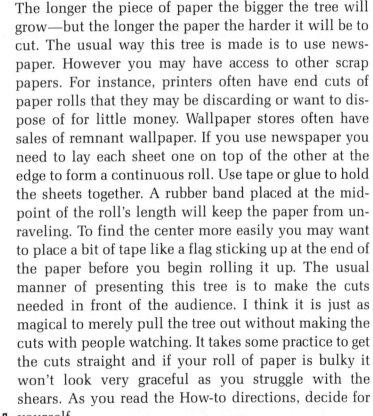

The longer the piece of paper the bigger the tree will grow—but the longer the paper the harder it will be to cut. The usual way this tree is made is to use newspaper. However you may have access to other scrap papers. For instance, printers often have end cuts of paper rolls that they may be discarding or want to dispose of for little money. Wallpaper stores often have sales of remnant wallpaper. If you use newspaper you need to lay each sheet one on top of the other at the edge to form a continuous roll. Use tape or glue to hold the sheets together. A rubber band placed at the midpoint of the roll's length will keep the paper from unraveling. To find the center more easily you may want to place a bit of tape like a flag sticking up at the end of the paper before you begin rolling it up. The usual manner of presenting this tree is to make the cuts needed in front of the audience. I think it is just as magical to merely pull the tree out without making the cuts with people watching. It takes some practice to get the cuts straight and if your roll of paper is bulky it won't look very graceful as you struggle with the shears. As you read the How-to directions, decide for yourself.

HOW TO:

1. Grasp the roll of paper at the bottom and make three cuts, vertically, to the center of the roll.

2. Peel the cut paper back, as though you were peeling a banana, one layer after another.

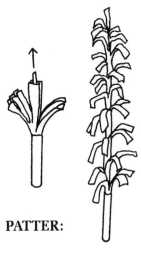

3. Reach into the center and pull up the tree.

4. After telling your story and "growing" your tree, lay the tree on a table or the floor or put the tree into a deep, narrow receptacle, such as an umbrella holder, wastebasket, box, or flowerpot. You will need to affix a vertical pole to the bottom of the container and slip your tubular tree over it, or use soft packing material, such as crushed newspaper, to hold the tree in place. I usually don't try to keep and reuse the tree; one of the children is always happy to walk away with it as a souvenir.

PATTER: After telling a story, simply say, "I have here the tree that I was just telling you about. It used to be only this big, but after hearing a story about itself it felt ten feet high." Pull out the tree and take your bow.

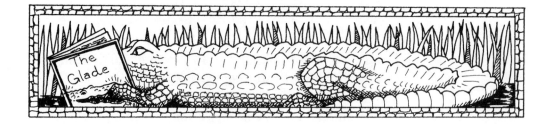

The Talking Tree

A Story from Vietnam

A merchant was coming home from a trip. He carried with him his clothes in one bag and his money in another bag. He arrived at a small village and sat down under a banyan tree. Road weary, he was soon fast asleep. When he awoke he was shocked to discover that his money bag was missing.

He started to yell and scream at the tree: "You took it. You took it." The villagers were worried. The man was acting very strangely. The local magistrate heard about the odd behaviour of the traveler.

The magistrate arrived and said, "What is all the commotion?"

"This tree has stolen a bag of money. I want it punished," said the man as he danced around the tree yelling, "You took it. You took it."

The magistrate ordered that a branch of the tree be brought to his home. He arranged with one of his soldiers to help him. The whole town waited for the trial of the tree.

The branch was brought into the magistrates chambers. "Beat it," commanded the official. As the tree was being beaten, the magistrate said, "Tell us. Did you steal this man's money?"

From behind the door, the soldier cried out, "Don't beat me. I didn't steal anything, but I know who did." The towns people were astonished to hear a tree talk. The thief who had actually stolen the money was terrified and decided that he had better confess to the theft.

The merchant thanked the judge and went home with his money and a story to tell to his family.

Growing a Money Tree

The paper tree from The Growing Tree trick can be used as a money tree, too, to accompany this Goha story from the Middle East. After sharing the story, simply show Goha's money tree. Another time, tell "Coyote and the Money Tree," found in *And It Is Still That Way: Legends Told by Arizona Indian Children* by Byrd Baylor (Scribner, 1976). Or, use this paper money tree when reading or displaying books about money and earning money.

The Money Tree

The Goha was poor. His neighbor was rich. One day Goha sat under the tree that divided his yard from his neighbor's yard.

"Dear Allah" he intoned. "I need 1,000 dinars now, today. Please send them down from this money tree." Nothing happened. "Oh, Allah. I hope you understood. I need the 1,000 dinars now—today."

Goha spoke loudly so that his rich neighbor could easily hear as he shouted again: "Allah, are you listening. Perhaps you didn't hear. I said that I need 1,000 dinars. I don't want less. Don't bother sending less than 1,000."

Of course, the rich neighbor heard the Goha. He called his wife over to the tree that divided their yard from the Goha's. "Listen to Goha. He's asking Allah for money. He seems to expect it to fall from this tree. I'm going to have some fun with him."

The rich neighbor, a merchant of great reputation, counted exactly 999 dinars into a cloth bag. He climbed the tree and sat in a branch directly over Goha's head.

"Please, Allah, surely you can hear me now. I need the 1,000 dinars right now. Remember, I need exactly 1,000 dinars, I won't even accept one dinar less."

The merchant chuckled to himself as he slowly threw handfuls of coins from the tree to the ground below. Goha immediately began scooping up the coins. He made piles of money under the tree and started to count it. There were only 999 dinars. Goha counted again and then again. Surely, there must be some mistake. When he carefully counted a third time, he sadly said, "Allah, I don't want to seem disrespectful, but I think you have made a mistake. I asked for 1,000 dinars and you have only sent 999."

The merchant whispered to his wife, "You see I have tricked our friend Goha. Now he will want to return the money to Allah and I will confess that it was me all the time." But, the rich merchant had waited too long to make his move.

Goha simply said, "Thank you Allah. We all make mistakes. 999 dinars will be quite enough for now. Perhaps when you get a chance you will send me the last dinar." Goha walked into his modest house to enjoy the money.

Naturally, the merchant was furious. He stormed over to the Goha's house and demanded his money back.

"What money?" Goha asked innocently.

"The money that I threw down to you from the tree."

"Oh, that money. The money from Allah's money tree. Those coins were given to me."

Outraged, the neighbor ranted and raved that Goha had stolen his money. A crowd collected in front of the two houses. "This must be settled by the magistrate." said one of the men.

"Yes, but how can I go to town to see the magistrate. My donkey is lame . . ." said Goha.

"Don't worry," said the neighbor. I will lend you one of my horses."

"But what about a coat. I have only a thin shirt and it will be cold riding to town."

"Don't fret", said the neighbor, "I will lend you a coat."

There was the Goha riding to town on a fine silver-grey horse wearing a wool coat. The magistrate came outside to greet Goha and his neighbor.

"This man has stolen 999 dinars from me," the neighbor complained.

"It is sad, is it not?" said Goha. "My esteemed neighbor has lost his mind."

"What do you mean?" asked the magistrate.

"Ask him whose coat this is," said Goha.

"Mine, of course" said the indignant neighbor.

"You see," said Goha. "How can it be his coat when I am wearing it? Now, ask him whose horse I am riding."

"Don't bother," said the neighbor. "The grey is mine. I raised him from a colt."

"You see what I mean," said Goha, "It must be my horse if I am riding him."

"I am beginning to understand," said the magistrate. "And the money?"

"Goha was praying to Allah for money and I threw it down to him from a tree," said the frustrated neighbor.

"Isn't that ridiculous", said Goha. "No one would waste Allah's time with such a ridiculous request and who would ever believe in a money tree?"

"I am sorry", said the judge, "but I must agree with Goha. Your story sounds preposterous. Case dismissed."

As you can imagine, the Goha's rich neighbor was very unhappy. However, Goha, although a trickster, was not a mean man. When the two men got home to their own homes Goha returned the coat. He also returned the horse and he handed his neighbor a money sack.

"Here is your money, my friend. Next time I sit under the money tree please make sure that you send down the correct amount."

Commercial Tricks

Magic suppliers have a unique aspect to their business. When they sell you tricks, they will not reveal how the trick is done unless you are serious about buying it. Usually, a magic-shop owner will demonstrate a trick. Then, after you have purchased the trick, the secret will be revealed.

If you have never explored a magic shop, or browsed through a magic-supplies catalog, you're apt to be fascinated by the sheer diversity of the tricks and effects available. When you visit a shop, ask to see some of the more popular commercially-produced tricks. You may want to buy a trick or two to use with your children, but be careful what you buy when first venturing into the world of magic. Many magicians end up with a closet full of unused magic tricks. It's important to make sure that the trick you choose will work for you. This is a list of some of the more popular tricks. Ask to see them demonstrated when you visit a magic shop.

Blendo: Three small colored silks change into a large silk, or flag.
Blooming Bouquet: Feather flowers bloom on a green stalk with a thumb tip. Used to produce or vanish small items.
Botania: A large pot of flowers appears from a silver tube.
Burning book: Open a book and flames leap out.
Color-changing silks: A colored silk changes color in a tube.
Coloring book: Black-and-white drawings turn into colored pictures.
Change bag: Used to produce or vanish small objects.
Dove pan: Used to produce small objects including real live doves.
Hippity hop rabbits: Rabbits change places.
Linking rings: Solid rings become joined by magic.
Nesting boxes: Used to produce a coin.
Spring flowers: Paper flowers are stored flat and spring into a bouquet.
20th century silks: A vanished silk reappears tied between two silks.
Wilting flower: A feather flower wilts at the will of the magician.

When you use magic in your book or story program, you might want to include these poems and word games:

Miraculous Mortimer

Miraculous Mortimer (Master Magician)
has sawn his assistant in two.
He can't recall how to reverse her condition—
has anyone got any glue?

by Jack Prelutsky

Magic

Magic is to count to ten
    before a car can cross the street
    and honk at you—or mornings when
    you can't let sidewalks touch your feet.

Magic is to jump the cracks—
    to touch whatever's made of blue—
    to cross your fingers with a friend
    who says the same thing you say, too.
                  by Myra Cohn Livingston

Magic Words

Every magician needs to have some magic words to make the magic work. Ancient magicians called this an incantation. Here are a few time-honored favorites:

    Presto
    Hocus Pocus
    Abracadabra

Challenge your children to think of some original magic words to use as personal incantations when they perform their magic tricks. Try these ideas to get them started:

    Peanut butter and jelly
    Lazy lemon lizard
    Purple pagodas

Quite a few word games and verbal jokes touch upon magical subjects, too. Use books and stories to introduce the following activities:

Rainbow Pencil: Read aloud or tell "The Magic Pencil" by Charlotte Hough in my *Celebrations* (H. W. Wilson, 1985). Then, show a pencil to your friends and say, "This magic pencil can write any color. What color would you like it to write?" If your friend says, "Red," take the pencil and write R-E-D. No matter what color is named, you write that word on a piece of paper. Hold up the paper, saying, "See, it really is a magic pencil and it can write any color."

Listen! Can You Follow Directions? When you tell or read "Watch Out!"

by Bruce Coville in this chapter challenge your group to follow these instructions exactly:

1. Touch a book inside and out without opening it.
(Ans.: Touch the book while inside, then go outside and touch it again.)

2. Leave the room with two legs and come back with six.
(Ans.: Bring a four-legged chair with you when you return.)

3. Jump across the room.
(Ans.: Walk across the room and give a jump.)

4. Stand two inches away from your friend without his being able to touch you.
(Ans.: Stand with the door between you and your friend.)

5. Put four chairs in a row. Take off your shoes and jump over them.
(Ans.: Jump over your shoes.)

6. Sing a song backward in the same length of time it takes to sing it forward.
(Ans.: Stand with your back to the group and sing.)

7. Ask a question that can never be answered with 'no'.
(Ans.: What does Y-E-S spell?)

Magic Resources

Organizations

The Society of American Magicians
P.O. Box 290068
St. Louis, MO 63129

The International Brotherhood of Magicians
103 North Main Street
Blufton, OH 48517-0089
    Both of these national magic clubs hold annual conventions and each publishes a journal (both are listed below).

The Society of Young Magicians
c/o John Apperson
2812 Idaho
Granite City, IL 62040

Magical Youths International
61551 Bremer Highway
Mishawaka, IN 46544
    These two clubs are primarily devoted to young magicians and both have news-letters directed to that audience.

Publications

Genii
P.O. Box 36068
Los Angeles, CA 90036
    This is from the owners of the Magic Castle in Los Angeles.

Good Life's Abracadabra
150 New Road
Bromsgrove, Worcestershire
B60 2LG England
    This is a British publication.

The Linking Ring
P.O. Box 89 Dept. G
Bluffton, OH 45817
    Published by the International Brotherhood of Magicians.

The Magic Manuscript
Louis Tannen
6 West 32 Street
New York, NY 10001-38008
    This firm also holds an annual convention.

Magigram
Supreme
64 High Street
Bideford
Devon EX 39 2AN
ENGLAND
    This is published by a magic supplier and includes explanations of many children's tricks.

MUM
11605 Victoria Drive
Oklahoma City, OK 73120
    Published by the Society of American Magicians.

The New Tops
Abbotts
Colon, Michigan 49040
   Published by Abbotts, an established magic supply firm that holds a convention annually.

Suppliers

Most of these mail-order suppliers charge a nominal fee for their catalogs.

Abbotts
Colon, Michigan 49040

Brad Burt's Magic Shop
4688 Convoy Street #109
San Diego, CA 92111

David Ginn
4387 St. Michaels Drive
Lilburn, GA 32047

Hank Lee
Box 789
Medford, MA 02155

Magic Hands
Postlach 1231 D 7033
Harrenburg
GERMANY

Rabbit in the Hat Ranch
1017 Crystal Ball Circle 2,
Casselberry, FL 32707-4536

Supreme Magic
64 High Street
Bideford
Devon EX39 2AN
ENGLAND

Louis Tannen
6 West 32nd Street
New York, NY 10001-38008

Selected Magic Books

For Adults

Many magic books are published privately and distributed through magic shops, so ask your local magic supplier for additional suggestions.

Adair, Ian. *Encyclopaedia of Children's Magic*. Art by Steve and Mavis Newby. Photos by Tim Cox. Supreme, 1991.
    Routines, promotion, patter, business advice for the children's magician. Adair is the general manager of the Supreme Magic Company (for which an address is provided in the above listings of resources).

Anderson, Gene and Frances Marshall. *Newspaper Magic*. Magic, 6082 North Lincoln Avenue, Chicago, IL 60625, 1988.
    A collection of tricks using newspapers compiled by masters of that art.

Behnke, Ed. Magic City Library of Magic. Magic City, Paramount, CA 90723, 1983–1990.
    Nineteen magic pamphlets on subjects including dove pans, change bags, cups and balls, and much more.

Eldin, Peter. *The Magic Handbook*. Simon, 1985.
    Excellent collection of magic tricks accompanied by color illustrations.

Fife, Bruce et al. *Creative Clowning*. Java, 1988.
    Ideas for using puppets, magic, juggling, and clown makeup.

Fulves, Karl. *Self-Working Paper Magic*. Dover, 1985.
    Magic tricks using money, cardboard, construction paper.

Ginn, David. *Kidbiz*. 4387 St. Michaels Drive, Lilburn, GA 30247.
    This is also the author of *Professional Magic for Children, Comedy Warmups*, and more of the very best magic books for adults interested in magic for children.

Hawkesworth, Eric. *Practical Lessons in Magic*. Supreme, 1984.
    This author also wrote *Conjuring* (Supreme, 1984), *A Magic Variety Show* (Supreme, 1984), and more. All are excellent short books with clear diagrams for close-up and stage magic.

Hooper, Edwin. *A Host of Surprises*. Art by Shawn Yee and Vanni Pulé. Photos by David Pusey. Edwin's Magic Arts (Bideford, Devon, England), 1990.
    The founder of Supreme Magic gives a clear explanation of commercial tricks as well as you-make-your-own apparatus and the effects they create.

Jeffreys, Michael. *The Enlightened Magician: The Best of the Best Powerful Magic*. Self-published, 1990 (available from: 1516 Purdue Avenue, #7, Los Angeles, California 90025).
    Interviews with Seigfried and Roy, Harry Blackstone, Jr., Billy McComb, and others.

Lamb, Geoffrey. *Illustrated Magic Dictionary*.
    Terms and names used by conjurors in stage magic.

Seabrooke, Terry. *Seabrooke's Book: Around the World with A Baking Tin.* Magical Publications, 572 Prospect Blvd., Pasadena, CA 91103.
Seabrooke is known for his fast-paced patter. This book has tricks, and also memories of his professional life.

Severn, Bill. *Magic with Paper.* McKay. 1962.
This book (appropriately published in paperback) is one of several by this author featuring easy-to-do magic using household props. Other titles are *Magic in Your Pockets* (McKay, 1968), *Magic Comedy* (McKay, 1968), and *Magic Across the Table* (McKay, 1972).

Sminkey, Donald C. *Handbook for the Magical Party Clown.* 2nd ed. Clown Capers, Bowie, MD, 1987.
A self-published book featuring marketing, magic, and balloon-sculpture ideas.

Smith, Samuel Patrick. *Big Laughs for Little People: How to Entertain Children with Comedy and Magic.* SPS Publications, P. O. Box 789, Tavares, Florida 32778, 1990.
Ideas for tricks and patter.

Zeikman, Robert. *Magic for Children—It's Magic.* Supreme, 1989.
Magic tricks and routines using commercial props.

For Children

Nonfiction

Bailey, Vanessa. *Rainy Days Card Tricks.* Watts, 1990.
Clear, easy-to-follow photographs show exactly how to perform simple card tricks.

Baker, James W. *New Year's Magic.* Art by George Overlie. (Lerner, 1989).
One of the Holiday Magic Book series from Lerner, which includes *Valentine Magic/Presidents' Day Magic* (1989), *April Fool's Magic* (1989), *Birthday Magic* (1988), *Halloween Magic* (1988), *Thanksgiving Magic* (1988), *Christmas Magic* (1988), *St. Patrick's Day Magic* (1990). These are excellent small-size books chock full of easy-to-do theme magic.

Barry, Sheila Anne. *Tricks and Stunts to Fool Your Friends.* Art by Doug Anderson. Sterling, 1984.
Tricks to do with a calculator, cards, and numbers.

Broekel, Roy and Laurence B. White, Jr. *Now You See It: Easy Magic for Beginners.* Art by Bill Morrison. Little, 1979.
Instructions for forty tricks.

Fleischman, Sid. *Mr. Mysterious's Secrets of Magic.* Art by Eric von Schmidt. Little, 1975.
Instructions for twenty-one tricks.

Marks, Burton and Rita. *Give Me a Magic Show.* Art by Don Madden. Lothrop, 1977.
Instructions for twenty-one tricks plus how-tos for making your own costume and wand.

Sheridan, Jeff. *Nothing's Impossible! Stunts to Entertain and Amaze*. Photos by Jim Moore. Lothrop, 1982.
Clear photographs and easy-to-follow text teach tricks and stunts in a picture-book format.

Stargl, Jean. *Paper Stories*. Davis S. Lake, Belmont, CA, 1984.
Short stories using paper cut-outs.

White, Laurence B., Jr. and Ray Broekel. *Math-a-Magic: Number Tricks for Magicians*. Whitman, 1990.
Magic with numbers.

_____. *Shazam! Simple Science Magic*. Art by Meyer Seltzer. Whitman, 1991.
Directions for simple effects based on scientific principles.

Wyler, Rose and Gerald Amers. *Magic Secrets*. Art by Arthur Dorros. Harper, rev. ed., 1990.
An I-Can-Read book featuring easy-to-do magic.

Fiction—Picture Books

Alexander, Sue. *World Famous Muriel and the Magic Mystery*. Art by Marla Frazee. Crowell, 1990.
World Famous Muriel solves the mystery of the Great Hokus Pokus . . . at the library. The perfect example of magic keyed to books.

Baker, Keith. *The Magic Fan*. Art by Keith Baker. Harcourt, 1989.
Yoshi finds a magic fan, but finds that there is magic in himself. The fan is artfully depicted with paper cut-outs.

Bohdal, Susi. *The Magic Honey Jar*. Tr. by Anthea Bell. Art by the author. North-South, 1987.
Julian dreams about a honey jar that has lost its magic power.

Delton, Judy. *Brimhall Turns to Magic*. Art by Bruce Degen. Lothrop, 1979.
An early-reader featuring stories about a bear turned magician.

Dubowski, Cathy East and Mark Dubowski. *Pretty Good Magic*. Art by authors. Random, 1987.
Presto shows the town of Forty Winks a pretty good magic trick.

Eliot, T. S. *Mr. Mistoffelees with Mungojerrie and Rumpelteaszer*. Art by Errol Le-Cain. Harcourt, 1991.
Mr. Mistoffelees uses his magical skills to confound his drawing room audiences.

Houghton, Eric. *Walter's Magic Wand*. Art by Denise Teasdale. Orchard, 1990.
Walter's magic wand works when he says the magic words.

Johnston, Tony. *The Badger and the Magic Fan*. Art by Tomie dePaola. Putnam, 1990.
A badger steals a magic fan from three tengu, the goblin children of Japan.

Kraus, Robert. *Phil the Ventriloquist*. Art by the author. Greenwillow, 1989.
Phil, a rabbit, can throw his voice into objects or people.

Lagercrantz, Rose and Samuel. *Is It Magic?* Tr. by Paul Norlen. Art by Eva Eriksson. R&S (Farrar), 1990.

Pete gets a magic wand, an old hat, and a special book that finally proves that "magic's something you must try your whole life through."

McPahil, David. *Pig Pig and the Magic Photo Album*. Dutton, 1986.
Pig Pig finds himself transported inside of photographs.

Fiction—Longer Books

Cresswell, Helen. *Time Out*. Art by Peter Elwell. Macmillan, 1990.
The use of a book of spells makes it possible for a family from 1887 to vacation in 1987.

Edmonds, I. G. *The Magic Dog*. Lodestar/Dutton, 1982.
Beauty, a dog, works with the Great Lafayette. She can make people appear and disappear with a wave of her wand.

Fleischman, Sid. *Mr. Mysterious and Company*. Art by Eric von Schmidt. Little, 1962.
A family of traveling magicians encounter adventure in the 1880s.

Jones, Diana Wynee. *The Lives of Christopher Chant*. Greenwillow, 1988.
Christopher trains to become the next Chrstomanci (head of magic control). Also of interest from this author and publisher are *Charmed Life* (1989) and *Witch Week* (1982).

McGowan, Tom. *The Magician's Apprentice*. Lodestar/Dutton, 1987.
Tigg, a pickpocket, is apprenticed to an enchanter.

Morrison, Dorothy Nafus. *Vanishing Act*. Atheneum, 1989.
Joanna is looking for the perfect rick to perform for the talent show.

Roberts, Willo Davis. *The Magic Book*. Atheneum, 1986.
Alex uses a book of magic spells to try and outwit the class bully.

Schwartz, Alvin. *Tales of Trickery*. Art by David Christina. Farrar, 1985.
Short trickster stories.

York, Carol Beach. *Rabbit Magic*. Art by Irene Trivas. Scholastic, 1991.
Ms. Lavender finally finds a trick she can perform at The Good Day Orphanage for Girls.

Magic Videos

Be a Magician. 60-minute video. Evansville, Ind.: Imagination Tree, 1985.
Featuring Martin Preston, this included magic presentations and a box of materials.

Flora, Brian. *The Balloon Video*. 55-minute video. Flora & Company, 1988.
Fifteen basic balloon sculptures are demonstrated.

Ginn, David. *It's About Time*. 55-minute video. 4387 St. Michaels Drive, Lilburn, Ga. 39247, 1990.
David Ginn's magic and comedy performances for schools are featured. A book is included with the video.

_____. *Live Kidbiz*. 60-minute video. 4387 St. Michaels Drive, Lilburn, Ga. 30247, 1988.
  In live performance and backstage, David Ginn shares his magical comedy routines.
  A book is included.

Starring the Universal Nut Bev Bergeron. The Magic Division of U.S. Toy Co. Masters of Excellence series. Vol. 3, 1988. Birthday party magic.

Chapter 14

Playing with Books

You've just given a book talk to a boy scout troop, or maybe you've just described the vacation reading program. Now you have a little extra time to play a game with the group, or enlist their help in a book project. The ideas in this section can be used to enliven a skills lesson, can be developed into a full program on book and word games, or can help you become better acquainted with a new group of children. Browse through this section and see what might be fun to try today.

Pen Pals

My friend Johanna Hurwitz and I have been exchanging letters on a regular basis, weekly, for over thirty years. In addition to being my pen pal, Johanna is a professional writer of popular children's books. But, long before her first book was published, I could have told you she was a writer. Her letters have always been full of "stories." She could take the simplest incident and turn it into an amusing anecdote and she freely acknowledges that her letter writing has been wonderful practise for writing books.

I encourage children to find pen pals while they're young. Children who regularly write letters or write in a journal develop strong writing skills. Although letter writing has suffered in this electronic age of telephones and fax machines, I have several other faithful correspondents, as well. I write to contacts in North Dakota, Mississippi, and England, each of whom I have met just once, and in our letters we exchange professional information, book recommendations, and news of family and friends. All three of these women have entirely different life styles than I do, which makes their letters, filled with details of their interests and activities, seem like serial novels.

As teachers and librarians working with children, we too often think of a pen-pal project in terms of foreign correspondents, seeing the letters as a way for our children to meet youngsters from other cultures. Initiating and maintaining that kind of project, though, can be quite ambitious, as most children find it difficult even to write letters to friends on vacation or family members who live at a distance. (My letters to my parents from camp are identical to those we received when our daughter was away at camp: "Dear Mom and Dad, How are you. I am fine. Love, Hilary.") Writing to a perfect stranger who lives in another country and whose English might not be proficient can be a real challenge. The first letter is easy, as we can tell about where we live and with whom, about our school and hobbies. The next letter gets harder, particularly since many teachers assume the correspondence will just naturally develop, and let children fend for themselves in writing letters. Many become discouraged and just stop writing. But, with support and encouragement over the rough spots, long-term pen-pal relationships can be wonderful. I recently met a woman who was making a trip to Japan to meet her pen pal of forty years standing for the first time. They had been corresponding since grade school. My friend Susan Guisti returned to the United States from several years working as a librarian in an International School in Rabat, Morocco. She has now initiated a pen-pal project with her American students and the Moroccan school. They exchange video tapes, which allows them to learn and strengthen speaking, writing, photography, and art skills while enjoying their project.

Among the many successful "domestic" pen-pal projects I've seen in my travels around the United States, two stand out: Mark Murphy, a first-grade teacher in Waldo, Ohio, has his children exchange letters with children in the same grade, but in another school in the same town. The students from the two schools are paired and they write letters each month. The teachers suggests topics for their letters, so that one month they may write about their favorite spot, another time about their families. At the end of the year, the two classes of first-graders meet for a half-day of festivities.

Susan Avery, a fourth-grade teacher in Kendallville, Indiana, has her children write to residents in a local nursing home. Each child is given the name of one of the elderly residents and the child initiates the correspondence. During the term, the class visits the nursing home and each child meets his or her pen pal. Susan reports that some children continue their friendships long after the end of the school year and, of course, the nursing home residents are delighted. The children learn about old age, sickness, and even death. This is an essay written by Amy, a student in that class:

Pen Pals

When we went to see our pen pals, they were so happy to see us. One was clapping her hands. My pen pal saved all of my letters and everything I gave her. We mean a lot to our pen pals. Most of the time they're lonely and sad.

Two of my pen pals died and I was sad. I learned that old people need us. Sometimes, they tell about the past and you learn about the "olden days." Sometimes, they tell about their family and friends. When we go we learn and have fun.

I hope we get to visit again. I learn something every time, but I wish I could stay longer. We never have enough time to visit with them.

When both of my grandpas died it was sad, but it's not the same with your pen pals. It's sad, too, but it doesn't feel the same. It just feels weird.

Mrs. Ruth Groh, my pen pal, died on Valentine's Day. That was really sad because Valentine's Day is supposed to be happy instead of sad. Now, I only have one pen pal, Mrs. Fern Pecci. I just wish we could visit again soon.

To Find a Pen Pal:

Although local nursing homes, boarding schools, and other residential facilities are always good sources for pen pals, the following organizations will also help find pen pals for your students. Be aware that some of these groups have a minimum age limit for members or charge a nominal fee for processing requests. For more information on their policies, write to these addresses:

Caring for Children
International Pen Pals
220 Montgomery Street
San Francisco, CA 94104

Kids Art and Mail Project
PO Box 274
Mount Shasta, CA 96067

League of Friendship
PO Box 509
Mount Vernon, OH 43050

Letters for Peace
238 Autumn Ridge Road
Fairfield, CT 06432

World Pen Pals
1690 Como Avenue
St. Paul, MN 55108

Friends Forever Pen-Pal Club
Box 20103 Park West P.O.
New York, NY 10025

International Pen Pals
P.O. Box 6283
Huntington Beach, CA 92615

Student Letter Exchange
Waswca, MN 56093

Postcards

Postcards are a convenient, intriguing way of introducing children to books and writing projects, as well as making them more aware of history. Before the advent of cameras, postcards recorded events and details of town life.

When I lived in France, I joined other collectors at trade shows devoted to pre-World War I postcards. Many people were looking for cards depicting villages where they or their parents grew up. I was searching for pictures of Chantilly, the town in which we were then living. I was amazed to discover how many views there were of this town and how little it had changed in eighty years. The schools of Chantilly duplicated the cards for the children and held a contest to find the student who could identify the most buildings from the pictures on the old cards. On returning to Huntington Beach, California, from France I discovered that the local historical society had just published old postcards of the town in a calendar. Most of those buildings, though, have long since been demolished.

Now, when I travel, I look for postcards. Recently, on visits to Kansas and Maryland, I discovered that both areas have avid postcard collectors. Maybe your town has a collection of such old picture postcards housed in the town hall, library, or local museum.

To build a postcard collection with your children, you can request contributions of souvenir cards from your friends and your children's families, as well as writing a letter to the editor of your local newspaper urging residents of the town to send your reading group cards showing people and places.

Your students can also write letters to newspapers and chambers of commerce in other states to request postcards showing their local landmarks and sights. You may find your class inundated with cards to read and puzzle over. Postcards from strangers also provide great practice in deciphering quirky handwriting (when your group is involved in this project, share *Muggie Maggie* by Beverly Cleary, Morrow, 1990). Some other ways to use postcard collections creatively are:

Puzzles

Print the author and title of a book on the back of a picture postcard and add a description of the book in the section meant for the message. Cut the postcard into puzzle pieces and put them into an envelope, giving each child an envelope to work on. When the children have recreated their pictures, they can each flip their card over for a good read on the other side.

Story Starters

Give each child a postcard with questions and imagination-joggers on the back, such as: "This picture is an illustration for the story you will now write. Does it show the beginning, middle, or end of your story? Who are the characters? Is there any dialogue in your story? When your story is finished, give it a title." Then, you can exhibit the finished stories with their illustrations.

Research

Give each child a picture postcard and send the children to the reference collection to find out all they can, in a given time period, about the places, people or objects on the card.

Design a Postcard

Children can create their own postcards by drawing pictures to illustrate stories they've enjoyed reading or stories they've written themselves on 3½ by 5-inch pieces of posterboard. Then, they can send the cards to friends with suggestions of a good book to read or keep the card as a bookmark.

Plant a Card

Once the children have drawn pictures to accompany their favorite books and stories, have them write on the message side of the cards, "This is a picture I drew of my favorite book. Please write and tell me your favorite book." Leave a space for a rely, stamp each card and address it to your school or library. You or your children can leave them in phone booths, school buses, or on a park bench. See how long it takes for someone to return one with a good book idea.

Exhibit

Use picture postcards from all over the world along the border of a bulletin board. Attach strings or ribbons leading from each card to a map of the world in the center of the board, securing the other end of the string to the part of the world from which each card comes.

Stamps

Design a stamp. Children can draw pictures of illustrators, authors, or books they would like to see commemorated on a stamp. Send your group's best designs to the U.S. Postal Service's Citizens' Stamp Advisory Committee, 475 L'Enfant Plaza SW, Washington, D.C. 20260–6700. One of my own pen pals, an art teacher from Russia, sent me four stamps designed by her students that are now used in the Soviet Union. Maybe your children's art work or ideas will end up on a stamp.

Activities

Collect at least one postage stamp for each child in your group. Hobby shops and stamp shops are a good source of inexpensive canceled U.S. or foreign stamps. Another way of collecting stamps is simply to ask parents to save interesting commemorative stamps they receive in the mail.

1. Each child chooses a stamp at random (toss them in a bag, hat, or box held just above the child's eye level). The objective of this game is for each child to use the library's resources to find out as much as possible about the person, place, or event depicted on the stamp. You can help the children to find any poems that are appropriate to the themes of their stamps. Finally, the stamps can be used to illustrate the research materials the children have assembled.

2. Use stamps to make mosaics. Make an outline drawing and use the stamps to fill in the picture.

3. Use stamps to cover boxes, folders, lampshades, or wastebaskets.

4. Ask a representative from your local post office, or an avid collector, to speak to your students about stamp collecting.

Souvenirs

This is another reminder that stamps make great, easy souvenirs to accompany a poetry program.

Conversations with Book Characters

This game can be played with any number of players. It works best when everyone in the group has read several of the same books.

HOW TO:

Choose two players who leave the room. While gone, they decide which two book characters from a single book they will represent when they return. The book character-players return and have a conversation with each other about elements of their story. For example, one character might ask the other for ideas that will save him from being made into bacon. The second player's character might suggest spinning a web to help him. If one of the group of observers thinks they've guessed the characters' identities, they do not call out the answer, but join in the conversation as another character in that book, such as Fern from *Charlotte's Web* in the example above.

Book Title Telegrams

The game of telegrams was played when our mothers were all children. Here's an update using silly book titles. Everyone will enjoy this game and it can be played for as long as you like, since the game keeps changing with each set of letters, so it stays lively.

YOU NEED: Paper and pencil

HOW TO: Participants call out one letter each. (Decide in advance how many letters you will use. Since each letter corresponds to a word in the title, the more letters you use, the more challenging the game becomes.) Write the letters at the top of the page and set a time limit. Each player must create a book title in which the words of the title fit the anagram letters.

Example: Susie Triceratop *at the* Rodeo

Read all the titles aloud and vote for the most imaginative—or plausible.

Follow Up: You might suggest that the group write a collaborative story based on the winning title.

Book Title Memory Game

This is a memory game in which players sit in a circle. The leader begins by reading the first item on a list of book titles. Then, the player to her right repeats that item. If she gets it exactly correct, the leader reads item two, and the same player to her right repeats the first and second titles. The leader keeps adding one new title to the list, and the same player continues her turn as long as she can repeat the list from the beginning, giving all titles correctly and in order. When she makes a mistake, the next player starts from the beginning with the first title, building his list by repeating them in proper sequence. The winner of the game is the first person to repeat all titles perfectly. Start with a list of ten and then see how many more your group can remember.

You can try the game using these titles, or pick some of your group's favorites:

1. If You Give a Mouse a Cookie
2. If You Give a Mouse a Cookie, I'm in Charge of Celebrations
3. If You Give a Mouse a Cookie, I'm in Charge of Celebrations, Mufaro's Beautiful Daughters
4. If You Give a Mouse a Cookie, I'm in Charge of Celebrations, Mufaro's Beautiful Daughters, The Boy of the Three-Year Nap

Well, you get the idea. When you create your list using book titles for middle to upper grades, aim for amusing and unexpected sequences of titles and titles of varying lengths (more of a challenge to the memory than consistently long or short ones). Display the books for the children to browse through and read, after they play the game.

You can play the Memory Game using this poem by Eve Merriam, and after each verse the group can call in unison:

> What else did you see?
> Tell, tell, tell

Have your students create their own list of the moving van's contents.

Frying Pan in the Moving Van

A new family's coming to live next door to me
I looked in the moving van to see what I could see.
> What did you see?
> Tell, tell, tell.

Well,
I saw a frying pan in the moving van.
> What else did you see?
> Tell, tell, tell.

Well,
I saw a rocking chair and a stuffed teddy bear
and a frying pan in the moving van.
> What else did you see?
> Tell, tell, tell.

Well,
I saw a rug for the floor and a boat with an oar
and a rocking chair and a stuffed teddy bear
and a frying pan in the moving van.
> What else did you see?
> Tell, tell, tell.

Well, I saw a leather boot and a basket of fruit
and a rug for the floor and a boat with an oar
and a rocking chair and a stuffed teddy bear
and a frying pan in the moving van.
> What else did you see?
> Tell, tell, tell.

Well, I saw a TV set and a Ping-Pong net
and a leather boot and a basket of fruit
and a rug for the floor and a boat with an oar
and a rocking chair and a stuffed teddy bear
and a frying pan in the moving van.
> What else did you see?
> Tell, tell, tell.

Well, I saw a steamer trunk and a double-decker bunk and a TV set and a
    Ping-Pong net
and a leather boot and a basket of fruit
and a rug for the floor and a boat with an oar
and a rocking chair and a stuffed teddy bear
and a frying pan in the moving van.
> What else did you see?
> Tell, tell, tell.

Well, I saw a lamp with a shade and a jug of lemonade
and a steamer trunk and a double-decker bunk
and a TV set and a Ping-Pong net
and a leather boot and a basket of fruit
and a rug for the floor and a boat with an oar
and a rocking chair and a stuffed teddy bear
and a frying pan in the moving van.
> What else did you see?
> Tell, tell, tell.

Well, since you ask it:
I saw a wicker basket
and a violin and a rolling pin and vegetable bin
and a lamp with a shade and a jug of lemonade
   and a garden spade
and a steamer trunk and a double-decker bunk
   and a Chinese model junk
and a TV set and a Ping-Pong net
   and a framed silhouette
and a leather boot and a basket of fruit
   and a baseball suit
and a rug for the floor and a boat with an oar
   and a knob for a door
and a rocking chair and a stuffed teddy bear
   and plastic dinnerware
and an electric fan and a bent tin can
   and a frying pan and
THAT'S ALL I SAW IN THE MOVING VAN.

by Eve Merriam

Books/Activities Boxes

I've been traveling for my work during much of my daughter's lifetime. She has always been a good sport about my leaving. In fact, I sometimes thought she was just a bit too cavalier. "Bye, Mom," she would say with the greatest of glee. I would then wonder what Dad or the babysitter did while I was away that made it such a joyous occasion when I left.

Before leaving, I would try to organize the schedule of who-was-to-drive-Hilary-where-for-what, but I never left homemade goodies in the freezer or made sure that she had a supply of clean socks to last until I returned (in fact, I trained Hilary very early to consider socks unfashionable, so that I wouldn't have to wash and sort them). What I did worry about was who would keep her supplied with wonderful stories to hear and books to read in my absence. Rather than take a chance that Hilary would sit mesmerized in front of the TV for hours with her brain turning to mush, I'd prepare a stockpile of books to have read to her when she was very small, and later, some selections I thought she'd enjoy reading on her own. OK, so she didn't always agree with my selections or take my advice, but usually she'd eventually come to me and say, "Mom, do you remember how you said last month that I should read *Bridge to Teribithia* and I didn't. Well, I read it this week. You were right. . . ." (What more could a mother ask?)

As I wandered through airport gift shops during my trips (who buys those breakable grinning clowns, anyway), and the various shops in hotel lobbies, I would purchase an interesting postcard here, a puzzle or game there. If I found something on sale, I'd put it away in the "present closet" for that day when I'd need a gift. That someday-gift developed into the Mom's-Away Treasure Box. Though I never had time to do the laundry, somehow I always found time to wrap little individual gifts and always there were books among them—some that we owned, some that we borrowed from the library—to be opened every day of every week.

Another approach to this idea is the Home Sick Box. When I was kid, if

you were sick on a school day, you got to stay and home and be treated like a princess. Your mother would bring you a coloring book and a new box of crayons. You listened avidly to the radio soap operas and worried about the plights of Stella Dallas and Lorenzo Jones. Those are still pleasant memories for me (even if I did have the mumps).

Today, your mother might be working outside the home, and with divorce and remarriage a fact of life for so many families, she may even live in another town. A babysitter may be the one to stay home with you, or the sitter or a parent may just check in by telephone several times during the day. Lorenzo Jones has disappeared from your radio dial to be replaced by daytime television. No one brings you a coloring book, but school work that you missed is sent home with your big brother. Although no teacher wants a child to fall behind in her lessons, doesn't it seem that a child who's too sick to attend school may not be up to doing pages 36 through 39 in her arithmetic book? Instead of making the dreariness of being sick even worse, why not send home a surprise that's sure to cheer, entertain, and expand a child's imagination? Make up a Take Home Sick Box to send home instead of a "make up assignment."

The items below are good basics for stocking the Home Sick Box, and you can adapt these ideas to create a Birthday Box, Vacation Box, or to suggest to parents for the Mom's-Away Box mentioned above or for a Babysitter's Box.

Hint: Keep in mind that, as items may not be returned, you should include only those materials you wouldn't mind losing from your classroom, library, or media center.

Books: This one is the *must,* as something wonderful to read can help take a child's mind off how dreadful she feels. Paperbacks might be the best choice, but try to select a variety of fiction, non-fiction, and poetry titles that are appropriate for the child's grade level. When choosing the just-right books, consider what reading material is most appealing to you when you're not feeling very alert or energetic.

Blank Book: For today's busy children, a sick day can be the perfect time to discover the pleasure of writing in a journal or diary. A bound book with a pretty cloth cover is the most attractive choice and can be purchased at a stationery or book store. However, a notebook, a few pieces of copy or drawing paper, or even a packet of plain paper will all serve the purpose of providing the child with the means for writing down her thoughts. Treetop Publishing (220 Virginia Street, Racine, Wisconsin 53405) produces bound blank books for children containing just a few pages.

Crayons, Pencils, Pens: Including a pen for writing, a pencil with a good eraser for sketching or drawing, and as many crayons as possible, but at least

the primary colors (red, yellow, blue) and black will encourage a child to be creative and to experiment with some simple color mixing.

Pictures: Start collecting a stash of pictures to add to your Take Home Boxes. Greeting cards, stickers, postcards, photographs, pictures from magazines or newspapers can all be used to make collages or as story-starters.

Puppets: Whether you choose paper finger puppets, simple cloth puppets, or more sophisticated hand puppets, the child can discover a new friend as she makes up dialogue and enjoys the puppet's company.

Stationary: Writing paper, envelopes, and stamps are handy for letters to relatives, the school friend who moved to another town, or for the child who must be out of school for several days and wants to send a message back to her classmates.

Rubber stamps: These are widely available from stationers, in toy shops, and by mail order. One source, Stamper's Delight, 80 Lovering Rd., North Hampton, N.H. 03862, represents the products of eleven different stamp companies, so their selection is enormous.

If you wish, you can duplicate the following directions to enclose with your box of goodies to give it a personal touch or modify it to fit the stash of items

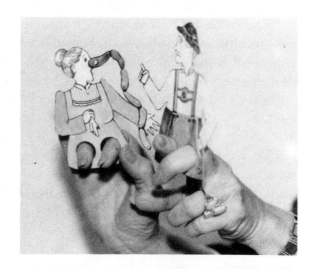

you've collected to be used (or distributed to parents who like this idea for suggested use) as a Birthday Box, Vacation Box, Babysitter's After-School Box, or the When-Mom's-Away Box mentioned above.

Surprise! Surprise!

Here's something to keep you company while you're home

Books: Look. Here are some books that were chosen just for you. After you have finished reading, write the title and author of the book you just read, along with the date you read and where you were at the time. Now, choose your favorite quote and carefully copy it into your new blank book. Make some notes concerning your favorite character in the blank book, too. Then, rate the book according to this scale:

10 points—an outstanding read

5 points—a good read

1 point—a boring book

If you would like to tell a particular friend about this book, jot that reminder down, too, noting the name of the person you'd like to share the book with in your journal.

Blank Book: Hello. I am your new journal. You can use me to write a story, ask a riddle, tell a joke, copy a favorite poem from a book—or write your own poem in me. You can tell me your secret thoughts and your observations and use me as a reading journal to record your reactions to the books you read.

Puppets: Here is a new friend. Who is it? It it a boy or a girl? Give your puppet a name. Have a conversation with the puppet and ask it questions: "What do you like to read?" "What are your favorite TV shows?" "What is your favorite season?" Now, have your puppet answer the questions in his or her own puppet voice. Act out the dialogue for a parent or babysitter.

Stationery, Envelope, Stamps: I am your writing kit. Use me to send a letter to your teacher or classmates, write to your favorite bookseller, or send a fan letter to your library.

Language Arts Quiz

These words graphs and word games are fun mind-joggers to get children thinking about the words they use. Try one or several of the word-pictures during a book break, then let your group make up some of their own.

1. | SAND |

2. <u>MAN</u>
    BOARD

3. <u>STAND</u>
    I

4. R|E|A|D|I|N|G

5. <u>WEAR</u>
    UNDER

6. CYCLE
    CYCLE
    CYCLE

7. R
    ROAD
    A
    D

8. T
    O
    W
    N

9. <u>MIND</u>
    MATTER

10. LE VEL

11. <u>O</u>
    M.D.
    PH.D
    D.D.D.

12. <u>KNEE</u>
    LIGHT

13. <u>i i   i i</u>
    oo   oo

14. CHAIR

15. DICE
    DICE

16. <u>GROUND</u>
    FEET
    FEET
    FEET
    FEET
    FEET
    FEET

17. T
    O
    U
    C
    H

18. DEATH/LIFE

19. ECNALG

20. <u>BELT</u>
    HITTING

21. HEAD
    LO   VE
    HEELS

22. ⌐ Z   Ƹ ∀ ⌐ ⊦

23. SYMPHON

24. NIGHT FLY

25. OOO CIRCUS

1. Sandbox
2. Man overboard
3. I understand
4. Reading between the lines
5. Long underwear
6. Tricycle
7. Crossroads
8. Downtown
9. Mind over matter
10. Split level
11. 3° below zero
12. Neon light
13. Circles under the eyes
14. High chair
15. Paradice
16. Six feet under ground
17. Touch down
18. Life after death
19. Backward glance
20. Hitting below the belt
21. Head over heels in love
22. Lying in wait
23. Unfinished symphony
24. Fly by night
25. 3 ring circus

Folktale Match-up

Duplicate the list of titles that follow, or compile your own list. Cut the titles apart at the spaces between words and put the slips into a box. Each player chooses a slip from the box and finds the person who has the other half of the title.

Example: **BEAUTY   AND THE BEAST**

This can also be played as a memory game. Toss the slips in a bag or hat and put all the slips face down on a table, or the floor. Players turn two slips face up. If they make a match, the two are removed. If they don't match they are turned face down once again. The next player turns one slip up. If she remembers where the matching name is she can turn that one up and make a match. The player with the most match-ups is the winner.

Hint: (for you to share aloud with your children): If you do not recognize these tales—go to the library and take out a collection of fairy tales. Sit down, READ and enjoy—and now you can play this game.

Folktale/Fairy Tale List

THE WOLF   AND THE THREE LITTLE PIGS
BEAUTY   AND THE BEAST
JACK   AND THE BEANSTALK
PUSS   IN BOOTS
HANSEL   AND GRETEL
THE BOY   WHO CRIED WOLF
SNOW   WHITE
THE PRINCESS   AND THE PEA
GOLDILOCKS   AND THE THREE BEARS
THE CAT   AND THE MOUSE
HENNY   PENNY
THE FROG   PRINCE
THE FISHERMAN   AND HIS WIFE
THE ELVES   AND THE SHOEMAKER
THE GINGERBREAD   BOY
THE WOLF   AND THE SEVEN LITTLE KIDS
LITTLE RED   RIDING HOOD
THE THREE BILLY   GOATS GRUFF
MOLLIE   WHUPPIE
THE GOLDEN   GOOSE
THE LITTLE   RED HEN
THE BREMEN TOWN   MUSICIANS
THE SUN   AND THE WIND
THE UGLY   DUCKLING

Personality Plus

   Make sure that your group knows the meaning of the words in the Personality Word List below before you start this activity. Cut the words apart and put them in a box. Have each person select a word from the box and assume that personality trait in a discussion. At the end of the time you have specified, have the participants guess what characteristic each member of the group was portraying. This game works well with five to eight people, affording each a chance to talk and "get into character."

While you can use any discussion question, I often choose to have children do this exercise after I have shared a picture book. I ask them to give their reasons (while expressing their allotted personality traits) why they would or would not recommend that the library purchase that book.

Personality Word List

ARGUMENTATIVE
POMPOUS
APOLOGETIC
SLEEPY
ANGRY
SHY
AGREEABLE
PICKY
SEXY
PESSIMISTIC
OPPORTUNISTIC
HUMBLE

MOROSE
IMPERTINENT
CONSOLING
DOMINEERING
AGGRESSIVE
EXUBERANT
EXULTANT
SEXIST
RECKLESS
SUSPICIOUS
MOTHERLY
GREEDY

NERVOUS
SLY
SCHOLARLY
DICTATORIAL
SLAVISH
DISORDERLY
OBSTREPEROUS
BORED
DECISIVE
EFFERVESCENT
RUDE
LAZY

SELF-INDULGENT
OBSEQUIOUS
COMBATANT
SOPHISTICATED
MACHO
SERVILE
PRECOCIOUS
FLIRTATIOUS
HAUGHTY

Spotting License Plates for Fun

Interpret these cryptic plates and then create clever messages with your group. (No 'answers' are supplied here; challenge the children to see how many they can figure out.)

GR8F1

KTZMEAU

LV2BGRK

RTZ BDWAY

DOINGRT

SONIQBM

BBQTOGO

ISKISNW

LYFSRAD

PP DOC (urologist)

IMFIRED

I LUV MNM

BATERUP

FACENME

4TUN8

2DM BIG

DOC 2B

PRFXSHN

HIOFFCR

SPOKN4

ZGR81

NJYNLF

DUUNOME

GN FISHN

NO WIFE

GTO 4U2C

ENGLLDY

MPECIBL

BALD P8

LVDOGYS

WRHVFN

SFTBLFN

IRDBKS

10SNE1

OOPS

RAG 4 FUN (on a VW convertible)

24HR FUN (on a sports car)

IHEPUC (optometrist)

CHOCKIS

RADPONY (on a Mustang)

1MB4MOI (on a mercedes)

MCDNIFE (on surgeon's car)

UCMEICU

GOSOCKS (Massachusetts sports fan)

SUPR DOC

OBAYB

IMZ14U

EZ4ME

2BRNT2B

SWMORDI (life guard)

KYT FLYR

CYCLNUT

Nonverbal Languages

Words are wonderful, but there are many other "languages" used for communication, including sign language, whistles, braille, fan language, and pictures. Share some of these forms of nonverbal communication with your children.

Sign Language

American Sign Language, used by the deaf, is based largely on finger spelling. Children learn this alphabet quickly and enjoy speaking in a "secret" language with special friends.

Braille

This alphabet was developed for use by the blind by a young blind boy in France, Louis Braille. Children enjoy inventing ways to create the raised letters. They can write full sentences and send messages using the sense of touch.

Train Whistles

Trainmen use their whistles to communicate. Pretend that you are a train "talking" to people watching you from trackside. . . . Here's how you'd sound and what it means:

Two long blasts, one short, one long
   To cars and people, STOP! The train is approaching a street crossing.
One long blast
   The train is coming to a station or a rail crossing.
Three short blasts (while train is standing)
   The train is about to back up.

You'll find lots more information in Helen Roney Sattler's *Train Whistles* (Lothrop, 1985).

Cartoons to Rate Your Reading

These expressive cartoon faces are easy for you or the children to use to visually describe reactions to a book or the characters in books or stories they read. You might suggest to the children that the cartoons are a good "shorthand" language for expressing their feelings in their journals or diaries, too.
   Start by tracing the figures, then practise drawing and interpreting them yourself. These examples are based on drawings from *Blackboard Cartooning for Teachers* by Eric Teitelbaum. The book and a video course are available from WE Productions, 40 Arboles, Irvine, CA 92715.

Tired   surprised   Worried   conceit

Reading Time

While the point of reading isn't how much you can read, but how much you learn from and enjoy what you do read, it can be useful to know how long a particular amount of reading will take, so that you know how much reading material you'll want to tote to the beach for the day or on vacation for a week. People like my daughter or my friend Bev, who read everything very quickly, aren't always the lucky ones: they just need to lug twice as many books everywhere they go! The following exercise is from *This Book Is About Time* by Marlilyn Burns

How Long Does It Take You to Read a Word?

Before you read the next section, get a clock or watch with a second hand so you can time yourself. There are three hundred words in the next section, not counting the title. Read it at your normal reading speed. Time when you start and when you finish. Then figure how many seconds it took you to read it. Divide three hundred by the number of seconds you took. That will tell you how many words you read in one second. Then you can figure how long it takes you to read one word.

The Tale of the Telephone Operator

There was a woman who was the only telephone operator in a small town. She did most of the work that is done automatically today. This was before there were any telephone talking clocks and when the sun was the chief timekeeper. So she did that job along with everything else. But it wasn't a big part of her work. Hardly anyone ever called her to check the time, except for one man. He'd phone late in the morning and ask this telephone operator for the time. She'd check her watch and tell him what the time was. This happened every day she worked.

Finally the woman was about to retire. She had been the telephone operator in this town for about thirty years. The time had come for her to quit. On her last day of work, the man called as usual. She felt she owed it to him to say goodbye. Besides that, she had been curious for a while about his daily call. So when he called, she told him the time as she always did. "But before you hang up," she also said, "I'd like to tell you that this is my last day on the job. And I've been wondering about something all these years that I've been here. How come you call every day at the same time, just before lunch, and ask me what time it is?"

He answered her with a question. "Do you know that every day the noon whistle gets sounded over at the firehouse?"

"Yes," she said. Everyone in town could hear the noon whistle.

"That's my job," he went on, "and I call you to check the time so I know when it's noon."

"Oh, dear," she said, "I've been setting my watch by that noon whistle all these years."

Favorite Book Exhibit

Mary Julien of Monterey, California, uses the National Library symbol to promote books. She asks the children to decorate the design with features, clothing, and background of their choice and to add the title of their favorite book. The result: a hallway lined with book suggestions for readers passing by. Here are some examples of their embellishments.

Book Art

When I worked as a children's librarian in public libraries and in school libraries, I seemed to always be desperately searching for attractive, book-related materials to hang on exhibit boards and to give to children. Now, I find I always need a supply of art to brighten seminar handouts and to distribute during school visits. The posters, book marks, badges, and bracelets drawn here can be reproduced in whatever size you need for your purpose and displayed or given as souvenirs to children who visit your library or have read a designated number of books. They also make good presents for all of the children you know and can be added to assignments, book lists or anywhere a touch of whimsy might help. When pressed for time, duplicate them directly from the book and post or distribute. When you have a bit more time (or the help of your class or group), mount them on poster boards and color as you wish.

TUNE INTO BOOKS

CELEBRATE WITH BOOKS

LOVE, LITERATURE

MAKE FRIENDS WITH BOOKS

LOOK! BOOKS

Putting It All Together

I first started "theming" when I moved from one location to another. As I unpacked my junk—I mean, educational materials—I tried to organize my materials into some kind of reasonable order. In the middle of the unpacking, I thought maybe I should arrange things by subject or theme. I put everything that dealt with holidays on one shelf, everything that had something to do with poetry on another. Then, I broke these large topics into genres, making little piles of stories, exhibits, poems, and activities for a variety of subjects. Without even planning to, I ended up with a complete program on dogs, one for Christmas, and another for Valentine's Day. You probably will find that you also have been collecting materials in subject areas that interest you and that children seem to enjoy each year. Even if you are a beginner at the Books-and-Children-Game, you may find that you have a box of miniature horses from your own horse-phase days or other treasures just waiting to contribute to—or inspire—a theme program.

In fact, I think the best way of putting together a program is to have it all just happen. Sometimes when you are looking for books and projects to fit into a particular theme program you might be tempted to accept mediocre materials in order to get the show on the road.

This can happen very easily when you are trying to accommodate a teacher or administrator who wants a program to tie into a unit in the curriculum. You may trap yourself by choosing a subject, perhaps a holiday, for a program commitment and then find that there just isn't enough good material available for a full-blown presentation. My favorite way of getting out of such a predicament is to include elements that may not have anything to do with the subject at hand, but introducing it so that it fits into the theme. For

instance, suppose that you have been asked to give a program on *Randolph the Rancher*. You are unable to meet the demand with the resources that you have or perhaps you are unhappy with the quality of the materials you've found. However, you do have a fantastic story about a cow or a cat. Why can't you simply say, "I'd like to tell you a story that I think Randolph the Rancher would have liked." The important thing is to introduce children to literature of distinction.

An easy way to put together a theme program is to make an outline of all the possible components and then fill in the blanks. Below are some of the elements you might consider when designing any program. Add components of your own, delete those that don't fit for you now, and fill in the blanks with materials from your own library.

Program Outline

Title: Your title should sound interesting, but also give participants at least a hint of what to expect.

Stories: Gather together all the stories that fit into the theme and then choose those that will suit the theme and your audience best. Depending on the age range your group encompasses, include a story for younger children, one for older children, and a participation story that everyone will enjoy. The literature can be presented as read alouds, reader's theater, or told in the traditional storytelling manner or with props. Don't forget to look at the nonfiction books to give balance to the program.

Poems. After reading a number of poems from a variety of anthologies, mix and match poems of different types and moods that are related to your theme. Use these throughout the program: to introduce the story, as transitional material between stories and to end the program.

Facts: Reproduce interesting facts and bits of trivia on your subject on handouts or to use as introductory material to lead in to the program.

Creative Writing: Is there a book, poem, story or fact that will serve as a springboard to a writing activity?

Creative Drama: You may want to direct a skit that fits into the theme.

Reader's Theater: Adapting a story or book excerpt using the reader's theater format is another way of presenting material, so that your program is varied and well-paced. Designating reader's theater as a separate entry on your program-option list will remind you that this is a possibility.

Activity: An activity, such as a word game, can involve everyone and become a major part of the program.

Craft: If you have the time, facilities, and a small enough group you can make something to take home.

Souvenir: Find something appropriate to give away as a memory of the program.

Exhibit/Bulletin Board: These ideas can be developed separately or combined with your other program elements to announce the event or serve as background and support materials to the program. Always display books that appear on the booklist. Artifacts also make a good exhibit. For instance, for a survival program, exhibit mountain-climbing equipment.

Book List: Collect books that feature the subject of the program and list them to post or duplicate to give the audience suggestions for further reading.

Afterword

And now . . . YOU read—just for the fun of It

Shh. Don't tell Judith, my editor, that I put this list here at the end of the book. I don't think she would approve. She'd probably say, "What does that have to do with children's reading? Where are the publishers and publication dates? What kind of bibliographic style is that? No."

But, now that you've read through this whole book and tried some of the ideas, I think you deserve some time to just sit in the bathtub and enjoy reading for yourself.

Actually, this list is the result of a letter I received last week. Marie Arnold wrote to ask for an update of a list I used to give out at my workshops. It was titled "Junk Reading: What to Read on an Airplane." I stopped distributing that list because at the end of the list I had asked for suggested additions to it, and I got very few responses to that request. However, with her letter Marie contributed her own list, and so this one is for Marie . . . and for you. I've included some titles from the earlier list that I find I still recommend heartily to my houseguests and I've added lots of new favorites.

First, though, please just skip this page if you find your tastes and mine don't agree. I *do* read "throw-away books" (books that you wouldn't pack up and move to your next house), as well as really good literature. My daughter says disdainfully, "How can you read that trash?" My husband, who will read everything, even a "women's book" doesn't comment. He just keeps reading—picking the books up as soon as I put them down.

At home, I usually confine my reading to the thousands of children's books that are published each year and with which I struggle to keep abreast.

But, on the road . . . I like Ken Follett, Dick Francis, Charlotte MacLeod, Wilbur Smith. I also reread Barbara Pym, Nevil Shute, Rumer Godden, and Thackery's *Vanity Fair*. My nonfiction tastes usually focus on the studies of the cultures and societies of countries where I've traveled for work or would like to visit.

Here are some books to pick up at the airport kiosk or from the library before a trip or vacation. You'll probably just grab them on impulse when you see them, so no, you don't need the publisher's name or the date of publication and they're in the order that they occurred to me, not arranged alphabetically (that's just in case Judith does peek at this page sometime). So, READ and have fun!

What to Read on an Airplane

Share of Honor by Ralph Graves.
> Big blockbuster, featuring expatriates in the Philippines in World War II.

A Green Journey and *Simon's Night* by Jon Hassler.
> Both are absolutely wonderful. In the first, a retired teacher travels to Ireland and meets Romance. In the second, Simon puts himself into a rest home.

The Ginger Tree by Oswald Wynd.
> Early twentieth-century Japan is the setting for the romance of a young girl from Scotland. An A+ read.

Getting It Right by Elizabeth Jane Howard.
> An innocent hairdresser meets two ladies and . . .

Walking Across Egypt by Clyde Edgerton.
> Impossible to describe, but lots of good food and interesting characters fill this one. An A read.

Crossing to Safety by Wallace Stegner.
> The story of a friendship between two couples. This is not junk, but rather one of the best books I've ever read. It makes the junk seem really junky. A+++

Cold Sassy Tree by Olive Ann Burns.
> Her only book, this has a memorable cast of characters. It focuses on "an old man growing young, a young man growing up."

The Empty House by Rosamunde Pilcher.
> By the author of *The Shellseekers*, which I loved, this short novel makes you feel good. Her work seems uneven at times, but I really liked this romantic novel of a lost love found.

Reasonable Doubt by Philip Friedman.
> A law mystery. My husband loved it; I like it, too.

Grass Roots by Stuart Woods.
> Sex, politics, crime, and a hero to admire—they're all here.

The Charm School by Nelson DeMille.
   A spy fantasy set in Russia.

Thus Was Adonis Murdered by Sarah Caldwell.
   A charming and sophisticated mystery set in Venice.

Hot Siberian by Gerald A. Browne.
   Two beautiful people: a Russian gem dealer and a British beauty in an amusing story. Fun.

A Knight in Shining Armor by Jude Deveraux.
   A "women's" book, but amusing. An American tourist meets a "knight in shining armor" from the sixteenth century.

The Evening News by Arthur Hailey.
   Complete junk, but a great inside view of the television industry.

The Arab of the Desert: A Glimpse into Badawin Life in Kuwait and Sau'di Arabia by H. R. P. Dickson.
   You will have to borrow this one from the library. It is 600 pages filled with everything you didn't even know you wanted to know about nomadic life in the desert. A fascinating study.

Out of Season by Barbara Gamble.
   An eccentric woman and her sixteen-year-old. Good fun.

An Inconvenient Woman by Dominick Dunne.
   New and old Los Angeles money clash in what would have been a great read, but the ending is "uncalled for."

Mrs., Presumed Dead by Simon Brett.
   A sixty-plus widow solves a murder in an upscale development. Brett wrote more about the same heroine in other books.

Bagdad without a Map by Tony Horwitz.
   Charming travel essays.

Any Four Women Could Rob the Bank of Italy by Ann Cornelisen.
   And they do—in Italy—which makes it even more intriguing.

Shining Through by Susan Isaacs.
   World War II women's spy story. I like Isaacs' snappy dialogue. If you haven't read *Compromising Positions*, her first book, start with that one.

Among Schoolchildren by Tracey Kidder.
   If you're in education, you'll enjoy seeing yourself and some of your students in this one.

First Among Equals by Jeffrey Archer.
   Two men vie for the position of Prime Minister in Britain.

An Indian Attachment by Sarah Lloyd.
   Amazing true story! This woman lived in a village in Pujab for two years and lived the life of the villagers.

Summer Half by Angela Thirkell.
   Gentle romance in gentler times.

The Watchers by Dean Koontz.
> This is the only Koontz book I've read, this features a super-intelligent dog—so, of course I liked it.

Video Nights in Kathmandu by Peter Iyer.
> How modern gimmicks (video and McDonalds) have reached Bombay, Tokyo, and Bali.

Happy All the Time by Laurie Colwin.
> Yes, it's happy.

His Third, Her Second by Paul Estaver.
> This chronicles a marriage between two nice people.

Overhead in a Balloon: Stories of Paris by Mavis Gallant.
> Short stories that make you want to take the next plane to Paris and sit in a cafe, watching these characters walk by.

The Prophet's Bell by Margaret Laurence.
> What it's like living in Somalia as an expatriate.

You Can't Be Serious: Writing and Living American Humor by Ralph Schoenstein.
> A humorist takes a look at American publishing.

A Year in Provence by Peter Mayle.
> The food. The people. The food. The place. The food . . . in France.

Where do I find books? In libraries and bookstores wherever I am and from my friend, Johanna Hurwitz, who sends me the titles of what she's read and enjoyed. What have you read lately—just for fun?

Happy Reading

Hugs,
  Caroline

Index